WOMEN'S LIVES IN COLONIAL QUITO

KIMBERLY GAUDERMAN

Women's Lives in Colonial Quito

Gender, Law, and Economy
in Spanish America

University of Texas Press, *Austin*

Library of Congress Cataloging-in-Publication Data

Gauderman, Kimberly
   Women's lives in colonial Quito : gender, law, and economy in Spanish
America / by Kimberly Gauderman.— 1st ed.
      p.   cm.
Includes bibliographical references (p.   ) and index.
         ISBN: 0292722230
      1. Women—Ecuador—Quito—History.   2. Women's rights—Ecuador—
Quito—History.   3. Women—Ecuador—Quito—Economic conditions.
I. Title.
HQ1560.Q58   G38 2003
305.4′09866′13—dc21

2003004064

In memory of my grandparents:

CHARLES W. STEELE
1915–1987

PEARL R. STEELE
1921–2000

For Ariela, la quiteña de mi corazón

Contents

Nothing Stays the Same

One City, Two Women

María's Story

María lived in Quito, a city nestled high in the northern Andean sierra in what is now the country of Ecuador. Quito is located almost exactly at the equator and, at 10,000 feet above sea level, it is the second-highest capital city in the world today. The earliest Spanish observers of the city and its surrounding area described its climate as "eternal springtime." Indeed, despite the burning morning sun and the afternoon hailstorms, the evenings there are pleasant, and many people leave their windows ajar to refresh their nighttime dreams. María, however, never did so. On the night in question, María, as was routine for her, carefully locked the outer gates of the stone wall surrounding her house, secured all the doors to the house, and locked the windows. As she probably would have told us, living in fear of violence affects the most mundane aspects of one's life, even the air one breathes at night.

María was a married woman with two children. Both she and her husband came from respected families. At the time of their marriage her husband was educated, trained in law, and seemed like an aspiring candidate to the professional sectors that were rising in wealth and influence in the city at this time. At some point in their marriage, however, her husband became an alcoholic and frequently subjected María to violent outbursts. Eventually he abandoned the family, leaving her alone to support herself and their two children, as she had been doing for several years before his departure. She didn't consider divorce an option. Although divorce was a legal possibility, it was a lengthy and expensive process. Most of all, from her and her family's viewpoint, divorce left the woman and her family shamed and disgraced. So though she lived separately from her husband, the couple remained legally married. Periodically she would hear that her husband was living in some other city, but he moved around frequently. Occasionally he would return to Quito, as he did the night recounted here.

Late at night María heard the thuds at the front gate, but she refused to open it. Her husband, however, climbed the wall and, as the doors were locked, broke a window to enter the house. Meanwhile, María sent word to the authorities to come, and she locked her children in their room. The authorities never came. This was not unusual; the law offered little protection in such cases. Once, when she had been badly injured by her husband, she tried to press criminal charges against him. The authorities explained to her, however, that wives legally could bring no suits against their husbands, including charges of physical violence. The reasoning behind this policy was to protect the integrity and privacy of the family from public interference. As María listened to her drunk husband scream obscenities at her from downstairs, she knew that her fear and pain would not be publicly acknowledged. The family, represented by the name and person of the husband/father, superseded all rights of the individuals it contained.

Ventura's Story

Ventura also lived in Quito, though at a different time. She was married with children and, like María, lived separately from her husband. Ventura's husband was physically abusive and, though she might have wished he would abandon her, it was in fact she who moved out of their house, relocating herself and their children to her mother's home. Although Ventura's husband traveled frequently outside of Quito on business, he continued to live in their Quito house and constantly menaced both Ventura and her mother when he was in town. He wanted Ventura to return to live with him, which she refused to do. Both women probably felt some relief when they learned that he again was leaving the city on business, this time to go to Lima. Any relief the women felt, however, quickly turned to concern when, the day after her husband's departure, Ventura received news that her husband had secretly come back into town with plans to harm her.

Like María, Ventura felt that she and her family were in imminent danger from her husband. Also like María, her long history of abuse at her husband's hands had led her to complain frequently to the civil authorities. This time, however, Ventura went before the authorities and insisted that they arrest her husband as a preventative measure to ensure her safety. At this time in Quito's history women could bring criminal charges against their husbands, and the authorities complied and sent out two armed men with orders to arrest Ventura's husband. The authorities found her husband with a group of armed men heading toward Ventura's mother's house. The confrontation between the officers and the group of men headed by Ventura's husband became violent, and her husband was killed by the pursuing officers. Ventura was not quite a merry widow (she sued the officer who killed her husband), but the legal and law enforcement systems had acted to protect her safety by intervening in an internal family matter at her request. Marriage did not eclipse her legal status as an individual who could actively represent her own interests as well as her family's. In fact, the success and status of the family depended on her ability to protect her own interests, even against her husband if necessary.

Comparisons

After reviewing these two women's lives, theorists and activists might be tempted to applaud the changes in society which produced such different circumstances for women. We might be inclined to see María as a victim of traditional gender roles, condemned by her sex to live under the perpetual tutelage and subjugation of a male. Ventura's ability to call on civil authorities to protect herself and her family from her husband's violence might be explained by more progressive and modern ideas concerning the status and rights of women in society. Such conclusions, however, would be ill founded; María lived in Quito in 1994, whereas Ventura's case occurred in 1685.[1]

Until the late 1990s María's juridical, economic, and social status, like that of all women living in modern Ecuador, was derived from legislation defining the family as a nuclear unit, impermeable to public scrutiny, and headed by a male. Family members did not have individual rights, because the family was considered a "community of common interests," interests represented by its male head. To legally reinforce the communal interests of family members, the Penal Code of 1971 specifically prohibited spouses and their children from suing each other. Women were legally obligated to practice total obedience to their husbands. Domestic violence was not considered a criminal act in the code.[2] The Center for Information and Investigation of Wife Abuse in Ecuador (Centro de Información e Investigación sobre el Maltrato de la Mujer Ecuatoriana, CEIMME) estimated in 1994 that over 68 percent of Ecuadorian wives were beaten and mistreated.[3] Economically, the Labor Code of 1970 placed women in the same category as minors and the mentally deficient in terms of contracting labor agreements. Any property or income women acquired was directly controlled by their husbands and legally guaranteed the husbands' debts. Husbands exercised complete authority in deciding where the family would live and how all property and income would be used. In addition, men had exclusive rights to custody of their children.[4]

When Law 103, the Law Prohibiting Violence against Wives and Family, was passed on 12 November 1995, it therefore dramatically altered the status of women in modern Ecuadorian society.[5] Not only did the law give legal protection to wives and children against male family members, but, in doing so, it redefined the family itself. Legally, the family was no longer viewed as a uniquely private sphere; it was now open to public scrutiny and intervention. Commentators rightly heralded the passage of this law as a triumph for women and the culmination of years of struggle on behalf of women. The right of wives to sue their husbands was seen as a sign that Ecuadorian women were finally overcoming their colonial heritage. This is a modern struggle, however, and colonial women such as Ventura would have few reference points to understand what the struggle was about.

In the seventeenth century the legal system governing the status and conduct of women was quite different from that in modern Ecuador. Ventura had a very different set of options open to her than those available to María. In the mid-colonial period, the family was open to community and legal scrutiny and intervention. Although it was assumed that family members held interests in common, individual interests were also recognized; spouses and children could litigate against each other. At that time, the legal system did not consider women minors or compare them to the mentally deficient. Women made contracts, became business partners, and engaged in civil and criminal suits in their own right. The property of a married woman was protected from loss due to her husband's debts and could only be used to guarantee her husband's business negotiations with her express approval. Women shared the custody of their children with their husbands and could determine where the family would live.

Ventura's options for living independently and supporting her family in the seventeenth century can be seen, in many ways, as more secure than María's, over three hundred years later. Recent legislation in Ecuador that allows wives to litigate against their husbands is not an example of a society overcoming its colonial past; instead, it returns to women rights they held several hundred years earlier. This book examines the legal, economic, and social status of women living in the seventeenth-century Audiencia of Quito. The history of these women may surprise some readers and will, I hope, promote a deeper discussion of how women's lives today are connected to their colonial past. A fuller understanding of women's colonial history might, indeed, raise the question of how modernity failed María, leaving her alone in a house full of broken windows.

Acknowledgments

Intellectual work is not a solitary endeavor but, indeed, is produced within a community. It is with joy and gratitude that I acknowledge the support that so many teachers, friends, colleagues, and family members have given me for these many years. The completion of this book is testimony to all their kindness and their faith in this project and in me. I am also very grateful for the institutional support I have received. The Social Science Research Council, the Fulbright Commission, and the University of California at Los Angeles offered crucial support for my doctoral research. I also thank the Feminist Research Institute at the University of New Mexico for providing funding for follow-up research in the United States.

The staff and the Director of the Archivo Nacional del Ecuador, in Quito, must be lauded for their diligence and courage in preserving Ecuador's national archival treasures. I would like to express my deep appreciation to the archival staff and especially to the Director, Grecia Vasco de Escudero, and her assistant, María Teresa Carranco, for the assistance and courtesy they so generously offered me. I was aided in my initial archival research by Christiana Borchart de Moreno, who kindly shared her time and expertise with me, and by Joanne Rappaport, who directed me to important holdings. Karen Powers has lent a compassionate ear and a guiding hand from the very beginning of this project. Thomas Davies, with his generous spirit, offered technical and personal assistance. A special word of thanks goes to Helena Saona, Assistant to the Director of the Fulbright Committee in Ecuador, who went far beyond the call of duty in her consistent support for this project. I also extend my thanks to the Facultad Latino Americano de Ciencias Sociales (FLACSO) for its technical assistance in making my stay in Ecuador possible.

Among the people who helped make Ecuador a second home for me, I would especially like to thank the Almeida and Fuentes families, Carlos Espinoza, Catalina León, Segundo Moreno, María Carmen Ulcuango, and my compadre Cristóbal Landázuri. Gabriela Torres, with her wit and compassion, brought laughter and sanity into my life. The good humor of fellow researcher Kris Lane eased many long hours in the archive. I will be eternally grateful to Mónica Calán, who helped me care for my daughter Ariela, who was still a nursing baby. With José Almeida Vinueza I learned the challenging and productive nature of intercultural and interdisciplinary exchanges, only one of the fruits of which is this book. To him go my heartfelt thanks for accompanying me through this project.

Long before images of cloud forests filled my mind, my journey to Ecuador began at the University of California, Los Angeles, where I had the good fortune of working with James Lockhart. His example of rigorous scholarship and devotion to students has been an inspiration to me and I thank him here for his years of guidance and unflagging support of my work. I also thank Ellen DuBois, who provided orientations and support at key stages in my doctoral studies and who consistently motivated me with her stimulating and accurate critiques of my work. My fellow graduate students—Julie Charlip, James Green, Rose Marie Pegueros, Matthew Restal, Pete Sigal, Lisa Sousa, Keven Terraciano, Erika Verba, and James Wiltgen—gave me good advice, friendship, and emotional support.

I have been helped along the way by many teachers and friends. Andrea Engelmann encouraged me to go to college, Daniel Pope and George Sheridan at the University of Oregon shared their love of history and teaching with me, and Luis Verano showed me the power of merging intellectual pursuits with social engagement. Jacques Kapuscinski convinced me to volunteer at the Latin American Cultural Center and, thus, sealed my fate as a Latin American scholar. I express my deep appreciation to Claire Finkelstein, whose friendship, since those days long ago when we scavenged the streets of Paris together, has continued to inspire me personally and professionally. Serge Blonkowski shared his home with me in Paris and endured long hours of philosophical discussion in broken French with me. I also thank Elinor Fuchs, whose support and encouragement facilitated my first research trip to Ecuador.

Most recently, my colleagues in the History Department and the Latin American and Iberian Institution at the University of New Mexico have provided me with an intellectually stimulating and personally supportive work environment. In particular I thank Melissa Bokovoy, Tim Moy, Pat Risso, Jane Slaughter, William Stanley, Samuel Truett, and the late Robert Kern for their encouragement and friendship. My fellow Latin Americanists, Judy Bieber, Linda Hall, and Elizabeth Hutchison, have provided me with intellectual insight, editorial advice, and emotional support. They have been wise mentors, good colleagues, and true friends.

The process of revising a dissertation into a book can be traumatic.

Fortunately, I have had the pleasure of working with Theresa May, Assistant Director and Editor in Chief at University of Texas Press. With utmost professionalism, patience, and good cheer she has guided my manuscript to publication. I also thank Carolyn Cates Wylie, Managing Editor, and Leslie Doyle Tingle, Assistant Managing Editor, for their help in the final stages of production of the book. I would like to thank Sonya Manes for her fine copyediting. Two anonymous readers at University of Texas Press inspired necessary revisions. Kenneth Andrien and Camille Townsend offered valuable insights on sections of this project. I also wish to thank Chad Black for his help in editing and proofreading the manuscript. It is with special gratitude that I acknowledge my appreciation for the geographical artistry of Larry Larrichio, who drew maps for this project. I also thank José Almeida, for his spatial understanding of the city of Quito and the country of Ecuador, and Joseph Sánchez, Director of the Spanish Colonial Resource Center, for sharing his wisdom about colonial maps with us.

My final thanks go to my family. Jenene Peterson, Joseph Gauderman, Scott Gauderman, Coreena Gauderman, and their children have given me joy and helped me to keep my academic pursuits in perspective. Charlene Peterson, my mother, has always inspired me with her strength and hard work, and I owe a special debt of gratitude to her. Laura Gauderman and Judy Gauderman have praised me consistently, despite my peculiar career choice. It is with great tenderness that I express my gratitude for the love and support I received from my grandmother, the late Pearl Steele. She was my steadiness in a mercurial world, and her home in Glenwood continues to be my refuge.

Since coming to Albuquerque, Larry and Alida Larrichio have opened their hearts, home, and boccie court to us. Aurora Morcillo and Charles Blieker have been true and constant friends. Sharon Howell, "Grandma Sharon," has helped me raise my daughter; I thank her for her endless patience with both of us. And to Ariela, born in the midst of this project, I thank you for insisting, sometimes rather loudly, that going to the park was more important than sitting at the computer. You were right. Finally, my deepest thanks go to Dan Harwig and to my comadre, Jayne Spencer. Their friendship has inspired and sustained me over the years; the completion of this book, and so much else in my life, would not have been possible without them.

WOMEN'S LIVES IN COLONIAL QUITO

1. The Audiencia of Quito, Seventeenth Century. MAP DRAWN BY LARRY V. LARRICHIO.

Introduction

Putting Women in Their Place

What did it mean to be a woman in colonial Spanish America? One way to answer this question is to look at how women of indigenous and Spanish descent from different social ranks were defined through custom and law. This book explores the lives of a spectrum of women from the Audiencia of Quito during the seventeenth century. It focuses on women's use of legal and extralegal means to achieve personal and economic goals; their often successful attempts to confront men's physical violence, adultery, lack of financial support, and broken marriage proposals; women's control over property; and their participation in local, interregional, and international economies. In a larger sense, telling these stories is a way of integrating women's lives into our understanding of Spanish colonial society.

One of the most surprising findings is that maintenance of social order during this period required women's relative independence from men. The logic of Spanish culture consistently undermined attempts to consolidate absolute positions of power at all levels of society, including the family and relations between men and women. The system of decentralized authority that structured Spanish colonial social and legal norms gave women—of both Spanish and indigenous descent—substantial control over economic and social resources.

The Audiencia of Quito was located in the northern section of the Viceroyalty of Peru. Although the city of Quito is now the capital of the nation of Ecuador, in the seventeenth century the city was the seat of the Royal Audiencia, a royal judicial court. The Audiencia's jurisdiction stretched north to Buenaventura, midway up the coast of modern Colombia, and south to Tumbez in what is now northern Peru. Eastward, the Audiencia extended from the Pacific coast across the Amazon to the frontier with Portuguese Brazil.[1] Although the Audiencia's jurisdiction was geographically large, effective Spanish control was concentrated mainly in the

Andean highlands, the region in which the city of Quito was located. Beyond the port of Guayaquil, which connected the region to the rest of South America and to Europe, vast areas of the coast remained unconquered until the nineteenth and twentieth centuries. The eastern Amazon region remained largely unexplored until the nineteenth century, and, even today, many argue that national governments have difficulties establishing an effective presence in this region.[2]

The seventeenth century was a period of prosperity for the Audiencia of Quito. While populations were dropping in the rest of Peru, the Spanish and indigenous populations in the region of Quito grew throughout the century.[3] This demographic growth provided the labor necessary to produce the agricultural and manufacturing surpluses that already by the 1580s had made Quito a major center of production and trade in Spanish Peru, following only Lima and Potosí.[4] During the seventeenth century, in fact, the diocese of Quito shared fourth place with the archbishopric of Mexico among all American sees in terms of wealth.[5] Despite the decline in silver production in Potosí (located within greater Peru in what is now Bolivia, the largest silver-producing district in Spanish America), the Quito economy expanded throughout the century, reaching its highest point for the entire colonial period in 1690. Quito's importation of regional and European goods was higher between 1640 and 1710 than it would be for the rest of the colonial period and even thereafter.[6]

The region's economy was noted for its diversity. The area around Quito was an important producer of tanned hides, sugar, biscuits (for provisioning the large ships which passed through the port city of Guayaquil), and gunpowder. Quito exported artisanal products such as buttons, fine lace, and rosaries. Beginning in the seventeenth century, it also became an important center in the production of art. Through the *Escuela quiteña*, an artistic style associated with the region, Quito was the source for paintings and sculptures shipped as far south as Chile.[7] The basis of the region's economy, however, was textile manufacturing. The quantity and quality of wool produced in the region and the availability of a large skilled labor force made Quito a major cloth producer in the Peruvian viceroyalty. Textiles were exported to Lima in the south and to the northern gold-producing regions in what is now Colombia.[8] The production and sale of wool and cloth involved all sectors of the region's population and included high levels of participation by women.

The hub of this economic network was the city of Quito. As an administrative, commercial, and social center, the city exerted its influence over the entire district but especially over the Andean region proper. Located high in the Andean mountain chain, several arduous days of travel away from the port of Guayaquil (which connected Quito to Lima and Europe),

2. *The City of Quito, Seventeenth Century.* MAP DRAWN BY LARRY V. LARRICHIO,
BASED ON COLONIAL MAPS AND DESCRIPTIONS OF THE CITY.

and far from any of the significant mineral deposits so sought after by
Spaniards, Quito seemed initially an unlikely place for an important urban
center. Travel to and from the city through the high mountain passes
was difficult in the best of times, but during the rainy season (October
through April) washed-out roads frequently made transportation impossible, leaving the city isolated.[9] The city itself was built on the flanks of
the active volcano Pichincha, its neighborhoods squeezed between deep
ravines that quickly became rushing rivers in the afternoon rains, typical
even during the dry season.

In his study of eighteenth-century Quito, Martin Minchom described
the city as a European center with a progressively more indigenous hinterland. The ravines crisscrossing the city acted as barriers between barrios,

or neighborhoods, allowing different areas of the city to develop their own cultural distinctiveness.[10] Although the city was founded as a center for the region's Spanish population, the unusual geography of urban Quito made physical expansion difficult. As its population climbed—estimated at 50,000 in 1650[11]—earlier attempts to racially divide the city's Spanish and indigenous inhabitants became impossible to maintain. The parishes of San Sebastián and San Blas, originally created in 1568 to house the city's indigenous population, were described in 1627 as racially mixed, along with all the other parishes in the city.[12] This integration of indigenous and Spanish populations exceeded that of some other major cities in Spanish America. Lima, for instance, retained its indigenous parish, Santiago del Cercado, through the seventeenth century, and Tenochtitlán and Tlatelolco remained indigenous communities within Mexico City into the nineteenth century.[13]

The proximity of Spaniards and Indians within the city did not, of course, erase the cultural distinctions between these groups. Indians and many mestizos continued to dress in traditional indigenous clothing, and almost all Indians and even some mestizos needed translators in order to testify in Spanish. Continual interracial contact, however, did provoke visible adaptations in both groups. Testaments show that wealthy indigenous women had their clothing made from Chinese silks and Spanish woolens. The households of wealthy Spaniards frequently contained articles such as tablecloths made from *cumbi,* the very fine indigenous fabric formerly used to clothe the Inca nobility.[14] The need to communicate between the two groups, not only for official governmental purposes but also in common official transactions, such as business agreements and land sales, produced a large and easily available corpus of translators. In addition to the material and administrative adaptations by Indians and Spaniards, there was also a blurring of ethnic boundaries as members of the two groups intermarried and formed permanent or casual unions.

The city of Quito was indeed a bustling Spanish metropolis, but the indigenous hinterland was not devoid of Spaniards. Even those Indians living in officially designated Indian pueblos often shared their towns with non-Indians. As we shall see later, royal policy prohibited Spaniards, mestizos, blacks, and mulattos from residing in Indian pueblos, but such mandates were largely ignored. The presence of poor Spaniards, mestizos, and Spanish officials in Indian communities was commonplace, a practice that helped connect these pueblos to the city of Quito through commercial and political networks.

The Audiencia of Quito is thus an ideal site for examining the situation of women in seventeenth-century Spanish America. The region's prosperity, demographic growth, and social stability make it possible to study colonial gender relations as they operated in a normal, mundane fashion, in a context relatively unmarked by the turmoil of conquest in the six- teenth century and before the centralizing forces of the Spanish Crown's fiscal and legal reforms reworked colonial social relations in the eigh- teenth century.[15] Because of the Audiencia's economic and political im- portance, the region's inhabitants produced a rich body of documenta- tion. Spanish, indigenous, and mestizo women left numerous traces of their lives in the historical record.[16] This study examines women's lives through records of criminal and civil proceedings, notarial records (in- cluding testaments, business contracts, and property rentals and sales), and city council records. These records from the Quito region itself are supplemented by Spanish legislation and commentaries on the legal status of women dating back to the seventh-century laws formulated as the Fuero Juzgo.

This broad range of sources, produced by and about women from the general population, permits a view of women involved in a variety of ac- tivities from a number of different perspectives. Because this study in- cludes women from different racial backgrounds, it also explores connec- tions between gender and racial categories in colonial society. Race, of course, has long been used as an analytical tool for understanding colo- nial society, and it is now commonly accepted that racial categories are socially constructed and fluid rather than purely biological and fixed.[17] Colonial legislative practice actually encouraged imprecise racial distinc- tions. Elizabeth Anne Kuznesof shows that although references to race appear consistently in colonial legislation, racial groups are not clearly defined. For this reason, "the courts themselves varied the criteria used to determine race in a particular case."[18] Racial categories were negoti- able and had practical legal effects, the most important of which were fiscal obligations. The major racial division in colonial society was be- tween Indians and non-Indians, and, as Olivia Harris notes, this was an economically grounded distinction. "The term Indian . . . became in the Andes fundamentally a fiscal category by which the obligations of the native population to the colonial state were defined."[19] In Minchom's study of Quito, he found abundant evidence of individuals who appeared to be culturally Indian but who sought Spanish or mestizo racial status to avoid paying tribute.[20] Racial categories manifested themselves saliently in the colonial economy, giving individuals financial incentive to mask racial/cultural identities that under other circumstances could have had great meaning for them.[21]

For the women in this study, racial status primarily became an issue in their economic relations. Women, regardless of their racial status, who sought to establish property rights or criminally prosecute men, engaged with a large corpus of Spanish gender legislation in which racial status was largely irrelevant. When women entered the economy, however, they were constrained by the same fiscally based racial distinctions as men. My research suggests that women's racial status, not their gender or marital status, was consistently used to determine the legal scope of their economic activities. The main economic distinction was between Indians and non-Indians, and, as in Minchom's study, women tried to position themselves on either side of this racial division in service to their economic interests. In the economic realm gender did become a prominent aspect of racial status in the indigenous population. As will be seen, indigenous women claimed financial advantages on the basis of both their gender and their race. Although people were obviously defined by both their racial and gendered status in colonial society, the importance of individuals' racial and gender identities varied according to the specific situations they faced.[22]

The book is organized around two central and connected arguments. The first is the premise that gender roles are culturally defined and that, therefore, the roles of women and men must be interpreted through the specific cultural matrix in which they were produced. Following this insight the book begins with an examination of Spanish social organization and argues that the constraints and possibilities governing women's lives in the seventeenth century were created within the system of decentralized authority that had historically characterized their society. Exploring how women were integrated into this system of decentered relations of power produces a perspective strikingly different from standard accounts of women's status in colonial Spanish America. Researchers traditionally use a patriarchal model to show how men, on the basis of their gender, held greater economic, social, and political power than women. As commonly used, the patriarchal model assumes that Spanish society was hierarchically arranged around a central authority and that this cultural framework also explains relations between men and women in society and the family. This work challenges that view by arguing that Spanish society was highly decentralized and that this social organization gave women more options for exercising authority than researchers have usually acknowledged.

Chapter 1 analyzes how the patriarchal paradigm has been used by historians and outlines the methodological and analytical inconsistencies generated by its continued use in the field of colonial women's history. This discussion is followed by an analysis of Spanish society based on the well-established body of historical scholarship on social relations and state structure in early Latin America. As early as 1947 Clarence Haring published the now classic *Spanish Empire in America,* an exhaustive analysis of virtually every level of administration within the Spanish colonial system of governance.[23] His research clearly demonstrates that administrative and judicial bureaucracies were not hierarchically arranged and that even the authority of the king was quite restricted within this system. (Haring, however, still held that centralization was the ideal organizational model that produced social order and that decentralization led to instability and corruption.) In the 1960s John Phelan drew on Haring's work to address the connection between decentralization and social stability in colonial Spanish America.[24] Although Phelan's own research on the Philippines and the Audiencia of Quito supported Haring's characterization of Spanish society as inherently decentralized, he argued against universally applying Western ideals of social organization. Instead, he argued that the contingency in relations of authority that so marked Spanish society actually produced a network of checks and balances guaranteeing that organizations and individuals, jealous of their own power, would control and limit abuses by others, thereby negating the need for a centralized figure of authority. Both Haring's and Phelan's work demonstrates that Spanish culture consistently worked against attempts to consolidate centralized positions of power, relying instead on multiple hierarchies with competing jurisdictions. Power relations were contingent; subordinates could impede the directives of superiors.

This decentralization marked all relations throughout the social and political institutions and practices of seventeenth-century Spanish America, including those between men and women, promoting asymmetry, disequilibrium, and difference, while at the same time ensuring authority and flexibility and, ultimately, social stability. Decisions within governmental bureaucracies and family networks were the result of tension and conflict, compromises made in realms where authority was always contingent rather than rigidly defined. Mutual surveillance was important in the maintenance of social order. Church and government officials watched and reported on each other; neighbors kept track of events in their part of the city; husbands and wives exercised authority over each other, and their property was under the watch of an extensive family network.

This system depended heavily on multiple, alternative channels of communication; social and legal mechanisms allowed individuals at any point to inform others about the conduct of those around them. This constant flow of information within all sectors of society made individuals accountable for their actions and thus did not require a centralized point of control. In fact, social stability required that individuals, including women, manipulate the inherent conflicts in the norms and laws governing social existence by, in essence, "playing the system."

These conclusions about Spanish social organization are reinforced by an examination of Spanish legal codes and the way they were used in Spanish America, as well as by a comparison of the status of Spanish American women with that of their female counterparts in Britain and France. Finally, a close look at legislation affecting women's control over the choice of marriage partners for themselves and their children demonstrates how gender relations in the colonial period changed over time. Women faced considerably greater limitations in their ability to control property and to influence political alliances between families toward the end of the eighteenth century than they had in the seventeenth century.[25]

The book's second central argument is that women were not sacrificial victims of a social order based on hierarchical, patriarchal relations of power, not because of notions of equality or fairness but simply because the system did not require such victims. Chapters 2 through 5 examine women of different ethnic and economic backgrounds through evidence of their legal and economic activities, showing women's active participation in civil society. Many of the women in this study took independent actions, but they were not seen as challenging the authority of colonial society. The system used women, but women also used the system to protect their social and economic interests and to punish the men who abused them. Women's rights, like those of other individuals and groups, were recognized and guaranteed in order to counterbalance and limit the authority of others. If women "hold up half the sky," in colonial Spanish America they did this precisely to keep men from claiming it all.

One clarification is perhaps necessary here: this study does not seek nor does it find gender equality in colonial Spanish America. Women's semiautonomous position in Spanish American society was not due to enlightened notions of women's rights or equality between the sexes. Women were not equal to men, but neither were men equal among themselves. An individual's status was influenced by wealth, occupation, special privileges (*fueros*) granted to members of specific groups (church officials, the military, aristocrats, students, guilds, Indians), and family status, along with race and gender. Social practice and legal reasoning emphasized the rights of people in different categories and virtually ignored questions of equality.

Given this fuero-based legal system, women readily accessed the legal mechanisms in defense of their rights. Chapters 2 and 3 examine women's use of the Spanish legal system. Chapter 2 examines the control of married women over property by analyzing the constitution of dowries and how women used this property. An analysis of a typical dowry contract, combined with examples from court cases, shows how women used their private estates to attain personal and family goals. Both husbands and wives faced legal restrictions on their ability to invest dowry property in economic ventures. Mirroring the general cultural logic of the time, marriage was a union in which the interests of wives and husbands at the same time merged and remained distinct, and this relation was reflected in their possession of both community property and separate estates. Wives independently invested in properties, and wives and husbands engaged in joint economic ventures, as we shall see in a detailed analysis of a contract between a wife and husband to jointly invest a part of her estate.

Women in colonial Latin America used the criminal justice system to protect themselves and family members from violent and unacceptable treatment by men. Chapter 3 describes the limitations women faced in resolving domestic disputes through the ecclesiastical courts. Although many scholars have recognized that church authorities failed to support women in domestic disputes, they have interpreted this failure as evidence that male adultery and physical aggression against female family members were socially acceptable behaviors. Legal records, however, paint a different picture. Adultery, physical aggression, and abandonment were criminal acts, and women routinely used the criminal justice system against men who abused them. An examination of court cases from the colonial period shows how and why women of different social rank and ethnicity sued men, the punishments men received, and why the royal government often supported women in domestic disputes.

The final two chapters shift the focus from legal issues to women's economic activities in the Audiencia of Quito. The region's rising prosperity and racial diversity are reflected in women's economic activities. Chapter 4 broadly discusses women's economic activities by examining the participation of Spanish, indigenous, and mestizo women in various sectors of the Audiencia's economy. The chapter begins with a detailed description and analysis of women's participation in textile manufacturing, the region's main industry, and goes on to consider women as urban and rural property owners, slaveholders, moneylenders, grocery store owners and operators, servants, bread bakers, and makers of *chicha* (a traditional, indigenous, fermented beverage). Case studies of women involved in these activities demonstrate that women, both married and single, operated their businesses and often invested their capital independently from the men around them. Women were not only economically active but were essential to the region's economic prosperity in this period.

Chapter 5 focuses specifically on the indigenous market women, known as *gateras*, who provisioned the city of Quito and surrounding pueblos with both staples and luxury goods. Information about their lives emerges from records of eighty years of litigation between these indigenous women and Spanish male grocery store operators and government officials, as well as from criminal records in which the women appear as defendants and witnesses. These records show that Indian women consistently won their cases and progressively expanded their economic activities throughout the seventeenth century. The chapter includes discussions of commercial law and its enforcement, the gateras' commercial activities in the city of Quito and in the surrounding pueblos, and the nature of the disputes generated through the gateras' economic activities. Surprisingly, the evidence shows that indigenous women faced few gender-specific constraints on their commercial or legal activities and that they claimed economic and legal advantages in market vending because of their racial status.

The final chapter draws together the various strands of analysis to reflect on women's status in colonial Spanish America. The fluidity of categories regulating relations of all kinds and defining gender roles and racial difference leads to a rethinking of traditional models that rely on hierarchical and patriarchal mechanisms of authority to understand the role of women in colonial Spanish American society. In rejecting this paradigm of female subordination, this study draws on a growing body of ethnohistorical research on this period. In traditional scholarship both indigenous peoples and women have been perceived as similar, subordinated historical subjects. However, revisionist work, especially since the 1980s, has sought to recontextualize the lives of indigenous peoples by including them as participants in creating and limiting authority in colonial society.

Bartolomé de Las Casas in the sixteenth century enshrined the image of Indians as defenseless, passive victims of Spaniards whose genocidal tendencies destroyed indigenous cultures, economies, and political systems.[26] This view of Indians in colonial Spanish America, also known as the Black Legend, endured from the postconquest period until the midtwentieth century. At that time, scholars increasingly became aware that this model could not explain why Indians retained so much autonomy in the central areas of conquest, Mexico and Peru.[27] Research indicated that the Spanish economic system depended on indigenous societies' maintaining a great deal of independence. Sedentary indigenous polities, operating within their own political, economic, and cultural systems, efficiently channeled the labor and goods that Spaniards required without centralized control by Spanish authorities. Spaniards and many indigenous societies, notably those who formerly had been conquered by the Inca and Aztec, in fact held similar cultural expectations that conquered groups would retain significant political and economic authority. As researchers began to explore how Indians, in many different ways, understood and interacted with the Spanish system of decentralized authority, they revised indigenous history. Researchers redefined the "paradigm of conquest," as Steve Stern so eloquently frames the process, and revealed Indians as active agents in manipulating competing legal jurisdictions, quarreling government officials, and the contradictory laws that constituted the Spanish system of governance.[28]

Spaniards were not promoters of cultural diversity. However, the shifting alliances and conflicts that quickened the Spanish concept of authority also created moments when Indians, like other social groups, could exert their autonomy. This book suggests that, like ethnohistorians, we Latin Americanists should reevaluate our research on women in colonial Spanish America by considering their lives within the context of traditional Spanish cultural norms that promoted contingent, decentralized relations of authority. As in ethnohistory such a move requires that we revise an entrenched paradigm that has structured, and in many ways crippled, our research.

This book argues that the patriarchal paradigm masks more than it reveals about the status of women in colonial Spanish America.[29] Spanish culture traditionally undermined the establishment of centralized positions of authority through which a patriarchal system might operate. By contesting the relevance of the patriarchal paradigm for understanding colonial Spanish America, I am not arguing that women were more liberated than they are today. Rather, evidence supports the conclusion that to the extent that women as individuals faced subordination in colonial society, it cannot be attributed to the Spanish legal system or to essentialized notions of gender within Spanish society. Patriarchy has structured many other societies, and continues to do so, but its emergence and resilience require specific forms of social organization. For this reason the patriarchal paradigm is a powerful tool for researchers, not because of patriarchy's timeless nature but because in many aspects of Spanish American life patriarchy is a modern creation.

CHAPTER 1

Ambiguous Authority, Contingent Relations

The Nature of Power in Seventeenth-Century Spanish America

Patriarchy Is Human?

"From the days of the primitive church to early modern times, patriarchalism was the underlying principle of all social relationships."[1] This sweeping statement brings us face to face with an assumption shared by almost all historians of gender in early Spanish America: patriarchy is a universal form of social organization. Under this "fundamental law of inequality,"[2] women were perpetual minors under the tutelage of fathers and then husbands. According to this view, men represented women in the public sphere and, within the family, controlled women's sexuality, reproductive roles, and labor power. The patriarchal paradigm has, in many ways, expanded the range of historical inquiry by asserting that gender organization is a fundamental aspect of all societies and therefore a legitimate subject of historical analysis. Using this model, researchers of women in early Spanish America have produced compelling histories, informing us of the important and varied roles that women played in their societies.[3]

A number of social scientists, however, question the usefulness of the concept of patriarchy as a model for understanding gender relations. Joan Scott argues that the analysis of patriarchy tends to be abstract, providing no material explanation for its appearance, nor any understanding of how gender inequalities affect or relate to other inequalities.[4] Indeed, Ida Bloom, general editor of the five-volume *Women's History of the World from the Earliest Times to the Present Day,* reports on the authors' "futile attempt to define a single theory of patriarchy and their struggle to avoid an overly eurocentric approach."[5]

Linking patriarchal analyses of Third World women to the maintenance of Western hegemony, Ruth Behar argues that the woman subject to such an analysis "exists in academic as well as mainstream reporting as a pretheorized reality, an already-fixed representation." She continues by quoting Chandra Talpade Mohanty, arguing that by representing the average Third World woman as leading "a truncated life based on her feminine gender (read: sexually constrained) and being 'third world' (read: ignorant, poor, uneducated, tradition-bound, domestic, family-oriented, victimized, etc.), Western feminists have engaged in implicit, discursive self-representation of themselves as educated, modern, as having control over their bodies and sexualities, and the freedom to make their own decisions."[6] By insisting on patriarchy as a metahistorical concept for understanding all gender relations, historians are complicit in constructing this "Third World woman" through the imposition of a single history for all women—one in which Western women have overcome many obstacles to equality with men while women in other societies, through their lack of "gender consciousness," remain tied to "traditional" female roles.[7]

Alison MacEwen Scott cautions against the use of stereotypes in the reconstruction of gender roles in Latin America. She compares gender analysis with class analysis, arguing that "although most societies are stratified according to some principles of class hierarchy, it would not occur to a good social scientist to portray particular classes in stereotypical form, nor to assume that their empirical manifestations were everywhere the same and immutable across time."[8]

Scholars in other fields thus critique the patriarchal model for its theoretical, political, and methodological limitations. Researchers of women in early Spanish America, however, continue to rely predominantly on a patriarchal model in reconstructing women's lives, and this practice has promoted methodological inconsistencies. Because patriarchy is considered a universal model of social organization, some scholars have assumed that the experiences of women are cross-culturally interchangeable. This belief in a universal historical trajectory has prompted some historians to substitute the experiences of other world regions, mainly the United States, Britain, and France, for the particular situation of women in Spanish America.[9] Others, asserting the stability and temporal continuity of gender roles, have used eighteenth- and nineteenth-century legislation, literature, and travel accounts in Spanish America (more numerous in these centuries) for interpreting gender roles in the sixteenth and seventeenth centuries.[10]

The reliance of historians of Spanish America on a particular model of family structure has been supported by early scholars in the discipline of family history, who formed generalizations about the nature of family life based on their research of northern Europe. The demographic historical work of the Cambridge Group for the History of Population and Social Structure, led by Peter Laslett, Jean Robin, and Richard Wall, while making pathbreaking advances in our knowledge of family structure, focused exclusively on northern Europe. Although their research demonstrates conclusively that the nuclear family structure predominated long before the advent of industrialization, rather than the extended or "classical family of Western nostalgia," there is a tendency to generalize about the type of authority generated within this nuclear family structure.[11] Laslett finds that residence, or the composition of individuals living in a particular household, is the defining characteristic of the domestic group.[12] Researchers assume that family decisions are controlled by one individual, the adult male, usually the husband.[13] This belief in the supremacy of male authority within the family also has been reinforced by social historians of the family, such as Edward Shorter and Lawrence Stone. Basing his work on England and France, Shorter finds that men represented the family in the public sphere, that women were traditionally confined to the domestic sphere, and that wives were expected to be passive and inferior to their husbands. This view of women's limited authority outside their households is echoed by Lawrence Stone, who uses prescriptive literature and literary sources that reflected elite and bourgeois aspirations in England.[14]

These generalizations about family relations, although accepted by many historians of Spanish America, have been increasingly challenged since the 1980s by historians of Iberian families.[15] Pierre Vilar, in his study of the family in Spain from the fifteenth through the nineteenth centuries, argues that northern European family models were not typical in Spain. His research shows that although families in most regions of Spain shared the nuclear structure of those in northern Europe, there are limits to interpreting social relations through this residential pattern. Spanish families shared economic, social, and political interests, and these extensive ties between households, rather than discrete living arrangements, determined social relations between family members.[16]

The practice of partible inheritance also plays a central role in structuring relations within and between households in Iberia. Unlike most regions in northern Europe, which practiced primogeniture (the transference of family property to a single heir, usually the oldest male child), Iberian families generally divided property among all children, both male and female. According to Vilar, the social impact of partible inheritance in Iberia was to decrease both the possibility of closed family groups and the importance of the patrilineal line.[17] Because children normally began new households with advances from their parental inheritance, the common interest in preserving and increasing family resources connected households together in an extensive family network despite separate residences.[18] Women's access to economic resources through partible inheritance gave women greater authority and responsibility for making financial decisions and publicly representing the family than would be typical in the male-headed households so prominently portrayed by family historians studying northern Europe. As Ruth Behar and David Frye conclude in their study of Leonese families: "Since both men and women inherit equally and retain their ownership of property after marriage, and since both husband and wife share in making basic decisions about the family economy, it is somewhat problematic to designate only the husband as household head."[19] The "traditional" family of northern Europe was not typical in Spain.

A Man's Home Is His Castle

Universalizing any particular form of social organization asserts that, in fundamental ways, all societies are alike. The general practice by historians of Spanish American women has, indeed, been to account for that group's particular view of family relations by situating Spanish culture within Europe's "Old Regime" societies. According to this model, all societies in Europe had identical social structures whose organizing principles of political order were conceptually based on hierarchical and patriarchal relations of power.[20] In this view society was organized as a well-defined hierarchy with a central figure of authority, the king. The structure of the family was organized through this same cultural logic: the absolute power of the father/husband over his children and wife was analogous to the authority of the king. Women were defined primarily by their relationship to a male authority, a father or a husband. Social structures mirrored this arrangement. Society was divided into public and private spheres; women were ideally confined to their homes and found little redress for their grievances in public opinion or law.

Researchers thus link gender norms to a specific form of political organization that, like patriarchy, is labeled "traditional." According to Steve Stern, "the metaphor of familial patriarch readily ran up the chain of rule to higher authorities, the metaphor of kingship readily ran down the chain of rule to husband-fathers, and the patriarchal family ruled by a father-elder was the fundamental unit of social survival and collaboration."[21] In short, social stability required that men occupy a political, social, and economic status superior to women. The capacity of men to "rule" over women within the family reflected the centralized authority of the king over his subjects.

There is, however, a well-recognized body of historical research on the organization of the Spanish state that demonstrates that royal authority was not absolute but was, in fact, highly decentralized. The work of historian James Casey shows that Spanish social and political structure diverged from the Old Regime societies that characterized France and England. During the Reconquest (711–1492) the Spanish Crown not only recognized the diverse legal jurisdictions of conquered peoples and ecclesiastical authorities; it also created new jurisdictions by ceding lands and populations to cities and to the military orders. Casey suggests that the development of feudalism was therefore truncated in Spain. Local customs and legal traditions, legitimated by the crown, limited the authority of feudal lords. Rural magistrates dealt directly with the crown without the intervention of the feudal lord or his officials.[22] This long tradition of local self-government also impeded the crown from centralizing its authority in Spain, because it had to negotiate at various jurisdictional levels to implement its policies. Opposition from local populations and even the royal government's own officials typically forced a compromise between royal and local interests.[23] Indeed, the crown expected its officials not to apply royal laws that were detrimental to local populations. Crown agents who applied the letter of the law could find themselves punished and suspended from their positions.[24]

The Role of Subordinates in Policy Making

Such elegance and efficiency attend a smooth chain of command that it is difficult to imagine a society with a different ideal of social organization. Indeed, historians of Spanish institutions, like those of women's history, expected to find a highly centralized society in which the authority of the king radiated downward through his councils, ministers, and officials, who then communicated the royal will to their subordinates. Scholars considered interruptions in this hierarchical chain of command to be flaws undermining institutional strength. The famous Spanish philosopher and essayist José Ortega y Gasset, for example, complained that Spain's lack of feudalism separated it from the historical trajectory of France and England, countries he considered modern and progressive. "Instead of a hierarchy of power and authority, stretching down from the throne to the people, this frontier nation had developed as a cluster of autonomous corporations—military brotherhoods, city states—with strong local roots." Such a system, according to Ortega y Gasset, only served to generate tensions and fragment society.[25]

The work of institutional historians in Spanish America, however, suggests how this decentralized system generated both authority and stability. Kenneth Andrien's study of the royal treasury in seventeenth-century Lima, for example, demonstrates that the authority of local officials to override crown mandates functioned to protect royal as well as local interests. Scholars traditionally view the decline in royal income during this period from Lima as a reflection of decreased economic activity in the

Viceroyalty of Peru. However, Andrien's research suggests that what caused the decline in the viceroyalty's remissions to Spain were decisions by royal authorities in Lima to spend an increasing percentage of the treasury's total income on local expenses. Crown officials stationed in Peru consistently refused to send the amounts of money stipulated by royal law. Instead, the officials spent ever greater amounts on the viceroyalty's military defense against pirates and the ongoing wars with the Araucanian Indians in Chile.[26]

The decentralization of Spanish bureaucracy allowed local crown officials to determine which goals were more important. In this case local officials decided that the military protection of the viceroyalty was more important than the remittance of funds to the metropolis. By delegating power to authorities at the local level, Spain was freed from the burden of militarily defending all parts of its realm; Spain spent no money for the defense of the viceroyalty of Peru. The strategy of decentralizing decision making extended rather than undermined crown authority, ensuring social and political stability through the creation of multiple centers of power able to respond to changing local and international situations.

The ability of local officials to assess the importance of crown directives in relation to the local situation and, on the basis of their evaluation, to impede the implementation of royal orders was codified in the formula "I obey but do not execute." As John Phelan explains:

The "I obey" clause signifies the recognition by subordinates of the legitimacy of the sovereign power who, if properly informed of all circumstances, would will no wrong. The "I do not execute" clause is the subordinate's assumption of the responsibility of postponing the execution of an order until the sovereign is informed of those conditions of which he may be ignorant and without a knowledge of which an injustice may be committed.[27]

This legal mechanism, by which authorities were permitted to postpone the implementation of royal orders, shows the positive role of subordinates in colonial policy making. Rather than simply executing orders handed down through a vertical chain of command, officials were expected to balance the objectives of royal authority with local concerns. As Phelan argues, the "I obey but do not execute" formula acted as an institutional mechanism for decentralizing decision making.

Overlapping Administrative Jurisdictions

Subordinates were thus able to influence and even impede the execution of the orders of their superiors. This disruption in a smooth vertical chain of command becomes even more problematic when we consider the horizontal relations between bureaucracies. Clarence Haring, in his study of colonial Spanish imperial administration in America, recognized that Spanish bureaucracy operated through checks and balances secured through a division of authority among different individuals or tribunals exercising the same powers:

> There never was a clear-cut line of demarcation between the functions
> of various governmental agencies dealing with colonial problems. On the
> contrary, a great deal of overlapping was deliberately fostered to prevent
> officials from unduly building up personal prestige or engaging in corrupt
> or fraudulent practices.[28]

By multiplying administrative centers, the crown maintained various channels of communication in order to receive information from a wide range of sources. The bureaucratic agencies of the viceroy, the archbishop, the Audiencia, and the local city council had overlapping jurisdictions and were encouraged to watch and report on each other. For example, in the first half of the seventeenth century, Dr. Antonio de Morga wrote continuously during his twenty-one years as the president of the Audiencia of Quito to inform the crown of what he considered the inefficiency and corruption of the viceroy of Peru.[29] In fact, all bureaucratic agencies could communicate directly with the king and his council without first passing through hierarchical controls. The city of Quito depended neither on the Audiencia nor the viceroy to favor its requests but kept its own agent in the king's court in Spain to represent the city's interests.[30]

The King and His Councils

Research on the organization of the Spanish state shows that subordinates could effectively block the execution of the orders of superiors and that administrative agencies themselves were caught up in constant acrimonious conflict. Still, it is possible that the king and his councils formed a centralized point of control over this network of contested authorities. In fact, both Haring and Phelan point out that the only centralization within Spanish administration was in the king and his council in Spain.[31] Yet the king's power was not absolute, and his power to command obedience was expressed in terms of reciprocity.

For example, in 1591 the crown insisted on establishing the *alcabala* (sales tax) in the Viceroyalty of Peru.[32] The king justified his request for this new tax by arguing that the crown had spent enormous amounts of money in safeguarding sea traffic, to the direct benefit of Peru. Because piracy was on the increase and the Viceroyalty of Peru had great wealth, the crown argued that it was now time for Peru to contribute financially to the crown's defense efforts. The sales tax had operated within Spain for some time and in New Spain (Mexico) since 1574. Despite repeated orders from the crown that the tax be implemented in Peru, however, two viceregal administrations had refused to promulgate it, using the "I obey but do not execute" clause to argue that the tax's imposition would cause instability and great harm to the realm. After repeated failures to impose the sales tax, the crown reduced its demand from 10 percent, the percentage due in all other Spanish kingdoms, to 2 percent.[33]

The people of Peru still rejected the tax. Like the crown, the people insisted that the basis of the relationship between the king and his subjects was one of reciprocal obligations. The Peruvian position was that the crown had taken no part in the conquest of Peru and therefore had no right to extract more money from its inhabitants. As one manifesto proclaimed in the name of all Spanish Peru: "[W]e state and confirm that we do not concede or consent, nor will we willingly subject ourselves to pay it [the sales tax] now or ever because in the conquest of these our kingdoms the king our lord, spent nothing."[34] The person who penned this manifesto and those who agreed with him claimed rights of possession to Peru because "our kingdoms" had been acquired without the aid of the king. They were claiming that the wealth of Peru pertained thus to their private estates, distinguishing this form of property from community property or wealth produced in common with the crown and to which the royal treasury would have a right. Invoking a large body of legislation and social practice concerning private estates (discussed in the next chapter, on married women's property), they insisted that the use of their estates had to be based on free will and that the nature of the economic transaction had to be advantageous.

The alcabala was seen as illegitimate for two reasons. First, the crown had not participated in the initial conquest, acting only later to ratify what had already been accomplished. This restricted the royal claim of copossession of the property of Spaniards in Peru. Second, invoking the principle of reciprocity, they perceived no benefit in obligating their estates to this new tax. The manifesto against the new form of taxation insisted on the need for reciprocity between the king and his subjects and the respect for individual property rights.

Royal authority, in theory highly centralized in the person of the king, was in practice significantly decentralized. Royal wishes were frequently disregarded and could, at times, be violently rejected. The legitimacy of the king's demand for obedience was conditioned by the monarch's ability to produce tangible benefits for his vassals. Royal requests for money were prefaced by enumerating the benefits the king had bestowed upon his vassals, the sacrifices incurred, and the resulting need for more financial contributions to the crown. If such arguments were not accepted by the populace, as in the case of the sales tax in Peru, rejection and even revolt could be seen as a legitimate response. Phelan concurs: "The 'absolute' monarchy of the Hapsburgs was a limited government in which local property interests exercised considerable influence."[35]

Conflicting Standards Analysis

Phelan explains how the decentralized Spanish state could still generate authority as well as flexibility by using the "conflicting standards analysis" first suggested by André Gunder Frank. Phelan outlines this model as follows:

More than one hierarchical channel of communication is maintained. Multiple and, at least, in part conflicting standards are set by superiors for subordinates. Conflict may arise among standards set within each hierarchy as well as among those set by different hierarchies. Subordinates are free to decide which of the conflicting standards to meet, if any. However, subordinates are responsible to superiors for their performance with respect to all standards; and subordinates may be held responsible for failure to meet any standard. The relative importance of standards is neither well, nor completely defined, nor is it entirely undefined. The priority among standards is ambiguous. Subordinates make their assessment of priority to guide their decision making and task performance. Each subordinate appeals to those standards which are most in accord with his incentives and the circumstances of the moment and to those which are most likely to be invoked by superiors in evaluating his performance. Superiors in turn make their assessment of priority to guide their necessarily selective evaluation of subordinates' performance and enforcement of standards. The entire process is continuous: superiors modify the set of standards to comply with their changing objectives; subordinates adapt their decisions to changing standards and to changing circumstances; superiors enforce standards in accordance with the changing priority.[36]

Frank's model, as used by Phelan, explains the internal mechanisms of the Spanish bureaucratic system outlined above. Embedded within the decentralized political system were conflicting crown policies, directives, and laws, whose very incompatibility forced individuals to determine which course of action to take at the expense of others. The lack of a single clear standard of conduct strengthened authority in the sense that, as any situation could be reprioritized and all rules could be invoked at any time, subordinates were forced to be sensitive to the objectives of superiors. Phelan notes that the emphasis in this system was on the achievement of task performance regardless of the means employed.[37] Authority, or the ability to make decisions and take action, was not the product of a vertical chain of command; rather it was produced within a broad network of pressures: "orders from Spain, local conditions, the peers and subordinates of bureaucrats, public opinion, incentives and penalties— served to create a whole complex of standards which guided and conditioned the conduct of colonial officialdom."[38]

Spanish governments, then, were not centralized bureaucracies representing activist, unitary states. The crown's main function was to legitimate the outcome of economic and social struggles occurring quite autonomously at local and regional levels.[39] By fostering both autonomy and interdependence in its bureaucratic agencies, the crown fashioned a web of partial control based on mutual surveillance, competition over shared jurisdictions, and conflict. The dynamism of this system depended upon each entity's ability to operate autonomously rather than within a hierarchical chain of command. Centralized control was disrupted vertically, by the ability of subordinates to subvert the orders of superiors, and horizontally, by the existence and competition of multiple administrative hierarchies. The power of the king was contingent upon his ability to balance demands for obedience with the redistribution of wealth and benefits to the population.

Decentralization not only marked relations between the crown and its subjects but defined local social relations as well. Let us consider an example. On an October night in 1696, Josef de Robles and Sebastián de Villegas went to the extramural parish of Santa Prisca on the northern outskirts of Quito and robbed the indigenous household of don Joaquín Rodríguez and his wife, doña Lorenza Fernández. A few days later, when Josef de Robles tried to sell a *lliglla* (an indigenous woman's cloak) in the center of Quito, a group of Indians from Santa Prisca recognized it as one of the items stolen from doña Lorenza and seized him on the spot. They took him and the lliglla back to Santa Prisca, where he was given over to the indigenous governor of the parish and locked up in the parish jail. A large group of parish residents, both Spanish and indigenous, went to look at him in jail and later, after he had confessed to the robbery, several accompanied the governor when he went with the thief to his house to recuperate some of the stolen goods. As they were going back to Santa Prisca to return Robles to jail, they happened to run into an official from the Royal Audiencia. After hearing what had happened, the official told them that the thief should be put in the royal jail, where he could be tried and punished by the Audiencia. After some further discussion, the Indian officials agreed to relinquish control over Josef de Robles to the Audiencia.[40]

What is notable about the criminal case against Josef de Robles and Sebastián de Villegas—who after more investigation were found guilty of a number of petty robberies against Spaniards and indigenous persons— is the initial lack of clear authority over the criminals. Santa Prisca, despite being located outside of the city, was clearly considered a part of Quito, both through its parochial status and by the residents themselves, who stated in their declarations that they were *vecinos* (citizens) of Quito. Despite being included within Quito's jurisdiction, the parish had its own form of government, an indigenous governor, and a jail. The actions of the group of Indians who originally recognized the stolen cloak show that parish officials were seen as the most appropriate authority. Rather than call on city or Audiencia authorities, they simply seized the presumed thief and took him back to the parish, where he was jailed and questioned by the parochial governor. It was only because of a chance meeting with an official of the Audiencia that Josef de Robles was turned over to crown authorities and thus enters the historical record.

Quito, despite being the seat of crown control in the Audiencia, did not exercise absolute power even within the city's physical boundaries. This lack of control was not due to a wayward population who challenged central authorities. The group of people who ran into the crown official did not try to hide what would today be considered vigilantism. In fact, the parish of Santa Prisca was organized as a separate center of authority with its own officials and system for handling criminals. The legal jurisdiction of the parish overlapped the jurisdictions of the city of Quito and the Audiencia. This independent and interdependent status of the parish of Santa Prisca in Quito characterizes the contingent nature of power relations within Spanish American society in general.

Fabricating Continuity: Spanish Legislation and Control over Marriage

Authority was both created and constrained within a network of contested power relations. The existence of multiple hierarchies, the tension between conflicting directives, and the ability of subordinates to disrupt vertical chains of authority were reflected in the peculiar form Spaniards gave their legal system. Spanish law incorporated several competing bodies of legislation, each of whose law codes remained in force literally for centuries. There was no vertical or cumulative trend within Spanish legislation, since more recent laws did not have precedence over older legal codes. Like the conflicting directives issued by crown authorities, any law promulgated as far back as the seventh century, though contradicted by newer legislation and often never enforced in practice, could be invoked at any time.

The use of older legislation to legitimate new conceptions of proper conduct was a common phenomenon and not one specific to gender legislation. An example of the generality of this tendency is the late-eighteenth-century attempt in New Granada (Colombia) to convince the people to construct and use cemeteries instead of burying their dead in churches. Testaments during the colonial period routinely direct that the deceased person be buried in a chosen church. The tradition of burying the dead in churches had begun in Spain in the ninth century. In the thirteenth century the practice was condemned in Alfonso the Wise's *Siete Partidas*. This legislation was never enforced among the populations of Spain and Spanish America. In 1789 the Spanish Crown issued a directive to all viceroys in Spanish America mandating the construction of cemeteries and prohibiting the centuries-old practice of burial within churches. In 1791, in order to legitimate this new practice in the treatment of the dead, a crown legislator in Bogotá invoked the thirteenth-century Partidas, laws never before enforced. However, at least through the nineteenth century, researchers have found no testament in New Granada in which the person directed that his or her body be buried in a cemetery rather than in a church.[41]

Because Spanish laws remained permanently viable, Spanish legislators could cite historical reference points in order to legitimate new requirements for social behavior. The use of the seventh-century Fuero Juzgo in the late eighteenth century is an interesting phenomenon in this regard. Although never abolished, the Fuero Juzgo was no longer in use by the fourteenth century. But, after five centuries of silence, the Fuero Juzgo reemerged in the Bourbon Monarchy with new force, and leapfrogging back to this body of legislation became a popular practice. In 1788 the crown restricted the rights of the church to the inheritances of members of convents and monasteries, thereby strengthening familial rights over property, and based its decision on the Fuero Juzgo. In the king's pronouncement it is specifically noted that the restriction on the church's right to its members' inheritances was contradicted by other laws within the Fuero Juzgo itself as well as by subsequent legislation. The mandate states, however, that despite the lack of use of these laws and the lack of their observance in common practice, the seventh-century legislation remained in force and the crown claimed the right to refer to this legislation as needed.[42]

The Bourbons also called on this seventh-century body of law to reform gender relations in the eighteenth century. The *Royal Pragmatic* of 1776, promulgated in the colonies in 1778, declared that all men and women under the age of twenty-five must obtain their parents' consent to marry. During this same time the father's authority was declared absolute in important family issues such as marriage decisions. The government ministers who designed this legislation cited the practices of other Catholic nations of Europe and two minor eighteenth-century Italian canonists, as well as Spanish civil law and the Toledan councils from the early medieval era. As Patricia Seed argues:

The completed Pragmatic . . . relied on the creation of a myth of "national" tradition. It cited the Fuero Juzgo, lib.III tit.2, and without specific reference to any subsequent legislation intimated that Spanish law had always followed this early precedent, when, in fact, it had not.[43]

Because any law within almost ten centuries of jurisprudence could be reprioritized and activated through social, economic, or political necessity, late colonial use of earlier legislation is not indicative of continuity in legal thought or social practice. Gender legislation changed throughout the colonial period; the apparent stability of patriarchal gender norms across this period is a fictive tradition reinforced by later legislation. Women faced greater legal restrictions in their activities in the eighteenth century than they had earlier. Simultaneously, men's authority over women and children was strengthened through control over their children's marriage decisions.

Throughout the colonial period the marriage of children was part of a family's overall strategy to extend its influence by means of an increase in wealth and status. "Practically all marriages were strategic alliances arranged with a view to improving the partners' wealth or social position. . . . Both partners were seeking the greatest wealth and the highest lineage possible in the other party."[44] Although the economic and social status of the original family and the children's future families were linked, throughout the sixteenth and seventeenth centuries parents did not have ultimate authority over their children's marriage choices. The Council of Trent in 1545 codified the right of sons and daughters to exercise free will in marriage choice and prevented their parents from disinheriting them.[45] Parents could still, however, refuse to give children advances of their projected inheritance in the form of donations and dowries at the time of their marriage. Such decisions over donations and dowries were left up to the parents individually. A wife could donate money to a son or dower a daughter in the event of their marriage without the approval of her husband. Or if she disapproved of her child's marriage, she could refuse to advance a child's inheritance, because her private estate could not be used in donations or dowries without her voluntary and express consent.[46]

The Council of Trent decreed that church courts had exclusive jurisdiction over marriage.[47] The doctrine of free will and the sacrament of marriage had long been upheld by the church, but the council sought to codify these traditions in reaction to the Protestant Reformation. Protestant doctrine relegated marriage to the control of civil authorities and mandated parental consent for children to marry.[48] The council's decrees, in contrast, were embraced by the Spanish Crown. "Philip II sent no less than 14 *cédulas* urging prelates, *corregidores* [officials in charge of *corregimientos* (territorial subdivisions of the Audiencia districts)] and town councils to observe the decrees of Trent."[49] The decrees were not, however, accepted by Protestant countries or even in other Catholic countries. In France the king refused to receive the decrees and issued laws that mandated parental consent for marriage.[50]

The cultural specificity of Spanish legislation that governed marriage during the majority of the colonial period has been largely overshadowed by the changes that occurred in the late eighteenth century. Through the Royal Pragmatic civil authorities gained control over marriage, and parental consent was mandated for all persons under the age of twenty-five. Such legislation was largely directed at controlling daughters, as most men married after the age of twenty-five. This decree was followed in 1783 by legislation preventing wives from making donations or bequests to children who had married without their fathers' consent.[51] The exclusion of women from independent participation in the formation of family alliances reflected a dramatic shift in women's property rights. The legal reasoning that formerly permitted wives to donate freely to their children considered that such donations were advances of inheritance, and, as a husband lost all control over a woman's estate when she died, a wife had full authority to both donate and bequeath to her children. The legislation of 1783, however, extended a husband's control over a woman's estate even after her death. By 1787 the Council of the Indies ruled that the father's veto of a marriage partner was absolute; even if children accepted disinheritance, the couple could not marry.[52]

Men gained control over family alliances in the late eighteenth century. Yet the idea that marriage "constituted a form of 'exchange of women' . . . with the purpose of strengthening the bonds between men," used by Florencia Mallon for describing nineteenth-century marriages, continues to be the dominant paradigm for evaluating marriage structures for the entire colonial period.[53] The definition of marriage as a daughter's "transfer from the wardship of father or guardian to that of a husband" did not hold true for most of the colonial period.[54] When fathers did gain legal control over children's marriage choices, they did so over both sons and daughters. This reflects the fact that sons as well as daughters continued to represent their individual families even after marriage; thus all children, not just daughters, were considered instrumental in the accumulation and reproduction of a family's social, political, and economic power.

In societies that cement alliances through the exchange of women, daughters are specifically marked as a form of gift property to be bestowed by their fathers. In exchange for a daughter, her family hopes to benefit from the new relationship to the groom's family but gives up its interest in the woman, her property, and her children, which now belong to her husband's family. In such social systems males do not become gifts and cannot be bestowed, because they remain within their original family, as do their property and offspring.[55] When women circulate as tokens that mark alliances between men, marriage is a foundational act that defines male power and distinguishes that social system as patriarchal. An example of this type of marriage practice is the British legal tradition of coverture, in which a woman lost her surname at the time of marriage and took that of her husband, symbolizing, in legal terms, her "civil death."[56] At the same time, she was severed from her original family's interest in her person and property; from that point on her husband legally represented her, and their children, who also carried his surname, belonged to him.[57]

Codified in medieval England through Common Law, coverture is the full expression of a patriarchal social organization and its investment of absolute authority in men.[58] Under coverture, a woman could not convey or contract real property to or from her husband; nor could she acquire property from or dispose of it to third persons without her husband's consent.[59] A wife could not draw up a testament, as she had no property to bequeath.[60] A woman's property was owned absolutely by her husband and was held liable for her husband's debts.[61] She could not engage in trade or business, sue, or be sued, and her husband was responsible for her debts and all other wrongful or injurious acts committed by her before or after marriage.[62] If a wife survived her husband, she was only entitled to the dower (one-third of his estate) until she remarried. Normal inheritance patterns left the estate to a single heir, the eldest son.[63]

Within the legal doctrine of coverture, a woman disappeared when she married—both literally, since she was prevented from engaging in public life, and juridically, because she was replaced by her husband in any legal processes affecting her. This "civil death" of wives within British legal tradition permitted their circulation between men who used women to cement alliances. Marriage within the Spanish tradition had very different consequences for women and served other purposes in society. Husbands did not automatically represent their wives, and married women continued to exercise legal, social, and economic rights independently from their husbands. In recognition of the fact that they retained identities separate from their husbands, women did not take their husbands' surnames upon marriage and could pass their surnames on to their children. Frequently, children of the same couple were given different surnames, some the mother's, others the father's, and still others the surname of some more distant relative.[64] In general, both men and women, as their social positions rose, sought out the most prestigious names throughout their extended families. Names were therefore not fixed; changing status resulted in changing names, and some people switched back and forth, never deciding which surname they preferred.[65] The fluidity of Spanish naming patterns reflects the importance of both men and women in promoting the social and economic success of their extended families.[66]

Social cohesion in colonial Spanish society was not produced through the exchange of women; the marriages of both daughters and sons extended the influence of their original families. Children's marriages, of course, had important consequences for their families, but for most of the colonial period men were not invested with the legal power to control these matches. Both husbands and wives had the capacity to influence and sponsor their children's marriages, though ultimately the child had to enter the marriage through her or his own free will. Power relations within the family were therefore similar to those at other levels of society; the prosperity of the family depended on the power of its members acting semiautonomously within a union in which their interests both converged and remained distinct. The growing power of the father in the family during the latter part of the colonial period, in fact, coincides with changes in the structure of crown authority. The increasing investment of authority in husbands and fathers was a manifestation of a general trend toward attempts to centralize Spanish American society. By the beginning of the eighteenth century, a single body, the Council of the Indies, controlled appointments and promotions for both ecclesiastical and royal officials in Spanish America.[67]

Conclusion

The general practice by historians of women has been to situate Spanish culture within Europe's Old Regime societies. In this model all societies in

Europe had identical social structures, collectively considered traditional, whose organizing principles of political order were conceptually based on hierarchical and patriarchal relations of power. The definition of Spanish America as a traditional society greatly facilitates a certain kind of historical research that draws on generalizations from other cultures, likewise labeled traditional, to explain the specific situation of women in Spanish America. The alleged inability of traditional societies to incorporate fundamental changes into their social structure legitimates historians' use of information from better-documented later periods to interpret the experiences of people living centuries earlier.

This tendency to posit the king and the father as central figures of authority unifies women's subordination in traditional societies and thus simplifies the analysis of women's status in Spanish America. Usage of patriarchal models has also, however, complicated the work of scholars in this field because their research clearly shows that women in Spanish America legally held and actively exercised rights that are incomprehensible within this framework. Although many researchers note the discrepancy between what societies with kingly fathers allowed and what Spanish American women were actually doing, scholars still attempt to explain the status of these women as a product of a social organization shared by all traditional societies. Because it was predetermined that Spanish culture, like all other traditional societies, was hierarchically and patriarchally organized, researchers tended to subordinate their own research on women to this widely accepted model of political and social organization. The result of this practice is that in many studies, the economic and juridical participation of women in society remains a mysterious quirk that disrupts the otherwise absolute power of men. For these scholars political organization and social organization are linked.

For at least one scholar, the discrepancy between her research findings and the presumed patriarchal organization of society was too great to continue this link between gender norms and political organization. Patricia Seed recognizes the accepted view, advanced by English family historian Lawrence Stone, that "authoritarian monarchy and domestic patriarchy form a congruent and mutually supportive complex of ideas and systems." However, she reasons that this link between political and familial organization is not appropriate for Spanish society because "[t]he Hapsburg kings had functioned as authoritarian monarchs since the sixteenth century, and yet, no imitative discourse of patriarchy in the family emerged until the early eighteenth century."[68]

This book attempts to reconcile the two views of the connection between gender norms and political organization. Like the majority of works of scholarship on women in Latin America, this book argues that political theory and social organization are linked.[69] However, this work supports Seed's research, finding little evidence that the status of women examined within the framework of this study was defined through patriarchal relations. The book's contention that these nonpatriarchal gender relations were mirrored in traditional Spanish political organization is supported by a body of respected scholarship in the early Spanish American field, which finds that for most of this period social stability relied on the exercise of authority through a network of decentralized power relations.

The object of authority was not to enforce the blind obedience of subordinates but to facilitate responses to changing situations. Because power was distributed among satellites within a network, contesting authority at any one point did not rupture the overall system. The structural generation of conflict between and within hierarchies produced mutual surveillance, which encouraged the flow of information throughout the network, preventing any position of power from obtaining closure or absolute control. The conflicts between parallel entities with shared and competing interests produced the tension which held the network together; in other words, social stability was the product of continual contestations of power rippling through a web rather than obedience generated through vertical lines of authority. It is only within this system, where power was created and maintained through dispersal amongst independent entities rather than infused in a centralized entity, that Spanish American gender relations can be properly understood.

This critique of patriarchal models does not mean that such paradigms should be discarded or that scholars cannot use conclusions from other regions but that patriarchy and other general models should not become a substitution for a lack of clear evidence or convincing arguments from local material. In colonial Spanish America there appear to be at least two displacements separating us from understanding women's status. The first is found in historical scholarship that frames the source material within a pancultural and transhistorical model of patriarchy. The second is found in the historical documents themselves, such as late-colonial legislation that cites far earlier legal codes, which reflect the conscious or unconscious agenda of their authors. It is through these displacements that the apparent stability and universality of patriarchy has been created.

CHAPTER 2

Married Women and Property Rights

Marriage was a sacred union eternally uniting the bodies and souls of husbands and wives. The merging of their property, however, was a different matter. If the church brought a man and woman together, civil legislation did much to keep their estates apart. The form of Spanish marriage practiced was indeed a paradox; joined in permanent unions, wives and husbands still loaned each other money from their private estates and expected their spouses to pay them back.[1] This chapter considers the organization of property within marriage as a reflection of the relations between husbands and wives. The focus on women within the family is not because women were relegated to the domestic sphere but because it is as minors and wives that women experienced the greatest limitations on their activities. Widows and single women over the age of twenty-five, like their brothers, were considered adults and could freely administer their properties, make contracts, and litigate.[2] The family is also at the heart of patriarchal models and is described as a domain in which husbands exercised absolute authority over their wives and children. An examination of how family members controlled and used their resources, however, suggests that the mutual restrictions and obligations imposed on both men and women cannot be accounted for within a patriarchal analysis.

The Dowry in Perspective

By the seventeenth century, Spaniards had accumulated several centuries of legislation and social practice concerning the rights of women to control property. Chapter 1 suggested that Spanish society was distinctive in its guarantees of female property rights. Gender legislation in England and the American colonies, built upon the doctrine of coverture, considered women as vehicles for the transference of property rather than property holders in their own right. In Spanish tradition the rights of married women to hold property in their own name was guaranteed legally through their possession of a dowry. Perhaps the most thorough study of dowry structure and rights in Spanish America is the work of Eugene H. Korth and Della M. Flusche, who examine how Spanish dowry and inheritance legislation affected family strategy in eighteenth-century Chile.[3] Within the limited scholarship on the dowry in colonial Spanish America, however, there is still disagreement over the significance of the dowry to society, to families, and to women themselves. Some scholars, using a British model of family organization, reduce the dowry to a mechanism primarily aimed at transferring wealth between men.[4] The research of other scholars, however, suggests that women's possession of dowry property usually was respected in Spanish America.[5]

Although many researchers do acknowledge the importance of the dowry to colonial Spanish American families, most scholars have not paid sufficient attention to the wider significance of the formal rules governing the dowry or the various ways women and families used this legislation to control property. Sophisticated work in this regard has been done for Portuguese American systems of inheritance and dowry. Linda Lewin's research on Brazilian inheritance laws links changes in the transmission of property to natural and spurious children (through bequests, dowries, and gifts) to shifts in attitudes about the role of the state, family structure, parental control, and patriarchal authority.[6] The work of Muriel Nazzari demonstrates that daughters, initially shown economic favoritism over their brothers in the division of parental property, became increasingly less important in the transmission of property between families in Brazil in the nineteenth century.[7] The increasing authority of husbands over wives, children, and family property in this same period is reflected in royal attempts to centralize the Portuguese state in the mid-eighteenth century, using British models of political and social organization.[8]

The research of both Lewin and Nazzari suggests that family relations in Portugal, like Spain, diverged from the standard model of the "European Family" described in Chapter 1.[9] Their work also shows significant differences in the concept of the family and the roles of women in Portugal and Spain. Although both countries shared the Iberian tradition of partible inheritance and the practice of advancing women's inheritance through dowries at the time of marriage, in the Portuguese legal tradition wives and husbands did not possess private estates. The Portuguese family was considered a corporate group unified around a community of interests. For this reason, a woman's dowry did not belong to her but was considered a part of community property.[10] This did not necessarily decrease her authority over family resources, but, as we will see below, the Spanish tradition differed from the Portuguese in that its recognition of both individual and community property encouraged open family networks rather than closed corporate groups and gave wives legal and economic identities distinct from their husbands.

This chapter considers marriages in which wives defined their property through a dowry contract. Many women, of course, married without dowries. Poorer women often married men who were equally destitute, neither spouse claiming any property at the time of their marriage.[11] At the other extreme were women of high social status whose families had fallen into poverty. These women, like their humble sisters, did not bring property or money into their marriages but used their status to contract marriages with wealthy men who, reversing the usual process, contributed dowries to their wives.[12] Despite these variations, it was generally true that an economically stable marriage required the contributions of both husband and wife and that the amount of capital a woman could bring into a marriage greatly influenced her marriage prospects.

Not all women at the time of marriage declared their economic resources as dowry property.[13] However, only property declared in an officially notarized dowry contract was legally recognized and protected in the Spanish legal system. This was to be expected in a legalistic society, where all transactions and relationships had to be witnessed and notarized in order to be legally enforceable. Even the church, when arguing against clandestine marriages, or marriages which took place without the specified witnesses, authorizations, and notifications, declared that though such unions might be valid they could not be legally enforced, because they were unverifiable through the prescribed procedures.[14] The requirement that a woman notarize the official worth of her estate at the time of marriage in order to maintain this property separate from her husband's estate, the value of which was also declared, and from their community property was a response to the general tendency in society to formally witness and document important transactions.

It is important to acknowledge that though all women of wealth carefully noted the content and value of their property at the time of marriage, poor women also possessed notarized dowry contracts. The humble María Gómez, for example, mestizo and an illegitimate child (*hija natural*), officially declared her house on the edges of Quito as dowry property at the time of her marriage.[15] The institution of the dowry thus not only affected the lives of elite women. As some of the cases below indicate, it was also a factor in women's property rights in the middle sectors, and, as in the case of María Gómez, it could even touch women living on the brink of poverty. In addition to the broad use of dowry contracts by a wide sector of the general population, dowry legislation itself was embedded in a complex network of legal theories and social attitudes that affected all women. Spanish courts upheld female property rights regardless of women's racial or socioeconomic status.[16] This investigation of how married women's private estates were constituted, used, and preserved will therefore shed light on the possibilities and constraints governing women's lives in general.

Women's Private Estates

Castilian private law was based on Visigoth, Roman, and canonical precepts and was reformulated throughout the colonial period. The seventh-century Fuero Juzgo, mentioned in Chapter 1, was based on Visigothic law codes that were modified, expanded, and recodified as the Fuero Real in the thirteenth century. The Siete Partidas, based on Roman and canonical law, were also compiled in the thirteenth century and formulated the legal guidelines governing the bridal dowry. Both the Fuero Real and the Partidas became the basis for the Leyes de Toro, enacted in 1505. The Leyes de Toro paid special attention to the status of women in Spanish society. This body of legislation outlined women's legal powers; the dimensions of husbands' authority; and the rules governing community property, inheritance, the dowry (*dote*), and the groom's contribution to the bride (*arras*).[17]

At the beginning of the sixteenth century and through the seventeenth, Spanish women owned, bequeathed, and inherited property on their own account.[18] A married woman's private estate consisted of her dowry, the arras, and any supplementary goods or capital obtained prior to or during marriage.[19] The dowry was the foundation of a wife's estate, and though administered by her husband, it remained her private property. In addition to the wife's holding of a dowry, a groom often gave his bride a gift of capital and goods—an arras, legally limited to 10 percent of his total worth at the time of marriage.[20] A wife was free to retain for her own administration any part of her estate not explicitly incorporated into the dowry or arras. The husband's legal authority over his wife's property was not absolute. Legislation spelled out that "his function as an honest, prudent manager was to redound more to the good of wife and family than to his personal aggrandizement and profit."[21] When the marriage ended, the husband was compelled to return the value of both the dowry and the arras to his wife's estate, and his private estate was forfeited if he did not meet this obligation.[22]

Legislation concerning married women's property was included in the dowry contract itself, a witnessed and notarized document in which the content and value of the dowry and arras were indicated along with the husband's pledge to abide by the laws governing the ownership and administration of his wife's estate.[23] The purpose of the dowry was declared clearly at the beginning of the contract: "to help cover the financial responsibilities of the marriage" (para ayudar a sustentar las cargas del matrimonio). After an itemized description of the wife's property and its value was included, her husband would declare that he "promises and obligates himself to maintain them in permanence and stability . . . as dowry property and capital of . . . his legitimate wife and her heirs without obligating them through any debt, criminal action or excess on his part or in any other way." He also would pledge to return the dowry to his wife or her heirs "whenever the marriage ends, either through death, annulment, divorce or in any other way legally permitted." He then obligated his own estate to guarantee the value of his wife's property.

As is clear from this legal format—followed by all dowry contracts— women's property was not simply transferred to husbands. The dowry was defined as the wife's capital and her contribution to the economic foundation of the family she was forming. In addition, her property was clearly marked as destined for her heirs, which gave her natal family permanent interest in the financial well-being of the new household. Goody explains that the result of this dowry practice was "to draw attention away from the conjugal bond and focus it instead on the relation between the couple and the wife's kin, whose rights towards the children of the marriage are guaranteed by the dowry."[24] The dowry contract shows that the meaning of family transcended that of the household by connecting the married couple to society at large through a broad network of legal, economic, and social relations. The economic foundation of the family was a notarial act that immediately opened up the family to legal scrutiny and intervention by extended family, preventing the family from collapsing into "quasi-autonomous household units headed by men."[25]

The dowry constituted a contract between the parties to the marriage, and thus a wife could sue her husband to compel him to return her estate to her control if he did not meet the stipulated conditions—for instance, by badly administering her property.[26] Doña Margarita Méndez Carrillo did just that in 1680, suing to retrieve her dowry from her husband, Andrés Molinero.[27] On a visit to Quito, she discovered that her husband owed money to a number of people and had mortgaged her hacienda, included in her dowry. Hearing that there was to be a concourse of her husband's debtors, she contracted a lawyer to represent her. In her statement she requested that all of the property included in her dowry be returned to her because the dowry contract "predated other contracts made by her husband, as well as the intrinsic legal properties of the dowry itself which, as dowry property, in any concourse of debtors must be preferred over all other creditors for the good of the commonwealth." In addition, she insisted that she had never obligated her property as guarantor for her husband's debts and "even if she had it would have no substance because wives are excluded from such obligations, and in the case that they do obligate themselves it is presumed that it is fraudulent and against their will because the legal presumption is that husbands against their will force them and use violence to compel them into such obligations." In her demand she stated that "because neither she nor her property owes anything to anyone in the mentioned contracts and afraid of being left poor, without dowry and without the property which she gave to her husband in dowry and marriage capital, and because she is obligated to defend her property for herself and her children against her husband, she is presenting the dowry contract signed by the above-mentioned Andrés Molinero."

Marriage might indeed have been a sacred union, but in terms of doña Margarita's financial relationship with her husband she made clear that she was his legally preferred creditor. Her dowry, as a signed contractual agreement, obligated her husband to preserve her estate. By causing her property to be indebted without her consent, he had broken the terms of their contract and violated the law. Under these circumstances she was obligated, as a responsible woman, to take legal action against her husband, not only for her benefit and that of her children but also, she claims, as a service to the commonwealth. For the good of society, or social stability, neither wives nor their property could be subjected to the absolute control of husbands. Wives continued to possess their property throughout their marriage and, since they were ultimately responsible for the preservation of their estates and their own economic well-being, they were legally empowered to litigate in their own names, even against their husbands. The legal presumption was that husbands would attempt to exercise authority over their wives' economic decisions. However, rather than being viewed as legitimate and an element of social order, this authority was seen as a disruptive force and a violation of the free will of wives; contracts in which the latter agreed to use their private estates to guarantee the debts of their husbands were invalidated.

The institution of the dowry was not just a legal fiction used to transfer funds through women to men. The possession of a dowry officially established the wife's ownership of her estate, obligated her husband's estate in favor of her property, and gave her the ability to legally defend herself and her property against her husband and his creditors. In fact, wives' property not officially declared within a dowry contract bore a greater risk of being subject to husbands' depredations. This was the unfortunate case with doña Francisca Tello, widow of Diego Jirón de la Chica, who tried to reclaim her property in 1672.[28] Diego pawned doña Francisca's property and then after eight years of marriage abandoned her and their three children. He died two years later.

The problem for doña Francisca was that though she claimed this property as her dowry, it was not officially registered in a dowry contract. She had married against the will of her parents, and as a result they had refused to dower her. When she left her parents' house, she took with her a chest of clothing and jewelry, the property her husband later pawned for 300 pesos. Doña Francisca presented her father's will, drawn up in 1671, as evidence that she had left the house with this property. Although she had married against the wishes of her parents, doña Francisca was not disinherited. In his will her father declared that she had left with goods totaling 1,000 pesos in value and stated that this sum should be deducted from her inheritance. The dowry was also computed as an advance on a woman's inheritance, and the dowries of her sisters and the donation given her brother when he joined a religious order were also deducted from their inheritances.[29] However, even though doña Francisca was able to document possession of this property at the time of her marriage, and though this property was being treated by her father in the same way as dowry property, her possessions were never contractually defined as her dowry. Since she was unable to present a dowry contract, neither her husband, his estate, nor his creditors were obligated to reimburse doña Francisca for the value of her property. After the court denied her demand, the best her attorney could do for her was to convince her husband's creditor to sell her property in order to pay the 300-peso debt and to give any excess proceeds from the sale to doña Francisca.

The possession of a dowry gave wives specific legal rights to defend their property. In 1682 doña Catalina Ponce Castillejo, widow of Juan de Salamanca, used the sanctity of her dowry to criminally prosecute Captain Pedro de la Vega Crespillo.[30] Her husband had died in prison and in manacles for the debts he owed to the captain. To recuperate this debt the captain seized cattle from Juan's estate, defining this action as a legal confiscation of property. Doña Catalina, however, claimed the cattle as owed to her dowry and defined the captain's seizure as theft. The courts agreed with her, and Captain Pedro de la Vega was jailed and ordered to pay a fine to the courts and return her cattle. What is noteworthy in this case is that Juan died in prison for debts despite the fact that he and his wife owned several parcels of land, houses, and hundreds of heads of cattle and sheep. He was obviously unable to use this property to pay off his debts and free himself, because, as his wife was able to successfully claim after his death, the property belonged to her dowry. Neither Juan nor his creditors could claim doña Catalina's property without her consent, and she apparently was unwilling to cede her private estate, even when her husband was languishing imprisoned and in chains.

The calculated use by wives of their dowries to the apparent detriment of their husbands is forcefully demonstrated in the demand of marriage annulment by doña María del Pino Argote.[31] One September morning in 1700, after over twenty years of marriage to don Josef Caballero, doña María placed a demand for annulment in the ecclesiastic courts, left her husband, and, with their two daughters, entered a convent. She also took the important action of legally confiscating all of his property in order to collect her dowry, which she claimed he had squandered. When don Josef sued to have his daughters returned to his custody, doña María responded that he was incapable of raising their children because, as she had seized everything, he didn't even have a house in which to live nor the hacienda with which to support them. His next strategy was to ask the court to accept his pledge of a financial guarantee in order to recuperate his right to administer the confiscated properties, but this was also rejected. Desperate because of his lack of success in the ecclesiastical court, don Josef demanded the return of his children and the administration of the hacienda in the royal courts. Doña María's lawyer was quick to respond that such maneuvers were invalid, since the same case could not simultaneously be tried in two different courts. Because the principal suit was marriage annulment, the ecclesiastical court had precedence over the civil court, and as child custody and the possession of the dowry were secondary cases arising from the demand for annulment, the ecclesiastical court also had jurisdiction over these cases. The Audiencia agreed with doña María, and our record of the case stops here; apparently, it continued in the ecclesiastical court.

It is not clear on what grounds doña María sued her husband for annulment, nor how the suit terminated. It is hard not to be impressed, however, by the surprise nature of her attack, which left her husband lamenting his "consternation in seeing myself in one instant deprived of wife, daughters and hacienda." Crucial to her strategy was her control over her dowry. By reclaiming her dowry, doña María removed from her husband's control funds that he could have used in his legal defense. She also thwarted his attempt to regain custody of their daughters by legally barring him from their house in the city and the hacienda in the countryside. Lacking a home and a means of support, his claims of child custody were significantly weakened. In addition, because she did have access to her dowry, she was able to support herself and her daughters within the convent. She also could afford to hire a skilled attorney, who was able to invalidate don Josef's demand for child custody in the Audiencia on technical grounds and force the suit back into the ecclesiastical court, the venue apparently preferred by doña María.

The suit between doña María and her husband demonstrates that possessing a dowry gave wives an economic independence that could be used as a legal strategy in itself. In the child custody case between them, don Josef claimed the *patria potestad* solely on the basis of being the legitimate father. Quoting from the Partidas, he argued that as the father he had the right to pawn his children in economic necessity and even to kill and eat them if hunger were driving him to the point of surrendering a castle that he was guarding for a lord or prince. Doña María, in her turn, instead of defining parenting as a gendered right, insisted that parents have duties in raising children and that it is the capacity to fulfill these parental obligations which must determine child custody. Foremost, she argued, is the economic capacity to raise and educate children in the best possible circumstances. Her attorney wrote:

[T]he laws expressly dispose that children should be raised and educated with the spouse that has better possibilities than the other even if that spouse were the one who was at fault in causing the divorce [in any case, she claims that her husband is the guilty party], and it is verified that the mentioned don Josef Caballero has neither a house nor the possibility of feeding their daughters because the wealth that he has administered and dissipated belongs to my client, and the land in Cusubamba which he was able to enjoy is confiscated and deposited by demand of my client for the detriment that he has caused her.[32]

Doña María redefined parenting as an economic responsibility. Her possession of a dowry and the disposition of authorities to enforce her rights to control her private estate became a legal tool with which she fought for the custody of her daughters.

The dowry gave wives a certain economic independence from their husbands as well as legal authority, but the dowry should not be seen only as a weapon that wives could potentially use against their mates. In addition, and perhaps more commonly, the wife's dowry was an integral element in a family's economic strategy. As a wife's property was legally separate from her husband's, it could not be seized by his creditors; nor could authorities claim her private estate or her half of community property as compensation for crimes committed by her husband.[33] The protected nature of a wife's property acted as economic insurance for the family and gave her husband a mutual interest in preserving the value of her private estate and in keeping her capital apart from his estate. The desire for a sound economic base for the family superseded the husband's individual interest in increasing his own private estate.

Laws prohibiting dowry property from being seized in the event of a husband's debts or criminal prosecution served doña María Gutiérrez Flores and her husband, don Juan de Villacreses, when an order for his arrest was issued in 1692.[34] A group of men, the Laras brothers, had kidnapped a young girl and, though arrested several times, always managed to escape. In their last escape, from the town of Ambato, don Juan was one of the men held responsible because he had pledged a financial guarantee for the guards, and he was ordered arrested and his property confiscated. Don Juan fled to a monastery; doña María hired a lawyer. She presented her dowry contract and sued to have the property returned as hers, which in fact it was.

The advantages of sheltering a part of the family's income from creditors and government confiscation encouraged some families to artificially inflate the wife's estate by increasing the value of her dowry. At the time of marriage, a husband would claim that his wife had brought with her more money than she actually had, sometimes even more than the entire worth of the couple, in order to safeguard the family income. Although such practices are normally hard to document, the situation of Juan de Rueda and his first wife, Gabriela de Salazar, provides us with an example of dowry inflation.[35] Writing his will in Quito in 1651, Juan de Rueda stated that at the time of their marriage neither party had any goods; he then admitted to forging a false dowry of over 1,000 pesos sometime after marrying his wife. He was counseled to do this by some friends, he said, because he was being threatened with a seizure of his property for a debt he owed on a piece of land he had bought from Captain don Cristóbal Núñez de Bonilla. At the time of writing his will, Juan de Rueda had become a successful silversmith, and the threatened piece of land shows up in his list of belongings, so the tactic was apparently successful.

Lockhart describes false dowries as a standard practice of Spanish Peruvian society during the conquest period; a specific example that he gives concerns an *encomendero* (recipient of a grant of labor and tribute from a specific indigenous community).[36] The case of Juan de Rueda and Gabriela de Salazar demonstrates that the manipulation of the dowry was a strategy known to lower social strata as well. Juan was an illegitimate child (*hijo natural*) with no capital at the time of his marriage, and Gabriela, in addition to having no property of her own, also lacked the title *doña*, which by this time even women of minimal social status often carried.[37] The fact that Juan was counseled by friends to falsify a dowry indicates that this practice was at least reasonably common. Finally, Juan and Gabriela's situation demonstrates that at a point of economic crisis in their family, it was Gabriela's supposed private estate which protected the family from foreclosure. One last note is that despite Gabriela's lack of wealth at the time of their marriage, Juan stated that all of the family's property, including the house in which he was then living, was the product of both their labor, thus showing that, at least in his mind, the success of their family had been the result of mutual effort.

The belief of men and women that the family's prosperity depended on their joint labor was codified in legislation concerning community property. In addition to the husband's and wife's private estates, they also shared community property, all property acquired jointly during the marriage.[38] When the marriage ended, usually at death, their joint property was divided equally between their separate estates. Husbands and wives bequeathed their estates separately to their children; the same legal guidelines for testaments applied to both. In the normal situation all legitimate children, regardless of their sex, inherited equally from both their parents.[39] If no children were living, the law mandated that the estates be divided between grandchildren, parents, the surviving spouse, or, in some cases, illegitimate children.

A wife's private estate, notarized in a dowry contract, was an important asset for the woman and her family in a time of legal or financial crisis. Wives retained their estates throughout their marriage, were entitled to half of the community property in recognition of their contributions to their family, and bequeathed their property to their heirs separately from their husbands. Wives sued husbands, creditors, and the state itself to recuperate their estates, and the legal and justice systems supported wives' demands by issuing judgments in their favor, returning confiscated property, and arresting creditors who seized wives' property. Spanish legislation, the constitution of the dowry contract, and the actual use of the dowry by wives and their husbands demonstrate that though husbands might administer wives' estates, their control over this property was at all times limited and by law could be completely negated.

A License of Her Own

The focus, until now, has been on wives' estates as static property, property which had to be preserved and whose major effect was as a protected stable entity which could be recuperated in a time of crisis. But wives also actively invested their properties in the economy, despite the legal restrictions on wives' economic and juridical activities, which seem, at first sight, quite daunting. Legally, a wife needed the license of her husband to make contracts or engage in or defend herself in lawsuits.[40] This legislation seems to have granted husbands the authority to determine their wives' economic and legal pursuits. Such a requirement that wives seek their husbands' approval before investing their properties or litigating in their own name would create vertical relationships between husbands and wives and centralize decision making in the husband.

This establishment of patriarchal authority within the family is more apparent than real, however. Like the structure of the state, vertical lines of authority within the family were disrupted by institutional mechanisms that enabled wives to limit and circumvent husbands' authority. As noted in Chapter 1, though a crown directive might seem imposing and absolute, in fact it was almost certainly contradicted by other directives. In addition, all directives passed through a network of authority, which could modify their content and impede their implementation. In a similar manner, the ability of husbands to restrict wives' economic and juridical activities was modified and contradicted by other laws. The objective of Spanish legislation that defined the status of married women was not to guarantee the patriarchal authority of husbands but to preserve and increase wives' estates. The power of the husband legally was sacrificed to the integrity of his wife's property. Spanish legislation held women ultimately responsible for their property by legally enabling wives to remove their private estates from their husbands' management, as discussed above, and to engage independently in economic and juridical activities.

There were a number of ways a wife could take part in economic transactions without resorting to suing her husband for the return of her dowry. She could receive a general license from her husband or the courts in order to represent herself.[41] Such powers of attorney between husbands and wives appear frequently in notarial documents and follow the same legal format as powers of attorney between any two parties. A general license to a wife gave her the power to represent herself legally and manage her property economically.[42] But many men gave their wives power to represent their husbands in legal and economic affairs as well. Juan Bautista Ramírez, for example, not only gave his wife, doña Teresa de Aldanaz, full power to contract and litigate on her own account but also gave her license to obligate his personal estate for the sizable sum of 4,000 pesos.[43]

If a married woman engaged in economic or legal activities without a license from her husband, there were legal ways to legitimate such actions. She could receive a retroactive license from her husband ratifying what she had already done.[44] If a husband refused to give his wife a license, the courts could compel him through fines or imprisonment, and if this were not sufficient the judge alone could grant the woman a license.[45] In an even more direct statement of the preeminence of women's property over male authority, legal scholars of the period agreed that any action a wife took which was ultimately beneficial to her estate was automatically validated.[46] The legal justification for legitimizing wives' successful business transactions was similar to the presumption behind the "I obey but do not execute" clause used to impede crown directives. Just as the mandate "the king can will no wrong" was used to justify independent actions of officials, in the case of wives and their property the assumption was that the husband could will no financial disadvantage in regard to his wife's property, thus justifying wives' independent economic initiatives.

The intent of Spanish legislation was to safeguard wives' property rather than to preserve male authority within the family. A married woman could engage in economic activities that were beneficial to her estate. In cases where the economic advantage was perhaps more dubious, a wife could simply have a third person guarantee her transaction. This occurred between doña Jacoba de Moreta, a married woman, and her mother, doña Francisca de Moreta, a widow.[47] Doña Jacoba's son, the priest Alonso de Moreta, was attempting to sell property that had been traditionally held within the family. Under Spanish law, family members had first rights over inherited property, and doña Jacoba was exercising this privilege by preventing the sale her son had arranged with another person by buying the piece of land herself.[48] Lacking a license from her husband, doña Jacoba's transaction was still legally valid because her property was guaranteed by a person with no impediments to her ability to contract debts: her widowed mother. This example also demonstrates another form of limitation on a husband's authority within the family, by showing the continued interest and intervention that a wife's original family exercised in her affairs.

The constant concern in Spanish legislation for maintaining separate men's and women's estates within marriage is clearly shown when husbands and wives undertook joint economic ventures. Legally, a wife could not act as a guarantor for her husband's business transactions unless it could be shown, as in the case of her contracts with others, that the financial transaction was beneficial to her estate. In addition, it was specified that to be considered advantageous to the wife, the outcome of the business relationship with her husband could not simply be her physical maintenance, since he was obligated in any event to give her food, clothing, and other necessary things.[49]

The law concerning the ability of wives to act as their husbands' guarantors inspired great legal scrutiny in the sixteenth century. There were questions about the validity of contracts between wives and husbands, and it was decided that financial agreements between a married couple were only valid to the extent that they partook of the general rule governing a wife's ability to contract: that the economic transaction had to be financially advantageous, specifically to her estate.[50] It was also argued that the consent of her husband was insufficient to legitimate financial transactions that were injurious to the wife. In addition, it was considered inadvisable for wives to jointly contract with husbands, because of the pressure a husband might exercise on his wife to obligate herself in unjustifiable business transactions.[51] What is notable about the legal commentary of the time is that no jurist legitimated economic partnerships between married couples on the authority of the husband over his wife or her property. What determined the validity of their economic dealings with each other was the perceived utility of the arrangement to the wife, rather than the authority of the husband, which, on the one hand, was considered insufficient to overcome the legal mandate to avoid contracts which were to her disadvantage and, on the other, an influence that could unjustly convince her to engage herself in nonlucrative business activities.

A husband's ability to use his wife's private estate was not automatic; by law it had to be negotiated with his wife in a notarized and witnessed contract in which she agreed to renounce the legal protections of her property.[52] An example of such an agreement is the contract between Juan Cristóbal de Arce and his wife, doña Josefa Zambrano de Rivera, in Quito, 1656.[53] Their agreement follows the standard formula for legalizing husbands' and wives' joint economic activities. In order to acquire more liquid capital, Juan Cristóbal wanted to put a *censo* (lien) on a piece of property. This property belonged to his wife, however, as part of her dowry, and thus he needed her permission to use her estate.

In the first step of their contract, doña Josefa asked her husband for a license, which he granted and she accepted. They then both pledged that they were "acting together, with the voice of one, and each on his/her own account" (ambos, a dos de mancomun, y a bos de uno, y cada qual de ellos de por si). After a description of the land parcel and the conditions of the censo, they both declared that they guaranteed the arrangement with their respective property. At this point, doña Josefa renounced a series of rights protecting women, beginning with a general renouncement of the laws prohibiting women from acting as guarantors to their husbands ("leyes de la mancomunidad") as well as other laws pertaining to women ("las de las mas mujeres"). Her husband also had to renounce specific laws and rights which could protect him from honoring the debt.[54]

In addition to general renunciations, doña Josefa renounced specific laws in her favor whose content had to be legally explained to her.

The aforementioned doña Josefa Zambrano renounced the Law of the Jurisconsult Senate of Veleyano which was approved by the Emperor Justinian, the Laws of Toro and the Partidas of Madrid, which are in favor of women, whose content I the notary explained to her, and understanding the laws she renounced their protection, and because she is married she promised in the name of God and the Cross to have signed this contract and not to proceed against it to recuperate her dowry or arras or other rights, nor to allege that she was forced by her husband or any other person and declares that she enters into this contract of her own free will because it is to her useful and beneficial.[55]

To legalize this series of renunciations by each spouse, both signed the document. Because doña Josefa was unable to sign her name, a witness signed for her. Doña Josefa and her husband were then joined together as principals for acquiring a censo, and the rest of the document repeatedly refers back to each of them individually in outlining their rights and obligations within the contract.

This typical contract between husband and wife reflects a relationship quite different from the patriarchal model. It was not sufficient that the husband grant a license; the wife had to specifically accept it. It is clear, moreover, that the husband did not legally represent his wife. The ability to "act as one" was a specific contractual arrangement, not an automatic imposition acquired through marriage. The act of contractually joining together did not erase their separate juridical identities. Both of them had to obligate themselves individually as well as together, and each had to personally sign the contract. This process recognizes an organization of family property which included both individual and communal estates. It is notable that even though doña Josefa was unable to sign, her husband could not sign in her name; instead, a third person signed for her. In this contract doña Josefa did not cede to her husband her property or her power to represent herself; instead, she became his business partner.

Both doña Josefa and her husband renounced the protection of a series of laws which could protect each of them within a business negotiation. Their guarantor in this contract, doña Josefa's brother-in-law, also had to renounce the same laws as his brother, Juan Cristóbal de Arce, laws which could have limited his financial responsibility in this transaction. Protective laws were in fact an intrinsic part of Spanish legislation, a type of specialized justice to compensate for the accepted inequalities in Spanish society. It is wrong, therefore, to view legislation that protects women's property as designed specifically to limit married women's juridical and economic participation in society. As we have seen, the men signing this contract also had to renounce laws which served to protect their property in economic transactions. Protective gender legislation was only one example of a whole spectrum of laws designed to protect different groups in society. Juridical powers, obligations, and rights were all influenced by age, race, religion, occupation, and social status. Gender and marital status were simply additional factors in defining a person's legal options. Significantly, individuals, including women, were often given the power to renounce protective laws and the limitations such laws placed on their activities.

Several conditions had to be met for doña Josefa's renunciation to be valid. First, she had to have full knowledge of the content of the legislation in her favor. For this reason, the notary was obliged to explain the specific laws to her. Second, her participation had to be of her own free will, specifically emphasizing that she was not being forced by her husband. Third, the only given reason for entering into this contract was that it was to her financial benefit. Such criteria demonstrate that married women were expected to make decisions based on their knowledge of their general situation; the laws affecting women as a group, as well as their individual situation; the value of their property; and the nature of the specific business transaction in which they engaged. Accordingly, a wife was expected to use personal judgment in evaluating her options before deciding what action to take, a far different process than simply obeying the orders of her husband. In fact, an admission that she had been pressured by her husband would have legally invalidated their business contract.

Representing Women

In economic transactions affecting wives' property, husbands were not legally conceded the right to represent their wives' interests unless wives gave their informed consent for their property to be financially managed by their husbands. In the above cases, all wives represented themselves in litigation concerning the preservation and recuperation of their estates. In order for a husband to represent his wife in legal actions that involved her estate, she first had to grant him a license to act in her name. An example is the case of Magdalena de Ribas, who in 1625 granted a license to her second husband to represent her in a suit to recuperate the value of her dowry from her first husband's estate.[56] The argument that a wife could manage her property, either alone or in conjunction with her husband, only in transactions that were directly beneficial to her also justified wives' right to self-representation within the legal system. A wife could defend herself in court without license from her husband for the same reason that her own defense could only be to her benefit.[57] As we shall see in the following chapter, married women were specifically permitted to litigate against their husbands in cases of physical abuse, abandonment, and adultery. Legislation recognized that a wife's interests could significantly diverge from her husband's. The husband's ability to represent his wife was thus limited, and in many important situations he required the specific consent of his wife to act in her name.

Conclusion

This examination of control over material resources in the family demonstrates that a husband did not exercise absolute authority over his wife or her property. Legislation which could have potentially centered familial power in husbands was instead embedded within a broader network of laws and social practices that worked to check the consolidation of husbands' authority within the family. By focusing on a restricted set of laws, instead of the wider legal and social context in which they were used, researchers have fashioned potential patriarchy into a social reality, despite the evidence that social practices during most of the colonial period do not seem to have involved attempts at any level of society to centralize control.

Family property was divided into the husband's and wife's separate estates. This distinction between men's and women's property was not only respected at the time the marriage ended, when a final division of all assets was made, but was meaningful during the marriage as well. Although a husband could legally manage his wife's estate, he was limited in its use and could not treat it as his property. Through the possession of a notarized dowry contract, a wife became her husband's creditor, and he and his estate were legally obligated for the amount of her estate. Many wives lost their dowries due to their husbands' mismanagement, but wives were supported in the legal system when they defended their dowries against husbands, creditors, and the state.

Wives legally needed a license from their husbands to engage in economic transactions or litigate. However, even more crucial for the validation of a wife's economic contracts was the requirement that the transaction be of specific benefit to her. A husband's license was not sufficient to legitimate economically injurious negotiations; nor did lack of a license necessarily invalidate economic contracts made by wives. Contracts between a wife and husband jointly investing their properties were subject to the same requirements as her contracts with others: the transaction had to be to her benefit, she had to enter the agreement of her own free will, and she had to renounce protective legislation, whose content had to be explained to her. A husband could not use his authority to force his wife to invest or alienate her property; any coercion on his part would have legally invalidated the contract.

Looking at property rights within the family shows that men did not automatically represent their wives on the basis of their marriage. Wives continued to have juridical identities separate from their husbands. In order to act in the name of his wife, a husband had to have her notarized license granting him this right for a specific economic or legal transaction. A wife was also empowered to represent her husband on the basis of his license. That a husband would permit his wife to act on his behalf shows not only that he thought her personally competent but also that he believed that her efficiency in maneuvering the legal system would not be compromised by her gender. The maintenance of separate identities by husbands and wives does not, of course, signify their equality. Mirroring the larger society, relations within the family were not based on equality, but neither was power rigidly centered in the person of the husband. The stability and prosperity of the family required that both spouses exercise authority individually as well as together.

CHAPTER 3

Women and the Criminal Justice System

In 1662 Maestro Francisco de la Vega, priest in charge of the parish of San Marcos in Quito, testified that he was well aware of the illicit relationship between the married Antonio Carrillo and María de Castillo. Antonio's wife, Agustina de la Vega (not a family relative of the priest), frequently complained to him that her husband physically mistreated her, stole her property, and abandoned her to live with María de Castillo, a woman held in ill repute by most of the parishioners. After patiently listening to Agustina "ten or twelve times," he gave her a recommendation that might seem surprising coming from a priest. He did not encourage her to change her husband's behavior by setting a saintly example herself in the virtues of silent suffering, obedience, and patience. Instead, he advised her to sue her husband. Maestro Francisco counseled the aggrieved wife to go to the civil authorities because, he said, it was the royal justices who knew how to resolve Agustina's problems with her husband.[1]

Agustina took the priest's advice and brought before the royal authorities criminal charges against her husband for physically mistreating her and committing adultery. We too would be wise to heed the priest's counsel and move beyond the traditional view of the church as the main instrument of social intervention into the otherwise private realm of women's and men's intimate relations. Although scholars, such as Asunción Lavrin, recognize that both the state and the church had overlapping interests in regulating sexuality and marriage in colonial Spanish America, research on men's and women's intimate relations has relied primarily on church sources. Historians generally consider the state's involvement in men's and women's relations as limited to practical issues, primarily the enforcement of inheritance law. The church, however, because of its monopoly over the formation of legitimate marriages and its definition of marriage as a sacrament that affected the salvation of individuals' souls, has been seen as the primary arbitrator in intimate conflicts between men and women.[2]

Research using ecclesiastic sources, although it has illuminated the dar-ing and resourceful tactics women used to confront men's abuse, has reinforced the notion that society tolerated men's abusive treatment of women. Researchers have interpreted women's use of illicit means to resist abusive men, such as women's abandonment of marriages or their practice of witchcraft, as evidence that society denied women legitimate avenues for redressing their grievances with men.[3] By minimizing the state's role as an arbitrator in men's and women's relations, however, scholars have neglected an important alternative for women confronting physical abuse, adultery, and neglect: the criminal justice system. This chapter will examine how women used the criminal justice system to protect themselves and family members from violent and abusive treatment by men. The results put into question the belief that society accepted a sexual double standard for women and men and tolerated men's physical aggression against female family members. The last chapter discussed how women were legally empowered and socially expected to protect their property rights. These same institutions, social structures, and expectations allowed women to take action against violent and disloyal men.

Limitations of the Ecclesiastical Court System

The church held exclusive jurisdiction over the constitution and dissolution of marriages in colonial Spanish America. Chapter 1 discussed how the church could be quite liberal, and even socially progressive in a modern sense, in its firm support for free will in marriage choices. The church condoned, and even at times facilitated, the marriages of children who lacked parental authorization. Once a marriage had taken place, however, whether through the free will of the parties or through coercion, the church considered the union permanent until the death of one of the spouses. Only in very rare cases did it grant divorces or annulments. Divorce was conceived of as a separation of the spouses and their property, but the marriage was still considered valid in that neither person could remarry. An annulment cancelled the marriage and left both individuals free to marry. Marital continuity rather than marital bliss was the overriding concern of the church. Because of its emphasis on the permanence of marriage, the church was largely uninterested in establishing firm criteria for the conduct of spouses. Clearer regulations would have made things easier for individuals seeking separation, allowing them to sue their partners for failure to meet authorized standards of conduct. As it was, although the church did adopt egalitarian guidelines for the behavior of husbands and wives, these guidelines remained poorly defined, and the judgments by ecclesiastical courts were often contradictory.

In a foundational statement concerning the definition of marriage by Alfonso the Wise in the thirteenth century, both men and women were exhorted to live permanently and faithfully together, neither one to engage in carnal relations with another person.[4] The expectation that women and men had an equal commitment to each other was also mirrored in the fact that the official causes recognized by the church for which a divorce or annulment could be granted pertained to both wives and husbands. Divorce could be granted if one of the spouses committed adultery, was cruel, or physically mistreated or threatened to kill the other; if one of the spouses attempted to convince the other to commit crimes; if one committed "spiritual fornication" by engaging in heretical or pagan acts; if one contracted an incurable and contagious disease or suffered from insanity; or if one of the parties was infertile. Another acceptable reason for divorce was one of the spouse's entrance into a religious order, after having obtained the license of the other spouse. An annulment was granted only on the basis of an impediment that was hidden at the time of marriage, such as a prior marriage of one of the parties, or if the two individuals were prohibited from marrying because of a spiritual or blood relationship. Annulment could also be granted if one of the parties had taken a vow of chastity before the marriage, if the marriage had never been consummated, or if the proper procedures for the marriage had not been followed, for instance, if one of the partners had entered the marriage under force.[5]

Following these guidelines, it would seem that the church's expectations for conjugal life were egalitarian, demanding faithfulness and collaboration from both spouses, and that the ecclesiastical courts recognized a number of causes for legal separations. Especially for women, however, there remained numerous ambiguities. In the case of adultery, for example, though both spouses were prohibited from committing adultery, a wife's adulterous relationship was considered a far more serious offense than her husband's. This difference in the perception of wives' and husbands' adulterous activities was based, interestingly enough, on property rights. In the last chapter we saw how legislative practice limited husbands' liberty to administer family property, because of society's greater interest in preserving and increasing wives' property. Similarly, society also constrained wives' activities in order to protect her husband's and the family's estates. Because all children to whom a married woman gave birth were considered legitimate, sharing equal inheritance rights to both parents' private estates as well as to their community property, should a wife give birth to another man's child, that child gained illicit rights to property. If a husband should engender a child by another woman, no such confusion existed; that child legally had no claims to the legitimate wife's property and thus did not affect the preservation of family property.[6]

Other than adultery, the most common complaint of wives was domestic violence, and here too the church's position was weak. Although the church ostensibly discouraged domestic violence, in divorce cases it is clear that the church often recognized a husband's right to legitimately punish his wife in order to change her behavior. There was no actual legislation that allowed husbands to physically punish their wives, but domestic abuse was usually considered by ecclesiastical courts an insufficient cause for obtaining a separation. In Natalia León's study of divorce in Cuenca, Ecuador, for example, of the twenty-four divorce cases encountered for the period of 1750 to 1800, twenty-one of the demands for divorce were by wives, and in twenty of those cases the women cited domestic violence as their central argument. The ecclesiastical court granted only two divorces during this period, and in neither of the judgments was the wife's mistreatment cited as a factor.[7]

León's study demonstrates other factors that are important when considering the effectiveness of the church in regulating conjugal relations: divorce cases were exceedingly rare, and usually wives initiated the demands but lost. Arrom's study of divorce in Mexico City shows the same pattern. Between 1790 and 1856 Arrom encountered seventy divorce suits; of these cases sixty-three of the demands were brought by wives. In the wives' suits, sixty-two accused their husbands of cruelty, and fifty-seven claimed actual physical abuse by their spouses. The success rate in the ecclesiastical courts was low; in only 12 percent of the total number of demands was a divorce granted.[8] Throughout the colonial period, divorce was difficult to obtain, despite the church's official recognition of just causes for legally separating married couples.

The case of doña Rafaela Núñez de Valladolid, in the Quito District, exemplifies the difficulties wives faced in the ecclesiastical courts, even when they had ample evidence that officially recognized causes for divorce existed.[9] Doña Rafaela was the youngest of three sisters; her mother had died when she was quite young, and her father never remarried. Her sisters had already married, and she, having expressed a desire to live a life of chastity and religious devotion, had spent much of her life in the convent in Ibarra. On an outing to the family's hacienda, she was raped by her brother-in-law, an event that traumatized her and increased her determination not to marry but live her life as a lay sister in the convent.

Her desires for a quiet life in the convent, however, were destroyed when her sister, the wife of the rapist, who herself had taken refuge in the same convent because of physical mistreatment by her husband, was approached by two nuns who wanted to arrange a marriage between their nephew and doña Rafaela. This sister summoned the third sister to the convent and told her of the proposition of marriage for doña Rafaela; she in turn went home and presented the offer to their father. Their father favored the marriage because, as he later testified, he lacked the financial means to keep doña Rafaela in the convent. Doña Rafaela, however, rejected the offer and insisted that she never wanted to marry but desired to remain where she was. Several witnesses, including her father and sisters, testified that the family began a campaign of intimidation, threats, and violence to force doña Rafaela to accept the marriage. Her father threw her down the stairs and threatened to kill her if she didn't accede. When the intended groom heard of her rejection of his proposal, he withdrew the offer of marriage and claimed that he too desired a religious vocation.

At this point, it looked like the situation was playing out well for doña Rafaela. Then came the first kidnapping. Her father, claiming insult because of the withdrawn marriage proposal, rounded up the sisters, their husbands, and several domestic employees; kidnapped both doña Rafaela and the groom in the middle of the night; took them to a priest; and forced them to marry. The ceremony lacked the procedures prescribed by the church for legitimate marriages. No proclamations of the intended marriage had been read in the church in the preceding weeks, neither of the two potential spouses was interrogated by the priest in private to ensure that they were marrying of their free will, and no notary was present. After the ceremony, the two were locked in a room in a sister's house for the night. Both doña Rafaela and her then-unwilling husband claimed that the marriage was never consummated. As he later testified, she told him that she was not a virgin because she had been raped by her brother-in-law, and for this reason, and what he claimed was his desire to become a priest, he desisted in his attempts to consummate the marriage.

The two then went their separate ways; she returned to the convent, and again it looked like she might be able to enjoy a peaceful existence. Then came the second kidnapping. Her husband publicly defamed her by claiming that she was not a virgin at the time of marriage, because she was involved in an illicit affair, and he threatened to sue for annulment and divorce. Then he apparently changed his mind and wrote a letter to doña Rafaela's brother-in-law, claiming that he loved her and wanted to live with her as her husband. A plot was devised to get doña Rafaela out of the convent: a niece went to visit her and, claiming that another niece was ill, convinced her to come with her to care for the sick child. When she arrived at her father's house, she was kidnapped by a group of men, who also seized all her possessions. The men took her to Quito and locked her in a house with her husband. After a few weeks in captivity, she escaped through an open window, leaving behind her things, and made her way back to Ibarra and the convent.

Doña Rafaela sued for annulment and divorce. The ecclesiastical court ordered her husband to pay for her expenses in the convent during the court proceedings. He did not comply and instead began to sell the things she had left in Quito. Many witnesses claimed that, in fact, his intention to acquire her property was the sole motivation behind the kidnapping. Meanwhile, his aunts in the convent were tormenting her with verbal abuse and deprivation of food. The court ordered the women to stop harassing her. Doña Rafaela was in a precarious situation. She lacked financial support and was suffering in the convent. She was isolated and forbidden from communicating with family members. Despite testimonies by her father, sisters, neighbors, domestic employees, and even her husband himself, verifying her early vow of chastity, her desire for a religious vocation, the use of threats and physical force to compel her to accept the marriage, the procedural irregularities of the ceremony, and the acknowledgement by both of the partners that the marriage had never been consummated, the case was still under dispute nearly a year and a half later.

Although doña Rafaela's demand united all the major causes officially recognized by the church as invalidating a marriage, the initial judgment by the bishop's lieutenant in reviewing the merits of the case recommended that she be forced to leave the convent and live with her legal husband. The suit was allowed to continue over the lieutenant's objections, but it is not clear that the case was ever resolved. Her husband seems never to have responded to the demand for divorce and was cited with *rebeldía* (failure to appear in court). Doña Rafaela's side of the case was considered complete, and the last information about this case is her lawyer's request that the final judgment be issued on the basis of the information and testimonies compiled on her behalf.

Doña Rafaela's story exemplifies many of the limitations wives faced when using the ecclesiastical system of justice. The move to annul or divorce a husband was an extraordinary measure for a wife to take. Doña Rafaela's sister, who would seem to have had compelling reasons to divorce her own husband, a man who beat her and had raped her sister, took no legal action and instead took temporary refuge in a convent. Such de facto separations must have been quite common, and the church rarely intervened in such situations. Doña Rafaela had the expectation that she too would be left alone in the convent, both before and after her marriage, but such an attitude only provoked kidnappings by her family and her husband's accomplices. She was clearly desperate and determined to separate from her husband in whatever way possible. When her father tried to counsel her, she reportedly replied angrily that "she was not asking for his advice but for his favor in order to leave the oppression in which she found herself, and if she did not have any other refuge she would flee to regions where no one knew her, if no one in her family offered her any relief."[10]

Once a wife presented a demand for annulment or divorce in the ecclesiastical courts, she had to remain resolute in confronting the long, isolating, and costly process. The law stipulated that a woman making such demands had to be "deposited" in the home of a well-reputed citizen or in a convent, with the husband obligated to pay for her expenses. Even doña Rafaela, who deposited herself in the convent of her choice, complained of the isolation, deprivations, and harassment to which she was exposed. For poor working women, who would have been separated from their livelihoods, or for mothers, who could find themselves separated from their children, such a period of isolation would have been onerous if not impossible to bear. When one considers the length of the litigation (often over two years), the great expense of hiring attorneys and notaries, and the likelihood that a suit would be rejected, it is not difficult to understand why the ecclesiastical courts remained an option that only a few wives took. For most women, the church was an inefficient mediator in their conflicts with men.[11]

Defining Family

For the church, once a marriage had taken place, that family unit essentially became hermetically sealed; relations between the couple became a personal matter. The attitude of the church can be partly understood in that the only official action it could take once the marriage had occurred was to dissolve the union. Although the church might encourage moderation and collaboration between spouses, it lacked any mechanism for officially censuring or punishing individuals without putting in jeopardy the permanence of the union. The church could only intervene on the part of individual interests at great risk to the institution of marriage—and thus to its own powers—since an important aspect legitimating the church's control over marriage was its definition of marriage as a permanent union sanctified by God.[12] The church instead emphasized the importance of the couple's common interest, which it defined as the continuation of their union together. Goody explains that "by insinuating itself into the very fabric of domestic life, of heirship and marriage, the Church gained great control over the grass root of society itself. . . . Religion entered into the basic units of production and reproduction."[13]

The state also recognized the family as a source of social, economic, and political power. Unlike the church, however, it defined marriage as a union incorporating both individual and common interests, much like any other legal institution in Spanish American society. The government enabled family members to protect their individual interests in order to prevent families from collapsing into closed corporate entities. Husbands were *not* legally recognized as the sole authority over family resources. Wives possessed their own estates and sued their husbands in court. Because civil authorities could not dissolve marriages, no action they took, no matter how disruptive, could ever officially end the union. State policies were not partisan to one sex over another; rather, the state used individual suits to increase the permeability of all sectors of society to external vigilance and social intervention.

In the seventeenth century, in addition to being judged as immoral by the church, adultery and domestic violence were considered criminal activities by civil authorities. Women from all walks of life skipped over the church, with its difficult, expensive, and lengthy system of justice, and instead simply sued their husbands in the criminal justice system.[14] Just as it was overwhelmingly wives who brought demands for divorce to the ecclesiastic courts, it was also wives who used the criminal justice system to resolve conflicts with their husbands. There is no record of a criminal suit being brought by a husband against his wife for any reason in the district of Quito in the seventeenth century. The definition of adultery, wife beating, and seduction as crimes signifies that men who engaged in such acts risked more than the moral consternation of a few church officials. Men who were violent or dishonest in their relations with women faced imprisonment, fines, confiscation of their property, banishment, destitution of their public offices, and forced labor in public projects, the military, or textile mills.[15] These mechanisms for legally punishing spouses increased government authority by extending its influence over individual men and women, whom the church had permanently sealed together.

Governmental Controls

Personal relations were of public interest, and public interest was fostered by the extension of governmental authority into men's and women's private relations. Royal and local authorities accomplished this goal by independently monitoring and sanctioning personal conduct, both through legislation and through the *rondas* (patrols), as well as by prosecuting men accused by women of duplicitous and violent behavior.[16]

The Spanish conquest of Peru generated many conflicts, some of them marital, in that men going to Peru often left their wives behind in Spain for many years, sometimes indefinitely. The crown issued numerous directives mandating that men in the Indies either send for their abandoned wives or be shipped back to Spain.[17] Although most of this legislation was never enforced, a few men were indeed fined large amounts of money for delays in bringing their wives to Quito. The viceroy, for example, ordered the conquistador Rodrigo Núñez de Bonilla to pay 3,000 pesos of gold to the crown in 1556 for not having brought his wife from Mexico. The money was collected but was returned to him once his wife had arrived. That same year the viceroy ordered the carpenter Andrés Suara to pay 500 pesos for failing to bring his wife from Spain. Again, the money was returned to him once his wife had arrived in Quito.[18] Ten years later, the king ordered that neither the judges nor the president of the Royal Audiencia grant licenses for men who had left wives in Spain to remain in the Indies and that such men be immediately sent back to Spain.[19]

It is generally agreed that this legislation remained a dead letter, but the use of it to accuse men must have been frequent, because a special licensing process existed to grant men specified periods of time to be physically absent from their wives as they traveled to other regions of the Spanish Empire. The accusations and the threat of punitive action were deemed troublesome enough that at least some men did apply for such licenses from the royal government. In 1573, for example, the Royal Audiencia of Quito granted limited licenses to Alonso de Prada and to Benito González to remain in the district, ordering them to immediately send for their wives in Spain.[20] Wife abandonment and men's sexual conduct were not ignored but rather were considered royal concerns—so much so that men wrote directly to the king from Quito, denouncing others who had abandoned their wives and set up new households with other women.[21] Although these denunciations were doubtless motivated by rivalry, it is noteworthy that the accusers chose the particular issues of wife abandonment and adultery to target the men, showing that there was a general expectation that royal authorities would intervene when such situations were brought to their attention.

Government officials at the local level also independently involved themselves in policing the sexual conduct of citizens. As in all other major cities, Quito authorities organized rondas to guard the city at night. Municipal patrols were organized to prevent disorderly conduct in the streets, robberies, and illicit sexual activity. The objectives of the patrols demonstrate the general lack of distinction between public and private activities. Along with drunks and thieves, the patrols arrested unmarried people caught in bed together. Even before a wife formally charged her husband with adultery, frequently he had already been jailed by city officials. In the case of Agustina de la Vega, with whom we started this chapter, her husband and his lover had been jailed at least once for their illicit relationship by the city patrol before Agustina reported him to the authorities. Men arrested by the patrols for illicit sexual behavior usually faced short-term jail sentences and moderate fines, but in some cases they received much more severe punishment. In 1695, for example, when patrols found Juan González in bed with his lover, he was sentenced to two years of exile thirty leagues outside of the city of Quito. If he violated his exile, an additional provision ordered that he be fined 100 pesos and that this sum be divided between the government court and the mill that supported the houses for abandoned women and children.[22] The unfortunate Josef Zagal is another example of a man prosecuted directly by government authorities, rather than through private accusations, when he was picked up by the municipal patrol for adultery in 1699. In a letter to the Audiencia, he complained that he had already spent four months in the public jail and that he was in manacles and being mistreated, and he asked that his case be transferred to the royal court, which it was.[23]

Fear that the government would take punitive action against those caught in sexually illicit situations was common. María Arroyo testified in jail in 1680 that she lived next door to where a murder had taken place, had heard the fight, and had seen her neighbor's corpse. She said that she had fled when authorities came to her house to take her testimony, because she was afraid that they would find her in bed with her lover. The official accepted her explanation for her suspicious behavior and freed her from jail.[24] The expectation that the government would prosecute sexual indiscretions must have been common enough for it to excuse what we might see as a greater crime, fleeing the scene of a murder. Private behavior was subject to public policy. Women expected the government to prosecute the men they accused, and the government indeed acted on the women's accusations.

Wives' Criminal Charges against Husbands

Wives in seventeenth-century Quito brought criminal charges against their husbands for adultery, domestic violence, abandonment, and lack of financial support. Many wives who accused their husbands of physically mistreating them also accused them of adultery and, indeed, tended to attribute their husbands' violent behavior to their relationships with other women. In doña Francisca de Barrionuevo's suit against her husband in 1680, the presumed connection between domestic violence and adultery is made clear by officials themselves.

Nicolás de Escobar, married to doña Francisca de Barrionuevo, has been publicly living in sin with Alfonsa Grado for more than six or seven years with great notoriety and scandal, for which reason he is abusing his wife, treating her badly in words and actions. And so that such excess be rigorously punished, it is ordered that proceedings begin so that in respect to this official injunction witnesses will come forth and be examined.[25]

Several Spanish and mestizo women neighbors did come forth to testify that they had seen Nicolás and his lover both mistreat doña Francisca. All the witnesses, however, attributed Nicolás' escalating violence to doña Francisca's public complaints about his behavior. As one witness succinctly put it: "[D]oña Francisca always publicly complained that her husband was in an illicit relationship with Alfonsa, and this was the reason he abused his wife in both words and deeds."[26]

Witnesses commonly made the connection between male violence and female public complaints but not, as might be assumed, to imply that wives should accept their husbands' affairs and mistreatment and learn to be silent. Agustina de la Vega, who, as we saw above, sued her husband on the advice of her parish priest, believed that her husband's abusive behavior stemmed from his drinking, a vice he had learned from his lover.[27] Agustina was well known in her neighborhood for continually complaining about her husband's behavior. Of over twenty witnesses testifying in a separate criminal case, all of them had heard Agustina's complaints. The parish priest explicitly stated that Agustina's husband beat her because she publicized his mistreatment. The priest did not, however, counsel her to keep quiet either as a moral stance or as a practical measure to stop her husband's violence. Instead, he told her to make her complaints more efficient by taking them to royal authorities.

The frequent connection made by witnesses between escalating male violence and female persistence in publicizing their maltreatment indicates the general opinion that women's speech was powerful. Men knew that wife beating and adultery were not male prerogatives but, in fact, illegal acts. Wives who revealed their husbands' illicit behavior exposed the men to both public censure and governmental punitive action. It was generally assumed that husbands had a lot at stake in keeping their unlawful behavior secret and would use violence to silence the victims, their wives. The chatter of women was not idle. In doña Francisca's criminal suit against her husband, he was ordered arrested and his property confiscated on the basis of the testimony of her female neighbors.[28]

Wives who did not publicly air their grievances with their husbands were at a disadvantage when they brought formal criminal charges against their spouses, because they could not rely on the validation of outside testimony. Such seems to be the situation of doña Juana Requejo, married to Captain Andrés de Sevilla, whose suit is unusual in that she uses no outside witnesses but only the testimony of people in her own household.[29] Doña Juana claimed to have lived in physical danger for over twenty years because of her husband's violent temper. What seems to have provoked her into criminally charging her husband with multiple counts of physical violence and adultery was the forced entrance into her house by his steward, whom she sued one day before she filed suit against her husband. Even as a married woman, doña Juana was able to bring a criminal suit in her own name against the steward for physically endangering her and her household.[30] He broke into her house at five in the morning in order to search for a mulatto girl in her service who, he claimed, had cheated him in the shop he ran. The steward destroyed property and threatened to kill doña Juana, so doña Juana locked him in a room, called for the police, and had him thrown into jail.

Feeling empowered, or simply fed up, the following day she sued her husband. Doña Juana claimed that she and her husband had never lived a conjugal life together. Instead, from the beginning of their marriage he had mistreated her, beating her and even repeatedly trying to stab and hang her. On numerous occasions her mother-in-law and her servants saved her life by intervening to stop her husband's violence. She also accused him of having long-term affairs, first with a married woman, then with two widows, and finally with her own niece, who was also married. She said that he lavished expensive gifts, such as slaves, money, jewelry, clothing, and food, on these women and in this way had wasted her dowry and left her in poverty. In addition, he had stolen her property: a chest decorated with gold and even a dress of hers, which he had altered to fit one of his mistresses. By doña Juana's account her husband was a violent and dangerous man, and her charges are similar to, if not more severe than, those in other wives' suits examined above, whose husbands were punished.

Doña Juana's husband received only a reprimand from Audiencia authorities and an order to treat his wife better.[31] A main difference in her case is that whereas the other wives repeatedly alerted the public about their husbands' conduct, doña Juana made no mention of making such appeals to anyone outside of her household. Thus the only testimonies she could compile to corroborate her charges were from her own servants. Having kept silent for over twenty years and effectively isolated herself from her community, she found that her case against her husband was substantially weakened, and judicial authorities, though condemning her husband's behavior, did not intervene forcefully on her behalf.

Community knowledge about familial relations was an important part of the legal process, especially considering that wives who presented charges against their husbands were usually held to a lower burden of proof than claimants in other similar kinds of criminal cases. In other types of physical aggression, for example, the victim of assault, or a representative, called for a notary to certify the location and gravity of the wounds, their number, and probable cause. With or without eyewitnesses the notary's report was the official evidence that the person had indeed been the victim of an attack. In seventeenth-century Quito, wives did not present notarized descriptions of the injuries inflicted on them by their husbands. Other evidence substantiated their accusations. A strong case would include witnesses from the wife's neighborhood, whose testimonies would appear more disinterested than those of people within her own household.

By considering the testimony of neighbors as sufficient evidence to punish husbands, the legal system itself promoted the permeability of the family because this consideration encouraged wives to report on their husbands' activities to the community. Community members often responded to wives' public complaints by censuring the husbands who mistreated them. The mestizo neighbor of doña Francisca stated that she had confronted her neighbor's husband and admonished him for mistreating his wife.[32] Men's reputations were connected to their treatment of their wives. The testimony of Diego Nagales against his brother was discredited by an attorney because he was "known by all to have beaten his wife."[33]

Networks of acquaintances could also aid in the apprehension of wayward husbands. In 1697 the indigenous Gerónima Chuquillanqui complained to her nephew that her husband had abandoned her to live with another indigenous woman. She wanted to sue her husband and have him punished. Her nephew informed the Indian in charge of the hacienda's indigenous workers of Gerónima's intention to legally punish her husband, and the indigenous official then contacted the Spanish steward of the hacienda. The steward, together with Gerónima, went out to the mistress's house, seized the couple, and turned the couple over to royal authorities, who then ordered the lovers jailed.[34] Husbands were held accountable for their behavior by community members, who acted as an informal source of pressure on the men to modify their conduct and acted as agents in the formal mechanisms for apprehending and prosecuting husbands who mistreated their wives through physical violence and adultery.

The government's zeal in prosecuting husbands could exceed the original intentions of the wives they had betrayed. Cases of physical aggression, including domestic violence, required that the defendant be accused by the victim or her/his representative. The success of the case depended largely upon the willingness of the aggrieved party to continue the prosecution. Even murder cases could be resolved outside of the formal legal process. In a notarized agreement, called a "pardon of death" (*perdón de muerte*), a family representative of the deceased person officially pardoned the killer. The common reason given for the pardon was the inability to financially continue the case. In addition, though this was theoretically not a causal factor, defendants usually paid an indemnity to the deceased's representative. Pardons of death were frequently used, and women were legally empowered to make such agreements. Women pardoned the killers of their kin, including husbands, brothers, sons, and parents.[35] In comparison, then, though a wife had the authority to pardon her husband's killer and terminate the prosecution of the murderer, her pardon of her husband's adultery had no necessary legal consequences. Unlike physical aggression and even murder, adultery was considered a crime against the government. Governmental authorities could thus apprehend, prosecute, and punish adulterous husbands without the involvement of their wives.

The government's compelling interest in monitoring family relationships seems to have been motivated more by the desire to prevent families from becoming private enclaves than by a concern for women or the welfare of the family itself. Judgments against adulterous men could result in the destitution of their wives and the long or permanent separation of spouses. The objective of most wives was the correction and not the destruction of their husbands. For this reason wives could find themselves in the position of pleading for leniency for the men they had once criminally charged. An example of such a situation is the criminal case pursued by doña Angela Hurtado de Mendoza in 1662 against her husband, Francisco Gómez de Acevedo, for adultery.[36]

Francisco was a functionary (*escribano receptor*) of the Royal Audiencia and apparently incorrigible in his affections for his mestizo mistress, Petrona de Escobar. Francisco and Petrona had already been picked up by the patrols and jailed by authorities three times for being found in bed together, when, in March, they were arrested again because of a formal complaint filed by doña Angela. At the time of the arrest, testimonies were taken from several neighbors, including Petrona's mother. All the witnesses gave details of the relationship and voiced their disapproval of it. Many said that they had tried to intervene but that Francisco was a violent man and had threatened them and Petrona when she had tried to end the relationship.[37]

In April the court condemned Francisco to six years of exile in the army in Chile and deprived him of his office. Exile to Chile was commonly understood to be a death sentence because few men ever returned from the war the Spaniards were fighting with the Araucanian Indians. Doña Angela stressed this point in her letter to the royal court, asking that the sentence be suspended against her husband because "there was no hope that he would ever return from the war" and that therefore her husband's parents, with whom she was then living, would have no reason to continue to care for her. She also argued that the removal of her husband from office would leave the family with no economic resources. She complained that as she was the person who had denounced his adultery to authorities, it was unfair for them to issue a ruling so detrimental to her. Finally, she claimed that Francisco had mended his ways and was now living tranquilly with her. Francisco's parents wrote a letter on his behalf as well. Royal authorities did change their ruling, suspending the exile to Chile. Instead, Francisco was exiled to Ibarra for four years, fined 300 pesos, and still ordered to resign from his position with the Audiencia. Because Francisco was now destitute, his father paid the fine for him, and he was freed from jail.[38]

The following month, in May, Francisco was found naked in bed with Petrona by the senior judge of the Audiencia, who accompanied the regular patrol because of information he received concerning Francisco's continuing affair. This time the arrest and the time in jail would be far more severe for Francisco and Petrona. They were both shackled during the arrest and then were held continually in chains during their imprisonment of several months. After two months in jail, Francisco asked that his shackles be removed because his foot was being crippled, but this request was denied.[39] Doña Angela wrote another letter on her husband's behalf, asking again that his office not be sold, because it would harm her. The Audiencia, however, finalized the sale of the office.[40] During his fourth month of jail, Francisco claimed that he should be freed because of the general pardon given by the king in honor of the birth of his son. His request was denied because, as the royal court determined, such pardons were not for people who had repeatedly committed "scandalous crimes."[41]

In the court's final judgment, Francisco was ordered to comply with the exile to Ibarra, to the north of Quito, and Petrona was exiled to Riobamba, in the south. Francisco fled to Lima. At this point Francisco's father expected doña Angela to sue for divorce. In his certification of his power of attorney to represent his son in all financial and legal matters, he made special note of his ability to represent him in the ecclesiastical courts in the event that doña Angela should bring a demand for annulment or divorce.[42]

In doña Angela's and Francisco's experiences, one can see all the various mechanisms used to stop adulterous liaisons and the repercussions on the people involved. Francisco was first apprehended and jailed by authorities, and then formal charges were brought by his wife. The court's decision to exile him to the war in Chile and deprive him of his office, however, was life threatening to Francisco and financially disastrous to his wife. Doña Angela was then forced into the incongruous position of speaking in favor of her husband and pleading for a suspension of the court's ruling in the criminal case that she had originally pursued against him. Doña Angela was, in fact, no longer listed as the claimant, and instead the case was prosecuted in the name of the royal government. Despite doña Angela's assurances to the court that Francisco had corrected his behavior, after his father paid his fine and he was freed from jail, he was again apprehended with his mistress.

The definition of adultery by the government as not only a grave offense but as one committed against royal authorities becomes even clearer during Francisco's final imprisonment of more than five months. Not only did the government reaffirm its decision to exile him to Ibarra and divest him of his official government position; it refused to free him through the general pardon granted by the king. General pardons applied to all those who had committed common crimes, such as debtors, thieves, and most murderers. Exempted from such pardons were those who had committed particularly grave offenses, especially those against the king, such as treason, counterfeiting, resistance to authorities, heresy, and premeditated murder.[43] The royal officials of Quito, then, considered Francisco's crime of adultery as equivalent in gravity to those offenses which merited punishment without exception. Indeed, the magnitude of his crime warranted, for government officials, severe treatment in jail, where he was continually shackled at the risk of crippling him.

It seems clear that the government was not operating on promasculinist policies, but it is also evident that its firm stance against male adulterers was not motivated by a concern for women. Any basis for familial life that remained between doña Angela and Francisco was destroyed when government judgments eliminated Francisco's livelihood and separated the couple by exiling him first to Chile, then to Ibarra. The harshness of the verdicts provoked Francisco's flight to outside of the Quito District. Doña Angela was left alone, with no financial support and dependent on the charity of in-laws. If the expectation of Francisco's father proved true, the final act of this story would be the formal dissolution of their marriage, spurred in large part by government intervention. The issue for historians is not to determine whether Spanish government and society were promale or profemale but rather to what extent both women and men were used as extensions of social control through continually shifting positions of authority and subordination. Conflicts between men and women within the family, like conflicts in other institutions, were the point of entrance for social vigilance and control. In the struggle between keeping and revealing secrets, both husbands and wives could reinforce their positions of power in the family, or, indeed, they could both be destroyed.

Seduction

Married women used the criminal justice system to force husbands to honor their vows to physically protect, financially support, and faithfully respect their wives. Marriage was a witnessed, legally binding act, and therefore it might be expected that either spouse could sue if the other broke the terms of their agreement. Unmarried women who voluntarily engaged in sexual relations with men outside of marriage, however, had legal recourse as well. Single women used the legal system to condemn men for sexually seducing them with the promise of marriage or financial remuneration.

The promise to marry was a serious vow that, despite legal censure and church discouragement, commonly legitimated the initiation of sexual relations by the couple.[44] Marriage promises were usually not witnessed and therefore not officially verifiable, and yet they were legally binding. Men who promised to marry women as simply a technique of seduction could thus be criminally prosecuted. Ignacio Gómez, a functionary of the City Council of Cuenca and owner of a sugar mill and several African slaves, for example, seemed to be just such a man.[45] In 1676 the mother of doña María Sosa criminally charged Ignacio with promising to marry her daughter, seducing her, and then, after she became pregnant, refusing to marry her. Ignacio was ordered jailed and his property confiscated. In a similar case doña Margarita Ortiz de Alcócer sued on her own behalf, claiming that Gabriel López de Sequeira, the son of a justice official in the town of Alausí, had deceitfully promised to marry her in order to seduce her.[46] She said that after pursuing her for two years, he seduced her, and then a month later he broke his promise to her and planned to marry another woman.

These two cases have much in common. The women were minors in age, claimed to be virgins at the time of seduction, and came from less wealthy and politically less well-connected families than their seducers. Neither woman had much success in her suit. Doña María's case was still being pursued three years later, though now by her stepfather, as her mother had since died. There is no evidence that doña Margarita's case ever went beyond a legal denunciation. Although theoretically a criminal act, a broken marriage promise was hard to prosecute because, as a nonwitnessed, oral agreement, it was difficult to corroborate a woman's claims.[47] In addition, the government probably felt less compulsion to prosecute these suits than it did in cases of married men's sexual transgressions. The government treated marriage as an official area of interest, like other institutions in society, using internal conflicts as a way of extending its influence and preventing the formation of enclave centers of power. The conflicts between unmarried individuals, however, did not involve organized and potentially autonomous unions, and therefore the government had less to gain in monitoring and intervening in such sexual transgressions.

At any rate, engaging in sexual relations on the basis of a promise of marriage was a common, if high-risk, act. The inability to rely on the legal system to enforce marriage promises pushed some women to take justice into their own hands. Such was the case with Tomasa Morales, whose lover's broken promise of marriage goaded her into physically attacking Bárbara de la Vega in 1691.[48] Tomasa, a poor seamstress, thirty-four years old, and definitely not a virgin, had little probability of successfully prosecuting her lover, Manuel de León, for deceiving her with a promise of marriage. After two years of sexual involvement, Manuel apparently forsook Tomasa for Bárbara, another woman of humble origins and mother of four children.

After confronting both Bárbara and Manuel several times about their sexual relationship, Tomasa got word one night that the two were walking together in the streets. Tomasa then gathered together a male friend and an indigenous woman, and, as her accomplices held Bárbara down, Tomasa attacked Bárbara with a dagger. The attack left Bárbara with six serious wounds in her head. In jail, Tomasa attempted to reduce her culpability for Bárbara's injuries by claiming that she had not intended to wound her, but rather to cut her hair (an act commonly used to shame a female), and that it was only because of Bárbara's resistance that she had accidentally stabbed her. Tomasa claimed that as she had already tried other means to break up Bárbara and Manuel's relationship, her attack was warranted because Bárbara was responsible for Manuel's broken promise of marriage.

To prove the authenticity of Manuel's promise to marry her, she volunteered the information that she had been sexually involved with him for over two years. For Tomasa, Manuel's promise to marry her was a serious commitment that morally and legally bound him to her; her attack was justifiable because she was protecting her honor. This view that a promise of marriage was equivalent to marriage itself and therefore legitimated conjugal relations—and, in its violation, acts of passion in defense of the relationship—was shared by her male accomplice in the attack, who was also arrested. He claimed that after the attack, Manuel himself told him that "no matter what happens, Tomasa was his wife because he had prom-ised to marry her."[49]

The government prosecutor, however, was not sympathetic to Tomasa's interpretation of the events and, in addition to prosecuting her for physi-cally attacking Bárbara, used Tomasa's declaration to indict her for her illicit sexual relationship with Manuel as well. Not only, then, did the government refuse to enforce Manuel's promise of marriage to Tomasa; it prosecuted as a crime the relationship she believed was honorable because of that promise.

Cases in which women had more success in suing for seduction were, interestingly, against married men. In addition to being sued by govern-ment authorities and their wives, adulterous husbands were also prose-cuted by the unmarried women they seduced. In the two cases examined below, authorities prosecuted and severely punished the male offenders, despite the fact that both women admitted that they had voluntarily en-gaged in sexual relations with the men because of the promise of financial compensation.

In 1692 doña Juana Martínez Cabeza de Vaca brought criminal charges against the married Matías Correa for seducing her illegitimate daughter, Petrona Martínez Cabeza de Vaca.[50] Several witnesses testified that they had seen Petrona and Matías together often and noticed that the two hid whenever any of Petrona's relatives happened by. The indigenous doña María de Espinosa testified that she herself was in an illicit relationship with Matías. For this reason, when she saw the two enter a shop together, she informed Petrona's grandmother, who then went to get her grand-daughter. Petrona then disappeared. She claimed later that Matías deflow-ered her and took her to many different houses to prevent anyone from finding her. In her declaration she stated that she engaged in sexual rela-tions with Matías because he promised to pay her 200 pesos, of which he claimed he kept 100 at the monastery of the Franciscans and the other 100 in the city of Riobamba. He also promised to buy Petrona clothing and to financially support her. On the basis of this agreement, they had sexual intercourse, but then afterward, when she asked him for the money, he did not pay her.[51]

Royal authorities jailed Matías and confiscated his goods. In his dec-laration from jail, he claimed that Petrona had run away from home and, because he had found her and returned her to her mother's house, Petrona was fabricating lies against him out of spite. In his defense he produced witnesses who testified that Petrona was known in the neighborhood for behaving loosely. Various people testified that Petrona frequently left her house at night by herself, wore low-cut dresses to fiestas, and accepted gifts of food and money from men. Her virginity was suspect. Now it would seem that maligning the reputation of a woman of illegitimate birth who freely admitted to exchanging sex for money would have been an easy task, but this was not the case. And, indeed, Matías' legal defense became even more difficult when two midwives examined Petrona and declared that she was four months pregnant. The government did not accept his defense and condemned him to two hundred lashes, ten years service in a military post, and confiscation of all his property in favor of Petrona. Matías did not, however, wait around for his punishments to be carried out. He escaped the Quito jail, dressed as a woman and with the help of female accomplices, who smuggled women's clothing in to him. What surprised witnesses who saw him later before he fled the district was not that he escaped from the jail but that he had shaved his beard and moustache to do so. What was a Spanish man without hair on his face?

Witnesses on both sides of this suit testified that Petrona was a rather gregarious young woman. Indeed, though witnesses on her behalf believed she was a virgin before consenting to Matías' overtures, no one claimed that she had led a quiet and reserved life. She herself did not initially complain that she had been corrupted or left in dishonor by Matías, simply that he had not paid her. The one expected witness who never appears in the suit is Matías' wife, who could have provided some background on his character. She never testified and, though some people claimed to know her, no one gave any information about her; even her name is not known. The only reason we know she existed is that Matías was noted as a married man. But perhaps that is all we need to know; it seems at least that was all governmental authorities needed to know in order to prosecute and punish him with such vigor. The fact that he was married was a major element in the court's decision and seemed to weigh more heavily than even the fact that Petrona was left pregnant. As was seen above, leaving young women pregnant did not necessarily incur even the notice of government authorities.

It might be claimed that married men were considered generally suspect and easier to prosecute than single men. At least one woman took advantage of this situation to falsely accuse a married man of seducing her and fathering her child. Francisca Ruiz de Padilla concocted an elaborate story, which included incest against Maestro Josef Flores, that convinced the woman she lived with, neighbors, and government authorities.[52] Francisca was a young widow who, because her parents had died and she had no one to care for her, lived with her also-widowed sister-in-law, doña María de Salazar. Maestro Josef Flores was a former business partner of doña María's deceased husband and was a boarder in her house.

Doña María stated that at some point she began to suspect a relationship between Francisca and Maestro Josef Flores and that when she interrogated Francisca, she "tearfully admitted that she had been guilty, because he had promised to favor her and used persuasions and she was a poor woman."[53] The gravity of Maestro Josef Flores' offense seemed even greater when it was supposed that the first night he seduced Francisca was the night the volcano Pichincha erupted in Quito. As one witness lamented, "while Christians were making confessions and carrying out acts of penitence because they thought it was the end of the world, Maestro Josef Flores had Francisca locked in his room and was committing adultery all night long."[54] In addition to being accused of the crime of adultery, he was also accused of incest. Witnesses claimed that he kidnapped and deflowered Francisca's sister, Andrea, after she had left the convent only two days earlier (which would have been considered incest). Officials jailed Maestro Josef Flores, and things kept looking worse for him. Francisca gave birth to a baby she claimed was his, and his own wife showed up to denounce him publicly for hitting her three or four years earlier. Neighbors testified that they had seen him with both sisters. Nuns testified in favor of Francisca.

Maestro Josef Flores' guilt seemed certain, and after more than a year in jail he was still awaiting sentencing. Then Francisca confessed. She admitted that she had really been involved in a long-term relationship with a priest and, wanting to hide the relationship after she became pregnant, she accused Maestro Josef Flores of seduction. Maestro Josef Flores had never touched her or her sister, and, in fact, she had hardly even spoken with him. Citing her confession, the courts absolved Maestro Josef Flores.

The situation of Maestro Josef Flores suggests that elements which traditionally are thought to have made men invulnerable to prosecution by women might have in some cases made them more susceptible. As a man who had graduated from his studies in arts and theology with a masters degree, Maestro Josef Flores' social prestige should have made his declarations of innocence credible or his guilt possible to overlook. But, in fact, people were far more willing to give credence and defense to the young, penniless widow than to him. His status as a married man increased the gravity of his crimes and the likelihood of his prosecution. The eagerness of the community and government prosecutors to punish the unfortunate Maestro Josef Flores suggests that what researchers often dismiss as "male prerogatives" were considered disruptive and abusive and were condemned by society and by law.

Conclusion

The church was an important institution that affected many aspects of life and politics in Spanish America. However, its precepts and courts were not the only forces regulating conjugal relations. Once a marriage had taken place, the only option the church had for confronting marital difficulties was to temporarily or permanently dissolve the union, a course of action church authorities were highly reluctant to take. The church lacked any official mechanism for censuring and punishing spouses within the course of a marriage. It was overwhelmingly wives who sued for divorce in the ecclesiastical courts. The process was long, costly, and usually unsuccessful. For this reason, many wives chose instead to sue their husbands through the criminal justice system for domestic abuse, adultery, and lack of financial support.

The criminal cases of wives against husbands show that women were generally supported in public opinion and law. Witnesses condemned the behavior of violent and unfaithful husbands and were eager to volunteer incriminating evidence about the men's activities. Government authorities prosecuted husbands both independently and on the basis of wives' formal accusations. Through legislation, and especially through organized patrols, both municipal and royal officials showed an interest in regulating the conduct of married men. Although domestic violence, like other cases of physical aggression, required the continuing willingness of the victim to pursue prosecution, the government prosecuted adulterous men independently of and even despite their wives' sentiments. The government's punishment of men included imprisonment, fines, confiscation of property, loss of office, and long exiles. The impact of such severe judgments against husbands was often equally devastating to wives, who, attempting to salvage some part of the family income, found themselves defending the men they had originally charged criminally.

The aggressive prosecution and punishment of husbands by the government suggest that male authority in the household was not officially defended. It has been suggested here, in fact, that married men may have been targeted in particular because of the risk they represented in using family relationships to consolidate their power. The potential for patriarchy was recognized but was considered destabilizing and disruptive of the public vigilance and intervention used to regulate all other social groupings in society. However, policies that undermined male authority did not necessarily benefit women. As has been seen, judgments against husbands did not consider the possible negative impact on women or children and were even sometimes secured against the express wishes of female litigants.

Unmarried women who used the legal system to sue men for seduction also had some success, though again usually in suits against married men. Breaking a promise of marriage was an illegal act yet one hard to document and even more difficult to convince government authorities to prosecute. Women had more success in suing married men. Even women with questionable backgrounds, who stated that they had voluntarily en-gaged in sexual relations in the expectation of financial gain, won their suits against their married lovers. Again, it seems that the government was much more interested in prosecuting potential patriarchs than single men who did not yet head families.

■

CHAPTER 4

Women as Entrepreneurs

Women and the Economy

Women contributed substantially to the prosperity of colonial Spanish America through their economic participation. The breadth of women's commercial activities has, indeed, attracted the attention of numerous historians. The research of these scholars has not only increased our knowledge about the kinds of economic activities women participated in, but, as a collective body of scholarship, their work also shows the universal character of women's involvement in the colonial economy. What remains less clear in the literature, however, is how and why the social structure permitted and even encouraged women to become economic actors. Women's participation in the colonial economy has, in fact, been recognized as one of the most difficult aspects of women's lives to integrate into a patriarchal model. As Arrom points out in her study of women in eighteenth-century Mexico City: "[T]he most easily refutable aspect of the stereotype of the traditional Latin American woman is her isolation from economic activities."[1] Research on women's economic roles, however, does more than change our vision of women; it also forces us to reconsider our view of Spanish society itself. Women's commercial activities, both independently from and in joint ventures with men, defy division of society into separate gendered spheres—the private, domestic world of women and the public, economically driven world of men.

The women in the seventeenth-century Quito area were no exception, and Chapters 4 and 5 focus on women's participation in Quito's main industry—textile manufacturing—and the subsidiary economic enterprises it supported. This research suggests that women faced few gender-specific obstacles in their economic activities and that women's civil status (single, married, or widowed) was not a crucial factor in determining the scope of their economic activities. The diverse forms of labor, production, and investments by women from all racial backgrounds and economic sectors suggest not only that women's involvement in commercial enterprises was essential to the region's growth but also that women's economic roles were accepted and supported by colonial legal and cultural norms.

Textile Production

The basis of the region's expanding economy in this period was textile production, an industry which heavily involved women. Participation in textile manufacturing was extensive in the area. In 1681 the Audiencia estimated that over 30,000 people were dedicated to this occupation just in the district of the city of Quito.[2] Women were involved in both the production and commercial transport of the district's textiles, as owners of *obrajes* (the shops or mills where most of the textiles were produced); as laborers in the obrajes; as participants in commercialized domestic textile production that operated through the "putting-out" system (to be discussed later); and as investors in the transport of textiles to Lima.

Because textile manufacturing was the region's most profitable economic activity, it is no surprise that Quito's most illustrious families controlled the largest obrajes. The royal government initially granted obraje licenses to encomenderos, many of whom were involved in the original conquest of Quito. In the seventeenth century, licenses were given to families closely tied to the Royal Audiencia. Javier Ortíz de la Tabla estimates that in the seventeenth century six families controlled 50 percent of the licensed obrajes within the corregimiento (subdistrict) of the Audiencia of Quito.[3] Some of these families, originally using their encomienda grants to obtain forced indigenous labor for their obrajes, maintained their elite status through the eighteenth century, partly thanks to their close ties with the royal government and endogamous marriages between families.

Women within these elite families possessed obrajes through both inheritance and marriage and by using their status to directly obtain royal licenses to found additional obrajes. Doña Catalina Galarza, a member of an obraje dynasty dating back to the conquest of Quito, obtained a royal license in her name in 1607 to found a new obraje. A few decades later, doña María, from the same family, married don Francisco Villacís, who also came from an elite obraje-owning family. He had inherited an obraje in Machanga from his mother and another in Chillogallo from both his parents. When don Francisco died, doña María inherited both these obrajes from her husband. Doña María then married don Antonio de Ormaza Ponce de León, *oidor* (judge) of the Royal Audiencia. In 1686 the obraje that doña María inherited from her husband in Chillogallo was identified in a lawsuit as belonging first to her dead husband and then to her second husband, the oidor don Antonio. Don Antonio was identified as her husband, thus legitimating his connection to the obraje through her, but apparently in the operational definition he, and not doña María, the actual owner, was considered the person responsible for the obraje.[4]

It is difficult to know to what extent elite women were directly involved in the operations of the obrajes they owned. Certainly they, like their male counterparts at this high level of society, lived in the city of Quito, whereas their obrajes were located in indigenous communities many leagues away. Decisions over labor and production were left up to the *maestro* (administrator) of the particular obraje. Women in less lofty circles, though they still could possess considerable wealth and social status, ran smaller obrajes inside their homes; doubtless these women were intimately involved in day-to-day operations.

An example of such a women was doña María Brava de Quintanilla, who wrote her testament in 1700.[5] Doña María had been married three times, her third husband loaning her the large sum of 1,200 pesos in an official, notarized contract. She also owed a series of debts to other Spanish men and women, including a priest and the corregidor of Quito, as well as smaller debts to indigenous women. She must have used this money in the operation of her obraje, located in her home in the parish of Santa Bárbara in Quito. She operated the obraje with the help of her sister, doña Sebastiana de Quintanilla, who doña María stated knew what sums of money were owed to whom. It is, in fact, her sister whom she chose as the executrix of her testament and to whom she left all her property, rather than to her own husband. Doña María apparently did not expect her obraje to continue production after her death. She asked that all her debts be paid, that the debts the obraje's indigenous workers owed to her be collected, and that the cloth and unwoven thread be sold. Of note is that doña María was one of the very few women who could sign her name, as literacy was a rare accomplishment for women outside of convents in this epoch.[6]

The notably despotic doña Catarina Bravo de Saravia is another example of a woman who turned her home into an obraje and personally controlled the operations of her establishment. Doña Catarina's house in Achimbo, in the jurisdiction of the villa of Riobamba, incorporated her private jail and obraje.[7] As we shall see below, doña Catarina's simultaneous possession of a jail and an obraje was not coincidental. In addition to tribute obligations, which forced many Indians to work in the obrajes for specified periods of time, the other main coercive mechanism for supplying obraje workers was through the criminal justice system. Doña Catarina was noted for her harsh, hands-on approach to running her obraje. She possessed a black slave woman named Anita, who controlled access to the obraje and refused to let any family members of the mostly indigenous workers visit them or bring them food. Anita also reportedly whipped the indigenous workers on doña Catarina's behalf to control them.[8] Witnesses testified that doña Catarina also used another slave, the mulatto Isadora, to punish and control her workers.[9] Doña Catarina reportedly forced the workers to labor for long stretches of time with neither food nor rest. Her workforce was acquired through her son, the corregidor of Riobamba, whom she dominated to such an extent that doña Joana Rosa Conda, *cacica principal* (principal female indigenous ruler) of Achimbo, demanded that it be clarified who was the official corregidor, don Francisco de Meneses or his mother.[10]

Workers frequently accused obraje owners and their administrators of abuse during the colonial period. Conditions in the obrajes were reportedly so horrible that they provoked the exodus of indigenous families from their communities, the hiding of births, and the practices of abortion and infanticide to avoid the suffering these children would later experience as obraje workers.[11] Both the recruitment and the composition of the labor force left the workers vulnerable to deprivations by those in control of their labor. Ortíz de la Tabla suggests that during the sixteenth and seventeenth centuries, only indigenous males were contracted as obraje workers, citing the rigorous nature of the work, the completely enclosed area in which the workers labored, and the mentality of the epoch, which would have seen as scandalous the continual close contact between men and women workers.[12] Reliance on an exclusively male indigenous workforce might have been true for the large, royally licensed obrajes owned by the district's elite, the subject of his research. Smaller obrajes, however, typically employed both indigenous men and women, as well as some non-Indians, who had been sentenced to labor in the obrajes as punishment for crimes they had committed.[13]

Ortíz de la Tabla charts the composition of the labor force in the royally licensed obrajes that operated in the district of Quito in 1680.[14] His research indicates that the male indigenous labor force in these kinds of obrajes was acquired in two ways: through royal grants of *mitayo* workers, Indians who mandatorily spent several months working in an obraje as part of their community's obligation to the crown, and through voluntary mechanisms in which individual indigenous men contracted themselves as wage laborers. Among the obrajes considered by Ortíz de la Tabla is the royally licensed obraje in the indigenous community of Chillogallo, owned by the elite doña María Galarza, mentioned above. Doña María Galarza had inherited this obraje from her first husband, and it was one of many obrajes listed as her personal estate at the time of her second marriage. The Chillogallo obraje received no mitayo workers and instead relied exclusively on Indian men who voluntarily contracted themselves as textile workers. A 1686 lawsuit brought by the indigenous workers against their administrator suggests, however, that even "voluntary" wage laborers experienced a great deal of coercion and even abuse.[15]

In their suit the workers claimed that Lucas Gutiérrez, the administrator of the Chillogallo obraje, locked them up in the obraje jail for long periods of time, habitually whipped the workers, and on three occasions had hung some of them by their genitals for hours at a time. In physical examinations of the workers, officials found that though the Indians did have marks on their genitals, there were no signs on the rest of their bodies of being beaten. In his defense Gutiérrez claimed that the indigenous men had mutilated themselves in order to accuse him. He explained that though he had beaten the Indian men, it was because they were lazy workers and frequently tried to escape the obraje after they had been paid. It is hard to know whether the claims by the indigenous men were exaggerated, but Gutiérrez' defense indicates that a great deal of physical coercion was considered acceptable to motivate ostensibly voluntary wage workers.

The workforce in the smaller obraje of doña Catarina, connected to her home in Achimbo, was not exclusively male or indigenous; nor did her recruitment methods approach the category "voluntary." In addition to harshly treating her workers, as mentioned above, she also acquired her workforce in an irregular manner. Because of her control over her son, the region's corregidor, doña Catarina apparently considered the entire corregimiento as her obraje. When production fell behind in her house, she forced the pueblo's *gateras* (Indian market women) to weave for her, and she distributed cotton to be spun by women in other pueblos under her son's jurisdiction.[16] Workers claimed that she frequently trumped up charges against women and then ordered her son to arrest the women and sentence them to work in her obraje. This practice provoked the lawsuit in 1693 by the cacica principal, doña Joana Rosa Conda, who claimed that doña Catarina falsely accused her of seducing married men and then imprisoned her in the obraje.[17] Doña Joana complained that she was forced to work for long periods of time in chains, without food, and that she was never paid.[18]

The large female element in doña Catarina's workforce is attested to by the number of women who complained that they were forced to work with men inside her obraje, that they were frequently underfed and beaten, and that often they were not paid for their work or were only partially compensated. When an indigenous woman who was sentenced to work for doña Catarina for two years became pregnant in the obraje, Doña Catarina accused the woman of becoming pregnant as a way of escaping.

As punishment, she ordered one of her female slaves to whip her and shave her head. In another case, a mestizo woman who was pregnant and had been deposited in the obraje in anticipation of her marriage, as was standard practice, was given one hundred lashes when she attempted to carry out the marriage.[19]

A major difference between the royally licensed obrajes and the smaller obrajes was in the composition of the workforce and labor recruitment. The workforce of large obrajes was composed of indigenous men who worked for specified lengths of time as part of their community tribute obligation or who were part of a skilled cadre who contracted themselves as wage laborers. In smaller obrajes indigenous men and women worked side by side with non-Indians, and recruitment methods could be highly irregular. If at the highest levels of society, elite obraje owners, such as doña María, were able to use their direct connections with members of the Royal Audiencia to obtain governmental allocations of workers from indigenous communities, smaller obraje owners used their relations with appointed officials to target individuals. Doña Catarina reportedly used her son's position as corregidor to falsely accuse people and have them sentenced to work in her obraje. In addition, because of her authority in the pueblo, she was able to have women in the process of marriage or divorce, who had been temporarily removed from their homes by authorities, deposited in her house, in order to exploit their labor.

These examples of female-owned obrajes suggest that relations between obraje owners and governmental officials were extremely important. Elite obraje owners had intimate connections with members of the Royal Audiencia itself, as seen by doña María's marriage to one of the judges of the royal court. Both of the women who ran obrajes from their homes had relationships with corregidores, officials appointed by the Royal Audiencia.[20] Doña María Brava de Quintanilla was involved in business transactions with the Quito corregidor, to whom she owed money, and doña Catarina's son was the corregidor for the region in which she had her obraje. In addition to the difference in levels of the royal government with which the women were able to connect themselves, there was a marked difference in the involvement of the women in the operations of the obrajes. Doña María relied on an administrator, and her name wasn't even identified with the obraje she owned in Chillogallo. Both doña María Brava and doña Catarina were responsible for the day-to-day functioning of the obrajes they installed in their homes.

For the workers themselves, it seems that conditions within the obraje could be extremely harsh, regardless of the gender of the owner or administrator. Doña Catarina and her female slaves were as heartless with those in the obraje as the male administrator of doña María's obraje in Chillogallo. In addition, whether the work was on an obligatory or a voluntary basis, physical confinement in private jails and corporal punishment were standard mechanisms for controlling both male and female workers. In terms of the actual financial compensation workers received in obrajes, in all three of the cases considered here a worker's pay became a problematic issue. In Chillogallo, workers were apparently paid, but, as the administrator claimed, vigilance was increased at pay time to prevent them from fleeing. In Achimbo, workers complained that doña Catarina did not pay them or only partially compensated them. In doña María Brava's obraje in Quito, she apparently gave her workers advances on their pay, thereby making them indebted, which might or might not have served as a method of retention.[21]

In addition to owning and operating these large- and medium-scale obrajes, women also organized smaller-scale weaving operations by setting up looms in their homes and hiring Indians to weave for them. Because of the small volume of textiles produced, the few weavers employed, and the usually illegal nature of the enterprise, such operations were not defined as obrajes.[22] The profits from these small weaving centers could be substantial, however, and attracted the participation of a broad sector of colonial society. One person was doña Juana Méndez de la Higuera, who turned her possession of four looms into the center of a prosperous and far-reaching economic network.[23]

Doña Juana's prestigious social background in many respects seems mysteriously connected with her life trajectory. The legitimate daughter of Captain don Diego Méndez, from Spain, and doña Ana de la Higuera, of Quito, she contracted marriage with a man of equally high social status, don Josef Montero. It is at this point that the events of her life seem somewhat unusual. Doña Juana brought no dowry to her marriage, and her husband had no capital at the time of their marriage either. Although doña Juana claimed that her grandparents and parents bequeathed considerable amounts of property and money to her in their testaments, she was never able to collect her inheritance, largely, she stated, because of her sister's opposition.

The family supported itself through her efforts and work in textile manufacturing. She claimed that her husband owed her 1,000 pesos that she had earned by her own efforts in this occupation. However, she forgave him this debt and urged her son to do likewise because of don Josef's poverty and because he was the father of her three legitimate children, of whom don Antonio Montero, a friar (*religioso diácono*) in the Mercedarian monastery, was the only one to have survived into adulthood. Eventually, her marriage was officially annulled, though she does not indicate on what basis the church granted the annulment. At some point in her life, doña Juana had an intimate relationship with the socially prestigious Doctor don Gaspar de Morales Celhoy Gúzman, who was the attorney of the Royal Audiencia. The result of their union was the birth of her illegitimate daughter, doña Margarita de la Cruz, who married Antonio Palacios y Albarrán.

For various reasons, then, doña Juana was forced to support herself and her family, and, like a large percentage of the population, she chose to do this through textile manufacturing. Doña Juana bought both raw wool and spun cotton from indigenous women, and she raised sheep of her own. She gave her indigenous employees advances on their wages; their debts registered in her accounting books totaled more than 400 pesos. She sold the finished cloth to Spanish merchants, who marketed it in Lima. After her marriage was annulled, when she had already been involved for several years in textile production, doña Juana expanded her business enterprises by paying 5,090 pesos to buy a large estancia near Cotocollao, on which she put a lien in favor of the convent of the Limpia Concepción in Quito. On this property she raised sheep, whose wool she used in her textile production, as well as cattle and pigs, which she marketed along with the wood that grew on her estancia. She also grew potatoes, vegetables, lentils, and barley, and she devoted a large section of land to growing maize. The maize was used as the raw material for yet another business enterprise, the production of chicha. Doña Juana hired an indigenous woman to make and market chicha, providing her maize and utensils necessary for its fabrication. Both the indigenous *chichera* and her son were in debt to doña Juana at the time that she made her testament.

Doña Juana encountered personal obstacles in her life that many women must have faced. Although she came from a prestigious social background, she began her married life as a poor woman, married to a man who, despite his title of "don," was also unable to bring any capital to their marriage. As a married woman, she began textile manufacturing, an economic activity she carried out independently from her husband, who, in addition to his lack of involvement in his wife's enterprise, became her debtor. She used her success in textile manufacturing to acquire capital to diversify her economic activities. Her business expansion exemplifies how the textile industry in the Quito region supported secondary economic activities, some of which will be discussed below. Through her weaving operation she became involved with merchants operating in Lima, she bought land and invested in livestock, she most likely sold her agricultural produce in Quito's markets, and she became involved in producing chicha for an urban indigenous population. Indeed, the textile manufacturing that she had begun as a married woman not only maintained her in her independence but brought her prosperity. She placed her son in a prestigious monastery, she contracted a stable marriage for her illegitimate daughter, and she was a woman of wealth at the time that she made her testament.

Women also participated on yet another level of textile manufacturing through the more dispersed putting-out system. The system operated as a form of commercialized domestic production in which the owner of the operation provided the raw materials to workers, who then wove the fabric in their own homes. We have already seen how doña Catarina supplemented the production of her obraje in Achimbo with the distribution of cotton to indigenous persons in nearby pueblos to be woven in their homes. Commercialized domestic production could also be the center of women's economic activities. By 1644, for example, Gerónima de Tamayo had built up an impressive fortune by putting out cotton and wool for indigenous women to weave.[24] Gerónima's life reads as a colonial version of a rags-to-riches story and demonstrates that beyond allowing women to maintain or recuperate their social and economic positions, as we've seen in the above examples, textile manufacturing was one of the few occupations for women that allowed them upward social mobility.

Gerónima began her life in Lima, where for more than twenty years she worked as a servant. When she wrote her will in 1644, she was a resident in Quito and was able to invest the considerable sum of 1,500 pesos in a business venture in Lima with Alonso Crespo. When Alonso left Quito for Lima, she also acted as his guarantor for a loan he obtained from another woman, doña Ana de Aguilar, for 300 pesos. As Alonso's guarantor Gerónima gave doña Ana Spanish clothing, jewelry, and cloth in pawn; at the time of her testament, she wanted the debt paid off from her estate and the items retrieved and sold to say masses for her soul. Gerónima also owned a black slave woman, whom she requested to be returned to her original owner along with the 120 pesos that she owed him.

The basis of her wealth was textile production, using the labor of a large force of indigenous women who wove cotton and wool in their homes. Gerónima was aided in the administration of her enterprise by a female employee, María de Castro, who was in charge of keeping records of how much wool or cotton was given to the individual indigenous women to weave, as well as how much they were paid. The indigenous women wove both coarse and fine cotton and wool for Gerónima, who sold the fabric in bulk to merchants and provided smaller quantities at the request of individuals. For example, she owed debts of 200 pesos and 90 pesos, respectively, to two merchants for money they had advanced to her for different kinds of cloth. At the other extreme the abbess of Santa Marta owed her 3½ pesos for an arroba (twenty-five pounds) of woolen cloth that she had asked Gerónima to have woven for her. Although Gerónima supported herself through commercializing locally produced cloth, she herself dressed in clothing made from imported cloth, and, though she seemed to specialize in cloth woven especially for bedspreads, her own was made of imported damask. Indeed, through textile production Gerónima had raised herself from a potentially lifelong occupation as a servant, to a woman who dressed in fine clothes and in her business negotiated contracts with men and women involving large sums of money.

In addition to women's participation as owners and workers in the production of textiles, they were also involved in the sale of local cloth both inside and outside the region. In 1641, for example, Juana de Ascutia and her daughter, María de Bonilla, invested 200 pesos at 12 percent interest in a company with the indigenous Francisco García Guasi. The money was to be employed in acquiring locally produced cloth, which would be sold in Lima.[25] Francisco's participation in the company was guaranteed by another woman who was apparently related to him, doña Juana Guasi, and her husband, Antonio Prieto. The contract stipulated that the cloth be sold only in Lima and that the women investors assume all risks involved in its transport.

That same year another mother and daughter pair invested in the marketing of locally produced cloth in Lima. Isabel González and her daughter, Bárbara del Castillo, formed a company with Bartolomé González in which they invested 1,000 pesos, again at 12 percent interest.[26] As in the above contract, it was stipulated that the cloth must be sold in Lima and that its transportation was at the risk of the investors.

In 1652 María del Corro y Trejo formed a company with Luis de Vergara de la Serna.[27] For her part she invested 2,122 pesos, 1,336 in money, and the remainder in merchandise. Luis invested 1,000 pesos plus his labor in transporting and selling the cloth. The profits were to be equally shared. In this contract it was stipulated that the merchandise be sold outside of Quito. This agreement, like the one above, followed the pattern in which the minor investor was the more active of two partners, regardless of gender.

Women also invested in shops that sold locally produced and imported cloth and clothing inside the city of Quito. The indigenous María Caxal formed a company with the merchant Gabriel Falcón de Santa Ana in 1637 in which she invested 100 pesos at 12 percent interest.[28] In their agreement Gabriel contributed no financial capital, only his labor and his shop, in which he sold local and European cloth and clothing. The following year María was paid her 12 pesos in interest, and she decided to invest more capital with Gabriel. She added 70 pesos to her original 100-peso investment at the same rate of interest. However, the 70 pesos were not given to Gabriel directly; instead María transferred to him a debt owed to her by Sebastián de Escobar, for which she gave Gabriel power of attorney to collect. It is clear that María's rationale in investing in a company with Gabriel was to have a kind of savings plan. She stated that she was using money that she had saved for her funeral and burial because she was afraid that she would spend these funds in some other manner. She therefore requested that at the time of her death the principal be withdrawn to pay for her funeral and burial and that in the meantime she would use the interest to help pay for necessities.

María's business relations with the merchant Gabriel demonstrate that even people such as she, who described herself as a "poor, elderly Indian woman," received standard treatment in such negotiations. The interest on her investment was the typical 12 percent, the same as those investing larger funds. In addition, we can see that relatively humble people, including Indians, used their savings to participate in the sale of textiles. Taking into account the examples of the mothers and daughters above, who invested similar sums of money, one can suggest that the accumulation of small investments could have been an important element in the financing of the district's main commercial enterprise.

Provisioning

Women were involved in many aspects of the provisioning of the district with the staples that daily fed its growing seventeenth-century population. As we will see in Chapter 5, women completely dominated street vending. Although infrequently, women also owned and operated *pulperías* (general stores). The list of royally licensed shop owners in Quito in 1642 included two women of at least relatively high social status, doña Francisca de Varas and doña Clara de Peralta.[29] It was not uncommon for men of high social status, who claimed the title *don*, to own shops that were administered by men of much lower social backgrounds. The women shop owners did likewise; doña Francisca's shop was administered by the mulatto Pedro de Vega, and doña Clara's shop was run by a pulpero with the plebeian name of Pablo Sánchez.

Doña Francisca and doña Clara probably avoided involvement in the affairs of the shops they owned by simply renting the shops to the *pulperos*. This was the case of doña Francisca González Rengal, a widow who supported herself and her daughters through the rental of her city-licensed pulpería, located in her house.[30] Although she wasn't involved in the administration of her pulpería, in 1669 she as its owner was brought into direct conflict with the city council over her shop's designation as a municipally licensed establishment. She had been in possession of this pulpería since 1633, when it was first designated as one of the city's thirty licensed shops. However, the *regidor* (alderman), Manuel Fraile, of the Quito City Council, repeatedly closed her shop because he wanted his own pulpería designated as a municipally licensed shop. The city council was, in fact, embroiled in a dispute with the Royal Audiencia over these shops, the council claiming the right to redesignate the original thirty shops. The Audiencia eventually ruled that the municipally licensed shops must remain in their original locations, and doña Francisca, after over three years of litigation, won her suit.

There were also women of much lower social status who were directly involved in the administration of the shops they owned. Although little evidence is available about pulperas, it suggests that the women were generally poor, being drawn from the same social sectors as men who filled this occupation.[31] It is unclear how these women got started, though at least some must have inherited the business from their deceased husbands. Such was the case of the mestizo María de Eraso, who owned and ran the grocery shop formerly possessed by her husband, Gerónimo Sánchez, when she testified in a murder investigation in 1671.[32] Other women were not so forthcoming in revealing how they came to possess the shops they operated. Josefa González, widow of Antonio González, for example, owned her pulpería, but there is no information on how she acquired it. It is clear that she ran and provisioned the shop herself, as she testified that she was familiar with a larger shop that sold wholesale, which had been robbed, because it was there that she bought bottles of wine to sell in her own pulpería.[33] It is indeed notable that all of the pulperas that we have information about were widows, suggesting, though certainly not conclusively, that one of the main ways a woman entered this occupation was through inheriting the business interests of her husband. It is also noteworthy that although many male pulperos ran shops owned by others, as will be seen in the next chapter, in the few examples of women pulperas, all of them owned their own shops.[34]

Owning a pulpería did not decrease one's social status in colonial society, but the pulperos who managed these shops were of very low social status. The general low opinion of pulperos is exemplified in a 1647 criminal case in which the defendant declared his honest reputation by stating that "he had never held the occupation of pulpero or other low and base occupations."[35] It is therefore not surprising that the men and women who exercised this profession were themselves from the lower sectors of society, often from mixed racial backgrounds, and frequently of illegitimate birth. The low reputation of pulperos was universal and durable in Spanish America. In the 1760s in Santiago, Chile, pulperos were described as coming from "the dregs of the population, *zambas* [individuals of indigenous and African descent], Indians and mulatas."[36]

If the women who ran their own grocery shops lacked much social prestige, however, not all of them were poor. The widow Tomasa Sánchez, for example, the illegitimate daughter of Gerónimo Sánchez, deceased, and Catalina de la Muela, achieved moderate prosperity with the pulpería she owned and administrated in Quito.[37] Tomasa ran her pulpería with the help of her only daughter, Francisca de Reinoso, who was in charge of the shop's accounting and inventory. Tomasa and her daughter lived in the pulpería, probably in rooms behind the main shop. In addition to the merchandise in the pulpería, Tomasa had 600 pesos in cash at the time she made her testament. She claimed that she owed no debts but that many people, probably her customers, owed her various sums of money, which were noted in a separate memorandum. She bequeathed 300 pesos to the monastery of San Francisco in Quito to establish a *capellanía* (chaplaincy) and left the rest of her property and money to her daughter. Through rigorously administrating her pulpería, incurring no debts, and living frugally in the back rooms of her establishment, Tomasa was able to save a sizable sum of money, part of which she used to establish her name in all perpetuity through founding the capellanía. Indeed, Tomasa used her occupation as a pulpera not only to maintain herself and her daughter but also to make a claim on a piece of eternity.

In addition to owning and operating pulperías, women also supplied these shops with merchandise. Gerónima Morales, a married Spanish woman of humble economic means, for example, was involved in the wholesale of goods to retailers.[38] Part of her family's income came from agricultural land, whose produce Gerónima was in charge of marketing. As part of her commercial activities, she received credit from others on the basis of future harvests. In her testament, for example, she requested that her husband, Juan Fernández de Córdoba, pay the remaining 90 pesos she owed to a priest with the proceeds of the coming harvest, as she had promised. Gerónima was not only in charge of marketing her family's agricultural produce but was a broker for the goods of others as well. Antenorio Mitia sent her maize to sell in the pueblo of Mocha, near Riobamba, and a nun in the convent of the Limpia Concepción sent her biscuit to be sold to the pulpero of Mocha. Gerónima's business relationship with the convent in Riobamba suggests that women of all walks of life were involved in the production and circulation of goods of primary necessity.

Women also participated in wholesale networks by raising and selling livestock. Women were regular participants in the official *abasto* (provisioning) of meat to the city of Quito. The city of Quito, like all large metropolitan centers in Spanish America, sought to assure a constant supply of meat to its citizens.[39] Through the abasto the city granted weekly monopolies to individuals and organizations to provide the cattle that were slaughtered in the city's slaughterhouse. The city council, throughout the seventeenth century, regularly granted the weekly abasto to women of leading families, such as doña Mariana de Villacís, doña Gerónima Revelo, doña Mariana de Granobles, and doña Ana de Cepeda.[40] Lockhart's research on Peru in the mid-sixteenth century shows that at that time and place, women rarely owned agricultural land and livestock.[41] By the seventeenth century in the Quito area, however, women of all sectors of society owned and administered agricultural lands and commercialized livestock. The elite Spanish women above, who sold their livestock to the city through the weekly abasto, were joined by both indigenous and mestizo women who raised livestock commercially.

The indigenous doña María Gualupiango, cacica principal of the Caguasquí and Lita pueblos and widow of don Juan de Salas, cacique (male indigenous ruler) of Caguasquí, sold twenty-five head of cattle to the friar Francisco de Paredes y Salazar in Otavalo in 1641.[42] When the mestizo Catalina Sánchez, widow of Joan Yañes, dictated her testament in 1645, she was careful to include the diagram of the branding mark she used for her seventy head of cattle on her estancia in Latacunga.[43] In 1642, doña Rafaela del Calillo agreed to sell one hundred arrobas of raw wool produced from her herd of sheep to Juan Gordón for 225 pesos, of which she received an advance of 170 pesos.[44] The indigenous María de Mendiola, *vecina* (citizen) of Quito, bought sixty-nine head of sheep to raise commercially in order to support two orphans she raised.[45]

Women of lower social status were involved in the actual processing of livestock. As we will see in Chapter 5, the occupation of sheep slaughtering and marketing was filled by indigenous women *carniceras*. If indigenous carniceras possessed little status in colonial society, Spanish women involved in processing animals did no better. The unmarried María de Castillo, who claimed to be Spanish, processed cattle hides in her tannery located beside her house in Quito.[46] By 1660 she had been running the tannery for over twenty years on land that she originally bought from Gerónimo Aguilar. María ran her operation with a large contingent of indigenous men and women, many of whom lived on her property. That María garnered little respect or wealth from this occupation became apparent in a lawsuit of 1662, which was the culmination of a bitter land dispute she had with her neighbor, doña Marcela de Fuentes.

The fight began in 1659, when María claimed that doña Marcela and her married sister, doña María, took her to doña Marcela's house, beat her up, and stole her land deed. The next year, doña Marcela secretly channeled water into María's property, destroying many of her tanned hides. That same year a civil accord was reached between the parties in which it was agreed that María owned the piece of land on which she had her house and tannery and that doña Marcela would channel her water into the street. However, in 1662 tempers flared again, and María claimed that doña Marcela and her sister beat her up in the street, threatened to cut her face, and called her an "Indian whore" (*puta india*). In addition, the sisters reportedly declared that since they were wealthy, they could defend themselves, whereas she in her poverty would have to sell her cloak in order to pay the notaries, and she would still lose.

In María's litigation the only people who testified on her behalf were her indigenous workers and mestizo women who dressed as Indians and needed Spanish translation. Indeed, it seems as if the whole neighborhood held María in bad repute. Many testified that she was frequently seen drinking and gambling with her indigenous workers. It was widely known that she was having an affair with a married man, to whom, people said, she had transferred all her vices. The parish priest testified that she never obligated her indigenous workers to attend mass on Sundays.

Despite her low reputation, María's complaints were taken seriously by the court. Royal authorities ordered that doña Marcela and her sister be put under house arrest. The suit continued for several months, though the outcome is unknown. What is clear is that María's longtime occupation as a tanner had not raised her status in society, and she remained notoriously poor.

Urban Property and Slaveholding

Lockhart's research indicates that in sixteenth-century Peru, urban real estate and black slaves who functioned as house servants were conventional areas in which women concentrated their ownership and investments.[47] The women in seventeenth-century Quito continued to participate in these traditionally defined activities, and we've already seen several examples in which women controlled real estate and owned slaves. Women owned a great deal of urban property both for their residences and for renting out, and land transactions by women of all racial backgrounds are commonly found in the notarial records.

For example, Juana de Bohorques both bought and sold property in Quito on 6 September 1638.[48] She sold a thatched house on a small piece of property to another woman and bought a tile-covered house in the parish of Santa Bárbara from the indigenous Francisco Ladino, a tailor.

In 1638 as well, the indigenous Elena Yumipansa sold land that she had bought from the indigenous Juana Sumasa to Diego de Barahona, also indigenous.[49] Another example is the land sold by the indigenous Francisco de Chaves to the indigenous Juana de Valverde, a piece of land in the parish of Santa Bárbara next to the houses of the indigenous women carneras.[50] Finally, the married Francisca Mendiola bought in her own name a piece of property, also in the parish of Santa Bárbara, from the indigenous Ana Vilca.[51]

Women used their urban property as a form of investment. The married Juana de Goyones, for example, rented a house in the parish of San Marcos to Pedro Rodríguez de Consuegra, with the condition that he install a shop at street level and not leave it vacant during the duration of the yearlong lease.[52] Doña María de Aguilar, in 1642, rented out her house in Santa Bárbara, with the exception of a set of rooms for herself, for the large sum of 1,642 pesos for a two-year lease.[53]

Women also bought and sold slaves in the city of Quito. The married doña Marta de Bohorques Villamarín, for example, in 1642 bought twelve-year-old Catalina Criolla, mulatto, and the black nine-year-old Domingo, separating him from his mother, for the sum of 350 pesos, from a priest who had inherited them from his mother.[54] In 1641 Francisca Gerónima de Fuentes sold to doña Catalina de Escobar and her husband the twenty-nine-year-old Isabel Angola, a black slave, for 330 pesos. Slaves were both few in number and high in price in the city of Quito, yet they were frequently found as women's personal property, and it is probable that much of the buying and selling of slaves by women was speculative in nature.

Money Lending

A great deal of the liquid capital that circulated through the district flowed through the hands of women. As we saw above, women of various levels of wealth invested funds in the textile trade. Beyond investments, any woman who could gather together even small amounts of capital lent out funds at interest or in exchange for pawn items. The pawning of personal property was an important mechanism in loan transactions, and even wealthy women, who were able to loan out great sums of money at interest, combined this activity with smaller loans, for which they accepted pawn items. The Spanish widow doña Tomasa de Fonseca y Ponce, for example, lent 1,000 pesos to the merchant Captain don Juan de Albornoz, which she requested be collected with interest by the executors of her will.[55] She also lent 150 pesos to Antonio Vara in Latacunga, which she wanted collected with five years of interest. In addition to these large loans to men, she lent out much smaller funds to women in exchange for pawn items. The indigenous Rosa de Tapia owed 6 pesos and 1 real, for which doña Tomasa had a *saya* (skirt) in her possession. Rosa's sister, Manuela, also owed 6 pesos and 1 real, for which she had pawned a Spanish shirt. A Spanish woman pawned several articles of women's clothing in exchange for a loan of 40 pesos. Doña Tomasa requested that the money be collected and the items returned to their owners. Doña Tomasa owned no landed property, nor does she seem to have been involved in any business enterprise, which suggests that loaning money itself was an important part of her income, using capital that she probably inherited.

Loans and the extension of credit were an intrinsic element in the economic survival of the lower sectors. The testaments of humble women, frequently mestizos, commonly mention a series of small loans and debts. Juana Gascón, the illegitimate child of Gerónimo Gascón and doña Petrona Taquima, was owed small sums of money, most between 2 and 5 pesos, by ten indigenous men and women.[56] She herself owed 5 pesos to Bartolomé, a barber, to whom she had pawned a silk lliglla (indigenous woman's cloak). Mariana de Torres, the illegitimate child of Pedro de Torres Beltrán and doña Inés de Espinosa, cacica, owed small debts to ten men and women, including money loaned to her by a Spanish woman; she owed her largest debts, of 83 and 35 pesos, to her sons-in-law.[57] In addition, she had jewelry pawned to Gregorio, a tailor. An example of the frequency with which poor women extended small loans to others is that of Tomasa Morales, who declared her official occupation as seamstress. On the night she attacked Bárbara de la Vega, discussed in the last chapter, she was out collecting debts.[58] Her victim, Bárbara de la Vega, was also out collecting debts that night, one of her debtors being a blacksmith who owed her seven reales.

But to find women who are truly impressive both for the number of people they lent money to and for the multiracial networks they created, one must look to the indigenous community. The testaments of indigenous women, more than any other racial group, consistently record long lists of both debts and loans, and these economic transactions commonly included Spaniards, mestizos, blacks, and mulattos, along with other Indians. Some of the debts owed to indigenous women were reasonably large. For example, Isabel del Castillo, illegitimate child of Diego Collaguasu and Juana Asumasa, was owed 100 pesos that she had lent to the Spanish captain Diego Díaz de Paz in the city of Archidona.[59]

The widow doña Leonor Carxatigua needed several pages to record her economic transactions.[60] Fifteen people owed doña Leonor money, sums ranging from 4 pesos that a mulatto and black woman each owed her to 200 pesos she had loaned to another woman. For her part she owed an unspecified debt to a Spanish merchant, as well as to the guarantor for that debt, her compadre Alonso Andújar. Doña Leonor also formed a company with Andújar, in which they evenly split the costs and profits for wheat they sowed on her estancia and on lands they rented from other Indians. Doña Leonor was a wealthy woman, and she donated large pieces of land to her compadre and to the four orphaned children she raised. Just as any wealthy Spaniard would do, she also founded a capellanía, which she expected to continue "until the end of the world," naming her godchild as the first priest to serve in it.

Doña Leonor seems a bit exceptional in her economic success, especially as neither she nor her deceased husband was a cacique, he lacking even the title "don." Far more common were indigenous women who were owed small sums of money by long lists of people. Doña Juana Tosi, for example, listed twenty-seven debtors plus a memorandum which recorded other debts owed to her.[61] All her debtors were other indigenous women and men, the sums ranging from 2 to 22 pesos. Some of her loans were made in exchange for pawn items. One of these transactions was rather curious; doña Juana had in her possession an *anaco* (an indigenous woman's skirt) pawned for 4 pesos by doña Antonia, the daughter of don Bartolomé Sancho Hati, one of the most important indigenous families in the entire Quito region.

María Mendiola listed fourteen debtors for sums ranging from 2 to 12 pesos.[62] Francisca Chuitiguay was owed money by nine indigenous men and women, most of the debts amounting to between 1 and 2 pesos.[63] For the largest debt, 30 pesos, she held items in pawn. Showing that even family members weren't always trusted when it came to repaying loans, Ana Marchin lent her niece 11 pesos in exchange for the pawn of a silver bowl.[64] Finally, demonstrating the ubiquitous presence of debt in the indigenous community, Lucía Nasipansa was owed money by three people: a mulatto and an indigenous man and woman. Nasipansa owned several parcels of land but does not seem to have been particularly wealthy. She was, however, able to place her illegitimate daughter, Pascuala del Rosario, as a lay nun (*monja donada*) in the convent of Santa Clara in Quito.

Conventional Activities

Some occupations were conventionally assigned to women, the public extension of skills traditionally used in the household. These occupations were normally filled by women of lower social status, generally poor indigenous women. Most house servants, for example, were indigenous women, usually young and unmarried. The common term used to refer to these young women was *china,* the Quechua word for servant.[65] Servant contracts seem usually to have been oral, as it is rare to find written records of them.

An example of a written contract, drawn up between Martín Bereno and the unmarried, indigenous Leonor Méndez in 1638, however, shows the low financial remuneration of this work and the expectation that these women would be completely dependent on their employers during the length of the contract.[66] Méndez was to earn the total of 12 pesos for a year's work, plus her food; lodging; medical care, if she should become ill; and religious instruction. In return she promised to serve Bereno in whatever he should demand for the entire year, with no breaks, and if she should, for some reason, miss a day of work, she was to make it up at the end of the year. In homes which had black slaves, the work of indigenous women was usually overseen by slave women, who typically possessed more authority than their indigenous counterparts. In some cases black slaves were even assigned their own indigenous servants. The daughter of an indigenous chichera, for example, was the servant of María, the black slave of Maestre de Campo don Manuel Ponce.[67]

Bread baking in the Quito District was also an occupation solidly filled by women. All references to bread bakers were to *panaderas* (female bakers). In addition, bread baking was done largely by indigenous women; references to other women in this activity are rare.[68] As in other regions women bread bakers were frequently at odds with officials. Bread baking was supposed to be a controlled activity, and the Quito City Council regulated the price, weight, and ingredients of bread. In March 1654, for example, because of a particularly wet year that had destroyed much of the wheat in the areas surrounding the city, there were constant accusations that the panaderas were highly irregular in both the baking and selling of bread. The council discussed how the panaderas were reportedly adulterating the bread, decreasing the weight of the loaves, and selling bread at higher prices than stipulated by law.[69] The council demanded that the corregidor and his lieutenant be more vigilant in enforcing its decrees concerning bread. The officials were ordered to ensure that each loaf weigh eight ounces and be sold at the legal prices. Those who bought maize and wheat in order to resell these grains at higher prices were to be punished for contributing to the scarcity and high prices of bread in the city.[70]

But problems with the supply of bread in the city continued, and in August of that year, the panaderas were once again the focus of discussion in the city council.[71] Earlier that month the council had mandated that the price of wheat was 3 pesos per fanega (unit of dry measure, about 1.5 bushels) and flour 3½ pesos per fanega. Accordingly, the council publicly announced a new price scale lowering the price of bread, to begin in September, giving the panaderas time to use the flour that they had bought at a higher price. The new regulations mandated that eight loaves of bread, weighing six ounces each, be sold for 1 real. The panaderas continued to be the topic of discussion, and in February 1655 the council considered methods to control the wayward bread bakers.[72] Despite the fact that the council had been distributing wheat to certain panaderas to ensure that bread got sold according to the legal guidelines, the women continued to sell loaves that weighed only three or four ounces. The council thus appointed special deputies to oversee the city's panaderas, with the power to seize the bread of any woman selling it at lower than the stipulated weight and giving the bread to the poor in jail. To the consternation of city officials, the women simply ignored laws that restricted their commerce and apparently worked out an accord with deputies to overlook their illegal practices.

The production, if not the sale, of chicha was the exclusive activity of indigenous women. The preparation of this fermented drink made from corn, called *azua* or *aka* in Quechua, was a female activity through long pre-Hispanic Andean tradition.[73] The Jesuit Bernabé Cobo dedicated a whole chapter to chicha in his chronicle *Historia del Nuevo Mundo,* finished in 1656, in which he described its religious significance for Andeans, its alcoholic properties, the mode of preparation, and its use as a folk medicine.[74] The fermentation of this drink was produced through the saliva of the chicheras, who masticated the boiled maize, then mixed it with water and allowed it to sit for several days. Perhaps because of this tedious process, only indigenous women were culturally inclined to prepare chicha.

Some chicheras controlled both the production and marketing of their product, such as Pascuala Llapasa, who both prepared and sold chicha from her house in the village of Perucho. She combined this activity with selling food items and prepared food to her indigenous clientele.[75] However, it seems to have been common for chicheras to be hired by non-Indians, who then marketed the product themselves. Such was the situation in the pueblo of Sanbisa, in which the royally licensed pulpería sold chicha. The Spanish owner of the shop tried to have the chicheras of the pueblo prohibited from selling the beverage.[76] We've already seen that the Spanish doña Juana Méndez de la Higuera employed a chichera, supplying the maize and utensils for its preparation.[77] In yet another example the indigenous widow Lucía Cueva was hired in Quito by Manuel de Bastidas, in whose house she also lived, to prepare chicha.[78] Despite the fact that chicha required specialized skills in its preparation, the indigenous women who filled this occupation had little social status and were quite poor, often employees of Spaniards and living in the houses of others.

Conclusion

Research on women's economic activities in the Audiencia of Quito suggests that women in the middle colonial period, like women in the eighteenth century for whom we have more information, actively participated at all levels of the economy. For women in the upper sectors of society, regardless of their racial background, their control over their economic enterprises seems to have brought them independence. Even married women operated businesses and invested capital independently from their husbands. There were women's occupations of lower status, which were traditionally filled by humble people, just as with men. However, as we've seen, much of the participation in the area's economy, including its most important industry, textile production, was not determined by gender.

Women operated in a racially mixed economy. Indigenous women invested in Spanish enterprises, owned livestock, and lent money to Spaniards. Spaniards also were involved in traditionally indigenous enterprises, such as the production of chicha. In addition, commerce was highly regulated in the Audiencia, and the commercial success of women, as well as of men, depended on their connections to royal and local authorities who were charged with enforcing these regulations. Women of all social ranks, from elite Spanish doñas to the poor indigenous bread bakers, were generally successful at negotiating agreements with various levels of authorities, who held divergent interests in the women's enterprises. The argument is not that women's lives weren't defined to a large extent by their gender but that this definition still allowed women to claim, as did doña Juana Méndez de la Higuera, that she acquired her wealth through her individual solicitude and work.[79]

CHAPTER 5

Indigenous Market Women

The indigenous market women of the Audiencia of Quito are unique in the region's commercial history because the combination of their profession, gender, and racial status made them identifiable as a specific group of economic actors. Authorities regulated and punished the women collectively, and the indigenous women vendors themselves challenged authorities and made alliances with other social sectors as groups organized around the specific products the women sold. This chapter explores indigenous women's participation in marketing in the city of Quito, the smaller villa of Riobamba, and some of the outlying pueblos of these two sierran urban centers.

In 1654 in response to an ongoing lawsuit between male pulperos (managers of small grocery shops) and indigenous gateras (women market vendors), the government-appointed attorney for the indigenous women argued that they enjoyed the same freedom and rights to sell their products as the pulperos.[1] A few years later the attorney for the Jesuits also argued in favor of free trade, claiming that the prohibition on the sale of meat from Jesuit herds of livestock was a violation of their "natural and human rights."[2] Despite these early appeals for equality in the marketplace and respect for the supposed natural and human right to engage in economic transactions, commerce within the Quito District was highly regulated. Power to regulate the provisioning of the large city of Quito and the smaller *villas* and *pueblos* fell under the shared jurisdictions of the royal government and municipal councils. The commerce both in the pulperías (small groceries and general stores) and on the streets and plazas, as well as the production and transportation of goods, were subject to a host of competing laws ambiguously applied on the basis of the seller's racial status and the origin of the merchandise. Women involved in marketing exploited the confusion in economic legislation and the irregular enforcement of laws. The gateras successfully manipulated colonial definitions of gender roles and race in order to limit government regulation of their commerce and to successfully compete with male Spanish shop owners.

The Gato and Gateras

In the seventeenth century the streets and plazas of both Spanish and indigenous communities were filled with women, overwhelmingly indigenous women, selling products produced locally as well as goods imported from other parts of the viceroyalty and from Europe. Women dominated street marketing to such an extent that references to vendors in ordinances and litigation always referred to them in the feminine, as if no men ever participated in this occupation.[3] Within Spanish culture the poorest women had been vending their wares in the Iberian peninsula's marketplaces for centuries. It is harder to ascertain, however, if the overwhelming presence of women in markets also had roots in pre-Hispanic practices in the Andes. There remains, in fact, considerable debate over whether markets were even part of an Andean tradition or if they were a Spanish innovation. Unlike in early reports of Mexico, where the magnitude and complex organization of indigenous commerce impressed the first chroniclers, early Spanish reports from the Andes made no direct reference to any marketing activity within indigenous communities. It has been traditionally accepted within Andean historiography that the Indians of this region lacked any market tradition, relying instead on what John Murra describes as "ecological archipelagos."[4] Murra defines this system as "simultaneous access of a given ethnic group to the productivity of many microclimates. . . . This was achieved by attempting to settle one's own people on as many tiers as circumstances (military, religious, and kinship ties) allowed."[5] In this view access to resources was achieved through community membership rather than through commercial relations.

Murra's theory remains generally accepted for the southern and central Andes, the core of Inca-controlled territory, but is challenged for the northern Andes by the works of Roswith Hartman, Udo Oberem, and Frank Salomon, who demonstrate the presence of a far-reaching and active market tradition in what later became the jurisdiction of the Audiencia of Quito.[6] Salomon notes that a market was never officially created in Quito; instead the *tiánguez,* as the Spaniards called the indigenous market, using the New World Spanish word borrowed from the Nahuatl *tianquiztli,* seems to have already been functioning.[7] This early tiánguez, however, does not appear to have encompassed the main function of later markets—supplying basic necessities. The earliest mention of the tiánguez in May 1535 refers only to precious metals, gems, and pearls.[8] Indeed, the city council did not consider this original indigenous market essential to the maintenance of the city, for a month later, in June, Spaniards were altogether prohibited from entering the tiánguez, under penalty of 12 gold pesos; slaves who disobeyed the ordinance were to receive one hundred lashes.[9] It is important to note that these early declarations about the indigenous market make no specific references to women, instead referring simply to the "indios." Although this could signify that both men and women were vending in the indigenous market, it was quite common for Spaniards to refer to "indios e indias" when both sexes were involved in an activity.

Spaniards continued to use the term tiánguez to refer to markets throughout the sixteenth century. However, by the seventeenth century Spaniards and Indians referred to markets using the word gato, a Hispanized version of the Quechua katu, defined as "a market for things to eat."[10] A gato was usually a centralized market plaza, though its meaning could also encompass any site where selling occurred. For example, doña Francisca Pizuli, the mestizo cousin of the cacique (male indigenous ruler) of Cotocollao, was said to have set up her own gato, or stall, on the public street where she sold, among other things, bread, cheese, salt, and raw sugar.[11] The Spaniards' choice of indigenous Andean terms to describe market activities supports the contention that they were recognizing an already established practice within indigenous society rather than imposing new forms of exchange on the northern Andean population.

In the seventeenth century market women in the Audiencia of Quito were commonly referred to as gateras, presumably because they sold in gatos. There was a strange linguistic overlap, however, between the partly Quechua term gatera and the Spanish regatera, used in the thirteenth-century Partidas to refer to female vendors.[12] In thirteenth-century Spain, these market women were considered so "vile" that men of the aristocracy were prohibited from taking them, or their daughters, as concubines. The women's status was comparable to that of prostitutes; if an aristocrat procreated with a market woman, their child would not be considered illegitimate (hijo natural) but spurious (hijo espurio), a category reserved for children engendered "against the law and natural reason."[13] In the seventeenth century, regatera was replaced by regatona, both terms apparently derived from the verb regatear, to do petty retailing, hence to haggle or be mean and sparing. Although regatona was a general term for market woman, its use was still offensive. The gateras of Quito were insulted when the pulperos referred to them as regatonas, responding in their legal defense that if anyone merited being called by this name it was the pulperos themselves, who enriched themselves by buying bulk items, in addition to stolen goods, and reselling them at high prices.[14] The connection between theft and the resale of items was made frequently and suggests that for the Spaniards there was something criminal in retail selling in general.

Indigenous market women were also occasionally referred to as *mindaláes* in this period. Salomon's investigation of pre-Hispanic markets suggests that mindaláes were a hereditary group of indigenous merchants operating in the northern Andes, who generally dealt in luxury items.[15] The etymology of mindalá is unclear, possibilities ranging from a Spanish derivative to an extinct Chibcha language in the northern sierra. Modern definitions include "small and stingy," and "Indian women . . . who sell food, spices, vegetables etc. at retail."[16] Salomon's evidence indicates that in the sixteenth century mindaláes were usually male, specialized in the importation of extrasierran goods of high prestige and high value, and seemed to be part of the native elite of the city of Quito.[17] From the two references we have for the seventeenth century, the gender, prestige, and activities of mindaláes had changed considerably, more closely approximating the modern-day definitions above. In 1665, for example, a Spanish *tratante* (small-scale dealer) collected small debts from "some Indian women who are called mindaláes," in a section of the market where potatoes and salt were sold.[18] The mindaláes, then, were women selling sierran products of low value and were at least partially dependent upon Spanish financing for their commerce.

The second mention of a mindalá occurs in Ambato, south of the city of Quito. The indigenous María Criolla was described as a "mindalá vendor in the gato."[19] She was subject to the cacique don Pedro Pila and married to the indigenous Pedro de Geres. Both her husband and son listed their occupation as shearing sheep. At thirty years old she owned a housing compound in which various indigenous families lived, including her married son. Again we see the generally low social status of mindaláes. María lacked a typical Spanish or indigenous surname; Criolla was, in fact, a description for non-Spaniards undergoing a cultural transformation. She was counted as part of the tribute-paying population of her cacique and married to a humble indigenous man. Her occupation vending in the market does not seem to be a family concern, as neither her husband nor son was noted as supplying her stock, the activity the two of them would most likely be involved in. From these two examples, it is hard to determine what differentiated mindaláes from the general mass of indigenous gateras. What is clear is that these seventeenth-century mindaláes lived very different lives than the elite indigenous merchants of sixteenth-century Quito described by Salomon.

Whether adapting to a long-held Spanish tradition of associating women with market activities, or continuing a northern Andean custom

of marketing, it is clear that Indian women in the Andes actively participated in this type of commerce soon after Spaniards invaded the region.[20]
By the seventeenth century in the Quito District, indigenous women seem
to dominate this occupation. Although women of all racial backgrounds
were involved in marketing, with the important exception of Spanish
women, who are never mentioned as market women, it is difficult to
know very much at all about nonindigenous women.[21] The Indian gateras
monopolize the historical documentation, completely eclipsing the presence of other women in this occupation. The convergence of indigenous
women's gender and racial status gave them economic and legal oppor-
tunities that simultaneously encouraged their participation in the market
and promoted their entrance into the historical record.

Indigenous women faced few gender-specific obstacles to their economic activities because, as we've seen, Spanish law recognized and even
supported women's economic independence from men during this period.
Indigenous women were subject to the same gender legislation as all other
women in colonial society. However, indigenous women did have an economic advantage over other retail vendors because of their racial status.
As Indians they were exempt from paying the royal sales tax collected
from other social sectors. This racial division within the colonial economy will be discussed more fully in the next section. The gateras had economic advantages over their male counterparts as well. Indigenous men
between the ages of eighteen and fifty were legally required to pay tribute
to Spanish authorities, usually in the form of money or regional products but sometimes, in the Quito region, in specific periods of physical
labor, especially in obrajes (textile factories). Indigenous women legally
were not subject to this type of taxation.[22] Indigenous women thus lived
in an economic nether land formed at the intersection of their race and
gender.

Indigenous women's tax-free status, however, rather than allowing
them to disappear into an unregulated, informal economy, actually fomented intense legal battles with shop owners and the government because the women made every effort to stretch the limits of their peculiar
legal status within the economy. The racial status of the gateras had much
to do with the proceedings and outcomes in this litigation because, as
Indians, they had access to a court-appointed attorney, the Protector of
the Indians. Whereas pulperos, and indeed other women vendors, were
required to hire attorneys to represent their interests, the gateras were
not charged for representation by the Protector of the Indians.[23] Access to
free, competent legal representation was, of course, a significant advantage for the Indians. Minchom cites a 1695 lawsuit in Riobamba in which
Feliciana de Mora sued Antonio de Riofrío for 400 pesos. In his defense

Antonio claimed that Feliciana was a mestizo but was pretending to be an Indian in order to use the services of the Protector of the Indians.[24] The gateras' ability and willingness to litigate and their capacity to legally challenge laws that restricted their activities allowed them to participate in determining the content of economic legislation. Despite the fact that gateras were illiterate, unable to speak Spanish, poor, and members of a profession which generally garnered little respect, they were effective legal adversaries, tenacious in protecting and expanding their economic activities throughout the century. While market women of other racial backgrounds were silenced by their poverty, the gateras left a permanent record revealing many of the mechanisms they used to perform the vital function of provisioning the Audiencia of Quito.

Throughout the region, marketplaces were officially located in central plazas and were important social and political centers in addition to having economic importance. Salomon notes that by the end of the sixteenth century, members of the Royal Audiencia in Quito worried that they were excluded from the mainstream of city life because of their distance from "the plaza where the natives conduct their markets."[25] Indeed, proximity to the market could be such a priority that determining its location became a significant political act. Such was the case in the pueblo of Achimbo, near Riobamba. There doña Catarina Bravo de Saravia, who was said to control the justice system, also controlled the gato, which she had moved from its former location to the front of her house so that she could better monitor its occupants.[26] Residents claimed in 1693 that she profited from the market's new location by forcing the gateras to sell food to her at half the normal price and, when her obraje fell behind in its textile production, obligating the market women to weave for her.

What the Quito cabildo (town council) and doña Catarina recognized was that being near the market enhanced their ability to affect the pulse of public activity at its very heart. Throughout the week a major part of the local populace passed through the marketplace, and the patronage of the plazas reached even higher levels on holidays. Even on fiesta days the gateras continued to sell their wares and transacted with those who supplied them with goods and credit in the market square.[27] Government authorities took advantage of the swollen population on these days to proclaim regulations to the inhabitants of cities and towns.[28] In Quito the four main marketplaces in the seventeenth century—the Plaza Mayor, the Placeta of San Diego, the Placeta of the Recoleta, and the Placeta of San Blas—were commonly used to announce new resolutions and laws affecting citizens. The town criers were careful to note that "there were many people present."[29] In fact, proclamations in the market were considered to reach the entire population of the city. When the pulperos demanded that the prohibitions on certain forms of trade between market women and their customers be announced in the city "so that the law comes to the notice of everyone and that no one can claim ignorance," the government ordered that the law be announced in the four central marketplaces.[30] Markets were also where public punishments were carried out. The markets of Quito each contained a post for public whippings.[31] Officially designated marketplaces thus not only served to control the economic activities of the population but were also areas where the government exercised social and political authority.

Commercial Controls: The Alcabala

City councils tried to centralize market activity in an attempt to guarantee order, simplify supervision, and centralize tax collection. Unlike in other areas in the Viceroyalty of Peru, the economic transactions of market women in the district of Quito faced much regulatory activity on the part of government officials. Research on colonial market women in the city of Lima, for example, shows that these vendors provisioned the capital with little interference from the government. Indeed, when late colonial officials tried to levy the alcabala, or sales tax, on indigenous vendors, there was a public outcry.[32] Already in the seventeenth century, however, market women within the Quito District were involved in pitched battles with government officials over the latter's attempts to regulate and tax their commerce. An attorney for the district's Indians in 1714, in fact, complained that "in all of this kingdom of Peru, no one levies the alcabala on Indians; only in this province are they expected to pay the tax."[33]

Historically, the district of Quito had a unique relation to the alcabala since the royal government had imposed it on the Viceroyalty of Peru in 1591. As was mentioned in Chapter 1, Spaniards in Quito, led by the city council, revolted against this tax, and royal troops were required to regain control of the district of Quito. By the next year, however, the sales tax was being collected within the district, and Quito's officials were perhaps the most rigorous tax collectors in the viceroyalty. The alcabala was originally a 2 percent sales tax but was increased to 4 percent in 1627, when it was added to the Derecho de Unión de Armas, a tax to fund the royal galleons that protected Spanish fleets from pirates. Rarely if ever was the tax paid directly by buyers in individual transactions. The tax was prorated, and the city of Quito was responsible for paying the royal treasury a fixed sum every year.[34] Quito was often behind in its payments, which increased the incentive of officials to levy the tax aggressively. This was especially true because the wealthiest citizens, usually merchants, acted as guarantors for the city, risking their own private properties should the city fall short in its alcabala payments to the crown.[35] Because the alcabala was regulated by the royal government but owed and collected by the city, conflicts repeatedly arose over on whom and on what the tax should be levied. Interests could diverge considerably between the Audiencia and the city council, and even officials at the level of the city often found themselves in dispute over the collection of the alcabala.

The alcabala was theoretically imposed on all sales transactions, with the large exception that Indians and their products were exempt from the tax.[36] This distinction between Spaniards and Indians in the economy reflected the formal division of Spanish America into two sectors: the Republic of the Spaniards and the Republic of the Indians.[37] Spanish governmental administration in America was based on this model, which attempted to keep the Spanish and indigenous populations politically and geographically separate. Indigenous rulers retained local authority, and individuals from the Spanish sector were prohibited from living in Indian communities.[38] Pre-Hispanic rulers were responsible for channeling tribute and labor from their communities to the ruling entities of the former Indian empires; in the colonial period they were expected to use their authority to continue this practice for the Spaniards. Although the "two republic" model was never successful in keeping the two populations separate, the official policy of distinguishing between Indians and Spaniards was used by both sectors to promote their own interests. In Guano, an indigenous pueblo near Riobamba, for example, a group of elite indigenous women "cacicas" attempted to expel all Spaniards, mestizos, blacks, and mulattos from their pueblo in 1692. In their lawsuit they cited a royal ordinance issued in 1681 that repeated the prohibition of all non-Indians from living in indigenous pueblos.[39]

The initiative to divide Spanish and Indian economies in the administration of the alcabala was thus consistent with formal government policy. Spaniards were to sell more expensive, processed foods and imported luxury goods; Indians were to sell domestically produced subsistence items on which the tax was not paid.[40] The attempt to neatly divide colonial society into two parallel racial economies failed because of the complexity of commercial networks. Both Spaniards and Indians, for example, were involved in the commerce of subsistence goods. Spaniards were required to pay the alcabala, but Indians selling the same goods were exempt because of their racial status.[41] Spanish producers, because Indians were identified with subsistence items, were frequently accused of using Indians to sell agricultural products, meat, salt, and other items that would normally have been taxed. Municipal officials claimed the right to collect the tax from Indians who transported or sold subsistence goods produced by Spaniards.[42]

Related to the alcabala was a series of regulations on pulperías (small groceries). In 1642 twenty-eight royally licensed pulperías and thirty city-licensed pulperías operated in Quito. Pulperías were usually licensed by the royal government, though large cities such as Quito could be given a dispensation which allowed these municipalities to license a specified number of additional pulperías. In 1633 the Audiencia granted the city of Quito the right to license thirty pulperías. These city-licensed pulperías were still operating in 1669, when a lawsuit was brought to determine if the Audiencia or the city controlled the locations of these thirty shops.[43] None of these city-licensed pulperías appears in litigation against the gateras, adding weight to the complaint by those in royally licensed shops that their financial obligations to the crown made it difficult for them to compete with the market women. The pulperos (managers of the pulperías) stated that in addition to the 30 pesos owed every year to the crown for payment of the alcabala, they also had to pay for yearly inspections of their businesses, pay other tariffs, and make obligatory contributions to government-sponsored celebrations and that they were expected to accompany soldiers leaving the city as far as Latacunga, one hundred kilometers to the south of Quito. In total, the pulperos claimed, their obligations to the crown amounted to 100 pesos per person each year.[44]

The pulperos themselves came from the Spanish sector of society, including mestizos and mulattos. There is no record of any pulpería owned or operated by an Indian in Quito during this period.[45] Pulperos were poor and lacked much social prestige. Most who appear in the litigation records did not own their own shops. Although the owners of the shops were noted as a way of identifying the establishments, the litigation was brought in the name of those who ran the shops, the pulperos. The general low opinion of pulperos is exemplified in a 1647 criminal case in which the defendant declared his honest reputation by stating that he had never worked as a pulpero nor held other jobs he considered to be "low" or "base."[46] Both men and women owned and operated pulperías. Wealthier owners rented out shops to others, avoiding the actual management of the shop and the stigma attached to pulperos.[47] Although only male pulperos appeared in litigation against the gateras and seem to have dominated this occupation in Quito, as we saw in the last chapter, at least some women were involved in this profession.

Pulperos were given the exclusive right to sell a gamut of products because they legally paid the alcabala. As will be seen, a major dispute between the royally licensed pulperos and the gateras in the Audiencia was over the definition of these products. The pulperos argued that the market women should be selling only fruit and vegetables in the plaza and that by selling other items they were encroaching on the pulperos' privileges.[48] The gateras, because of their racial status as Indians, had none of the pulperos' financial obligations to the crown. The pulperos argued that because the Indian women had fewer overhead costs, they sold the same products at lower prices, thus undercutting the legitimate profits of the pulperos. Indeed, pulperos argued that they couldn't meet their obligations to the crown unless the market women were effectively limited to selling only subsistence items.[49] This commercial competition between the gateras and the royally licensed pulperos brought both groups to appeal repeatedly to the Audiencia for changes to and clarification of the district's commercial law.

Legal Battles over Goods

Lowry's study of the indigenous population of Lima, the viceregal capital of Peru, suggests that the city's indigenous market women specialized exclusively in selling agricultural products such as fruits and vegetables throughout the colonial period.[50] Many in the district of Quito wished the indigenous women there had similarly modest ambitions. Unfortunately for the pulperos, the region's indigenous gateras stubbornly sold a wide range of items that theoretically should have been subject to an official price schedule (*arancel*) and the alcabala, both of which were supposed to be enforced by the government officials who inspected the licensed pulperías.[51] The gateras sold virtually everything. Among food items were ham, cheese, raw sugar, salt, honey, rice, beef, fish, bread, pastry, and nougats (candy), as well as alcoholic products such as chicha (an indigenous drink made from fermented corn) and *punta* (a cheap liquor made from sugar). That is, they sold Spanish-style and specialty items as well as indigenous necessities. In addition, they sold many processed and imported items, such as soap, tobacco, dyes, ribbons, thread, silk, jewelry, leather cords, knives, daggers, paper, and even Spanish clothing.[52] Such a varied list of prohibited items was sold by gateras not only in the urban center of Quito but widely throughout the larger district.[53]

In 1642 the royally licensed pulperos of the city of Quito tried to thwart this enterprising spirit of the gateras. The pulperos appealed to the Audiencia to enforce existing commercial law, reminding the authorities that the gateras legally were allowed to sell only fruits and vegetables.[54] The pulperos claimed that they were going bankrupt because the gateras sold their items at low prices, undercutting the profits of the pulperos, who, because of the numerous financial obligations mentioned above, sold their products at higher prices. There is no evidence that the gateras responded to the allegations of the pulperos. That year, in response to the appeal by the pulperos, royal authorities ordered that no "Indian, mestizo, black or mulatto woman" could sell prohibited items. At the first offense they would lose all their merchandise, and at the second offense, in addition to losing their wares, they would be fined 6 pesos and receive one hundred lashes at the post in the plaza where they were selling.[55]

It is obvious that the indigenous women ignored this ruling, since in 1654 the city's pulperos again brought charges against the gateras. The gateras responded, claiming that their extreme poverty, their tradition of selling in the plazas since the foundation of the city, and the benefits that the Indians provided the district all gave them the same rights as the pulperos to sell their products. The Audiencia agreed, and no action was taken until a third appeal by the pulperos in 1666, who again claimed that the gateras should be selling only "herbs, vegetables, potatoes and corn and other things of this type."[56] In response to the pulperos' appeal, the Audiencia ruled in 1667 that "Indian, mestizo, black and mulatto women" could sell all comestibles and local products (*frutos de la tierra*) with the exception of silk, Spanish clothing, beef, soap, and salt.[57]

The 1667 ruling significantly expanded the rights of the women vendors to sell most products. Because salt, however, was not included as a comestible, the commerce of an important group of vendors was prohibited. The salt sold in the markets was mineral salt, and the royal Spanish government had long practiced regulating its production and sale. The Spanish crown traditionally claimed monopoly rights over salt because of the custom of royal control over subsoil rights.[58] The crown legally possessed all minerals within Spanish domains and leased out the rights to exploit minerals to individuals who would then owe a percentage of the profits to the royal government. The crown's monopoly over minerals guaranteed it a lucrative income not only from gold, silver, and mercury deposits but also from the humble salt mines and salt pans. The first geographical surveys sent back to Spain always noted where salt was located in the newly conquered regions. Although the crown had apparently abandoned efforts to enforce its monopoly over salt in the Viceroyalty of Peru early in the seventeenth century, local royal authorities continued to regulate its production and sale. The Audiencia's decision in 1667 to grant a certain sector monopoly rights to sell salt was thus a well-established practice within Spanish law.

The indigenous women salt sellers, however, were undeterred, and they collectively appealed the ruling by the royal authorities. The unity of this sector of the gateras might reflect pre-Hispanic traditions. There is some evidence that salt was a particularly symbolic item for indigenous communities in the northern Andes, even acting as an ethnic marker in its own right. Nineteenth-century visitors, for example, remarked that Indians divided themselves between those who were civilized and ate salt and the barbarians who did not.[59] Other commentators of the period noted that Indians identified mineral salt as a feminine product and that women were exclusively in charge of its production.[60] However, because the evidence is late and relatively scattered, it is difficult to determine whether the strong connection between women and salt was primarily based on a pre-Hispanic tradition or, rather, developed during the colonial period.[61]

During the seventeenth century in the Audiencia of Quito, for example, there is evidence that various sectors, including Spaniards, were heavily involved in the production and transportation of mineral salt. Although Spaniards were producing sea salt—the condiment preferred by Spaniards—on the island of Puná off the coast of Guayaquil, mineral salt was far more widely consumed throughout the district. Less affluent Spanish sectors found mineral salt more affordable, and Indians preferred it. In addition, mineral salt also had industrial uses: miners used it to extract silver from ore.[62] There is also evidence that indigenous men as well were involved in the production and transportation of salt. In a 1678 lawsuit, for example, a group of men stated their profession as salt bakers (*horneros*), and other salt bakers were also referred to in the masculine plural (unlike the market vendors, who were always referred to in the feminine), which suggests that at least some men were commonly involved in this activity.[63]

The group cohesion of the female salt sellers might have reflected an indigenous tradition that associated women with salt. Their solidarity might also have been formed through their shared experiences in vending the same product in the market. Indeed, gateras in general seemed to strongly identify with each other through their merchandise; when stating their occupation they were always careful to indicate what products they sold. Women selling the same products were located in the same section of the market, and they litigated as a group when the commerce of their particular merchandise was threatened. For the salt sellers their commercial specialization seemed to be an element of group cohesion in contradistinction with other gateras in the market, to whom they showed little loyalty. In the legal defense of their commerce, not only did the salt sellers flatly deny that they exchanged their salt for stolen goods, they volunteered that it was really the other gateras, those selling raw sugar and other comestibles, who dealt in stolen property.[64] Litigating as a group they claimed that they had been selling salt in the plazas for many years and had even been paying the alcabala on their product to the city officials, for which they presented receipts.[65]

Information on two salt vendors, María Sinaylín and Isabel Criolla, suggests that they were indeed well established in the plazas of Quito and that careers in the marketplace could last many years and be quite stable. María Sinaylín was mentioned by name as one of the litigants in the suit brought by the salt sellers in 1667, and she presented evidence that she had been paying the alcabala. She also showed up two years earlier as a witness in a criminal suit with another gatera, Isabel Criolla. They were selling salt in the plaza mayor of Quito in 1665 when they witnessed a fight between two men that later ended in a murder.[66] Both of the women were well known at the time, and on the day of the crime they were involved in business transactions with Spanish and mestizo suppliers. Isabel Criolla was, in fact, the first witness who testified for the court, because she had been talking to the accused killer when the fight broke out.[67] In her testimony we learn that she was selling in the section of the plaza dedicated to potatoes and salt, was forty years old, and was a widow. She was born in Quito and owned the houses in which she lived in the neighborhood of San Diego, next to the tile factory of the Jesuits. She specifically stated her occupation as gatera, selling salt and potatoes. Thirteen years later the murder case was reopened, and Isabel Criolla ratified her first declaration. In 1678 she still sold salt and potatoes in the central plaza, was still a widow, and continued to live in the same houses.[68]

The example of the gatera Isabel Criolla suggests that in 1665, when selling salt was prohibited to market women, a section of the Plaza Mayor was specified for salt and potatoes. As the receipts of two salt sellers indicate, the gateras had apparently worked out a kind of truce with local officials, paying the alcabala even though they were exempt as Indians. In the criminal case several men explained that they were present in the market in order to negotiate credit arrangements with gateras. The men stated that they were collecting payments from goods that they had already delivered to the women or were negotiating the price of goods yet to be delivered. The men's declarations suggest that the gateras' commerce attracted the investments of Spanish and mestizo men. We can also see that the careers of market women could be lifelong, that they specialized in specific products, and that they permanently installed themselves in a particular market, as by 1665 Isabel Criolla was already a well-known gatera and was still selling in the same plaza thirteen years later. Despite the fact that the pulperos often tried to portray the women as shady, indigenous vagrants who trafficked in stolen merchandise, market women were more likely to be stable members of their communities.[69] Isabel Criolla was born in Quito, worked in the same location, and owned and lived in the same houses for the entire thirteen years we can record.

The Audiencia's decision in 1667 to permit the gateras to sell all comestibles and local products, with the exception of salt and a few other goods, pleased no one. Both the gateras and pulperos appealed the ruling. The gateras who sold salt were opposed to the prohibition of their commerce. The pulperos, for their part, were angry that the ruling, though it prohibited particular items, had broadened in general the commercial rights of market women. They continued to argue, as they had before, that market women should not be allowed to sell the same kinds of items as the pulperos and should be limited to selling only fruit and vegetables. The pulperos also responded to the receipts that the salt sellers presented to show that the gateras had, in fact, paid the alcabala. The pulperos argued that the fact that the indigenous salt vendors had paid the alcabala did not warrant an exception, because the pulperos, in addition to paying the alcabala, were burdened with other financial obligations to the crown.[70]

On the basis of the appeals by the gateras and the pulperos, the Audiencia reconsidered its ruling. The court first considered the issue of the gateras' payment of the alcabala. The court determined that payment of the alcabala did not give gateras the right to sell prohibited items. Royal law prohibited Indians from paying the alcabala: Indians could not choose to pay the tax; nor was it legal for officials to collect the tax from them. The court therefore ruled that the amounts paid by the gateras be returned to them by the officials who had collected the tax.[71]

The Audiencia therefore agreed with the pulperos that in the administration of the alcabala, primarily racial status determined fiscal status. If royal courts refused to change the relationship of racial status to the alcabala, they would, however, reconsider the relationship of goods themselves to the tax. The second action the court took in its 1667 ruling was to redefine the official status of salt. The court declared that it reaffirmed its original ruling that permitted gateras to sell comestibles; however, based on the appeal by the salt sellers, under commercial law salt now was defined as a comestible.[72] The gateras had won their case; the redefinition of salt as a comestible, a category of goods legal for Indians to sell, permitted the market women to continue their commerce.

The Audiencia ruling in 1667 legitimated a broad and ambiguous category of products Indians could legally sell, the comestible. The next year, 1668, the pulperos asked the court to legally clarify which items were considered comestibles and which were items of pulperías.[73] There is no record that the government ever officially defined the category of comestible. As the pulperos apparently feared, the salt vendors' successful bid to include their product in this legal category set a precedent for indigenous vendors and transporters of other items. In 1677, for example, a group of indigenous men who made a living by transporting sheep argued that mutton should also be considered a comestible and thus legal for them, as

Indians, to sell. They specifically cited the case of the salt sellers in Quito to bolster their claim.[74]

In 1679 indigenous men who transported salt won a partial victory, also using the precedent of the salt sellers. The Audiencia decreed that the alcabala had to be paid on items transported by Indians acting as commercial agents for non-Indians "except for the comestibles that the Indian women sold by retail in the plazas or on products cultivated in their own lands or lands rented for that effect." The salt transporters were allowed four mule loads of salt twice a year exempt from the alcabala.[75] In this ruling, the racial status of the gateras determined the legal definition of the product itself. Salt produced by non-Indians, on which the alcabala was legally levied, became redefined as a comestible and not taxed if it was sold by Indian market women.

Eighteen years after the court's ruling on the gateras' commerce, the market women's success continued to impact commercial relations in the district. When a group of Indian women who sold mutton were imprisoned in 1685 for not paying the alcabala, they defended themselves by claiming that mutton should be considered a comestible, specifically citing the earlier litigation of the women salt vendors in Quito.[76] The success of the gateras in Quito in legalizing their commerce thus reverberated throughout the district for many years. The court's decision in 1667 asserted the primacy of racial status in determining the fiscal status of individuals under commercial law. Indians used their racial status to broaden the scope of their economic activities.

Buying and Selling

The gateras sold a wide range of items whose origins spanned the theoretical division between Spanish and indigenous economies. It is no surprise, then, that the networks they used to procure their stock ruptured the logic of parallel economies as well, encompassing men and women of all social categories who supplied them with credit and goods. Indeed, the women's commerce depended on their agility in piecing together supply networks that included Spanish merchants and fellow Indians in an economy severely affected by a lack of currency.

Pulperos repeatedly cast aspersions on the legitimacy of the gateras' commerce by accusing them of dealing in stolen goods. The men claimed that a major source of procurement for the women was through black slaves and indigenous servants who stole items from their masters.[77] Indeed, as we have seen, the gateras themselves accused each other of involvement with stolen merchandise. The pulperos did not escape suspicion either. Gateras accused pulperos of enriching themselves by buying bulk items, in addition to stolen goods, and reselling them at high prices.[78]

Small-scale retailers, such as the gateras and the pulperos, were particularly vulnerable to accusations that they dealt in stolen property, because the district's lack of small coinage forced them to accept items from poor people in their daily commercial transactions. Officials suspected that goods exchanged within this sector of society were stolen by slaves and servants from their masters and employers. Because of such suspicions authorities tried to control transactions that involved the exchange of personal valuables. In 1656, for example, the Audiencia ruled that market women could not buy or receive in exchange jewelry, jewels, or objects made from silver or iron from any mestizo, Indian, mulatto, black, or "muchacho" (male servant).[79] The ability of officials to control such transactions was limited. The extreme shortage of coinage in the district throughout the colonial period made truck and barter structurally necessary in the lower sectors of the economy. Indeed, the gateras defended their practice of exchanging goods as being beneficial for the poor, who could trade a little corn or bread for other things they needed.[80]

Although the district of Quito reached its highest level of economic prosperity in the seventeenth century, actual coinage was rare. This currency shortage was generalized throughout Spanish America.[81] Robson Tyrer suggests that the principal economic problem for the Quito District from the sixteenth through the eighteenth centuries was the lack of sufficient currency to conduct economic exchange locally.[82] The Quito cabildo tried various tactics to increase the amount of currency in the city. In 1646 the cabildo discussed forbidding merchants to exchange Quito's textiles in Lima for other products instead of returning to Quito with currency.[83] A few years later, in 1654, the cabildo proposed mandating the exchange of locally produced textiles for the Spanish clothing that merchants from Cartagena and the Kingdom of Granada sold in the city in order to stem the outward flow of currency, "which was destroying the commonwealth and leaving the citizens destitute of coinage."[84]

Those dealing in items of low value, products that cost only fractions of a peso, were deeply affected by the general lack of currency. The pulperos resolved this economic problem by allowing frequent customers to build up small debts, accepting pawn items as security. The gateras directly exchanged goods with their customers. The market women's reliance on goods exchange seemed to have added an air of criminality to their commerce. Pulperos capitalized on this perception, dramatically declaring in 1654 that the gateras were a threat to the commonwealth, inciting "great robberies and thefts in every house in this city."[85] In fact, however, only one case was found from the seventeenth century in which market women were officially charged with dealing in stolen property. In this case the property was not acquired from servants or through the exchange of goods in the market; nor was the property resold by the gateras.

In the 1690 criminal case, two gateras from Quito's plaza mayor, Catalina Barona, a salt seller, and Petrona Criolla, a fruit seller, admitted to buying indigenous clothing that they suspected had been stolen from a Spaniard, Josef Robles.[86] Robles had indeed stolen the items from an indigenous household on the edge of town. Both women immediately pawned the items, making a small profit on their investments. The rest of the stolen items were purchased by other poor Indians, who also pawned their purchases.

This criminal case suggests that though individual gateras were involved in dealing with stolen goods, these activities do not seem to be structurally related to their occupation as market women. The stolen property was not resold by the women in the marketplace, where, in fact, it could have been easily detected by its owners. From the list of numerous Indians who bought and pawned Josef's stolen goods, it seems that this activity was a mechanism which poor people in general used to increase their meager incomes. This example also suggests that one of the principal mechanisms used in the circulation of stolen goods was to pawn them, effectively taking the merchandise out of circulation and concealing it for months at a time. Those in occupations in which they habitually accepted pawned items, such as the pulperos, were thus structurally linked to the circulation of stolen goods to a much greater extent than the market women, who depended on the direct exchange of goods and whose commercial transactions occurred publicly.

Pulperos and officials often accused the market women of acting as fronts for Spaniards who were obligated to pay the alcabala. There is much evidence that Spaniards were, in fact, heavily involved in the market women's commerce through investments and by providing the women with merchandise. The indigenous women themselves often claimed that they bought their merchandise from non-Indians, who had already paid the alcabala, and therefore, the women argued, they should not have to pay it again. This was the case of the women who sold mutton in the plazas, mentioned above.[87] They described how they bought, killed, and carried on their own shoulders the meat they sold in the city of Quito. The women claimed that those who raised and owned the animals should pay the alcabala and had always done so. Their attorney added that since the hacienda owners already paid a yearly flat fee for the alcabala, neither the owners nor the indigenous women should be taxed twice. From the response of the official in charge of collecting the tax, it appears that some Indians were entering the city with over two hundred head of sheep, a very different picture from that of a few women buying a couple of sheep from the local haciendas and carrying the meat on their shoulders into town. In addition, the official claimed that the sheep came from haciendas outside of the city's jurisdiction and that therefore the owners of the animals were intentionally using Indians to avoid paying the alcabala.

Whenever Indians brought large quantities of merchandise into the city, officials suspected that Spaniards were involved, and many times their suspicions were confirmed. In the case of the Indian men who transported salt to Quito, mentioned above, officials claimed that one Indian entered the city with over 1,000 arrobas (25,000 pounds) of salt; others were noted as entering with 493 mule loads of salt and another group with 129 mules carrying salt.[88] The Indians were charged with transporting products owned by Spaniards who sought to avoid paying the alcabala. In the Indians' declarations they revealed that Spaniards and mestizos in fact were investing heavily in their commerce. One Indian stated that he was lent 100 pesos at interest by a Spanish lieutenant, and another stated that a candle maker, his Spanish compadre, lent him 40 pesos for each of six trips he had made. Various Spaniards testified that they had asked the Indians how they had brought in such enormous loads of salt. The Indians reportedly responded that Spaniards were funding their trips.[89] The case was resolved with a ruling that limited the number of mules loaded with salt that Indians were allowed each year and by fining the two Spanish investors named by the Indians "for inciting the Indians to commit fraud."[90]

Spaniards were involved in transactions with Indians who transported large quantities of goods to the city of Quito. But non-Indians also engaged directly with the gateras themselves, often dealing in smaller quantities and on a more irregular basis. In a criminal case, mentioned above in relation to the gateras' selling salt, three men were among the witnesses questioned about events that led to the murder. The three men explained that they were present in the market that morning in 1665, arranging business transactions with the gateras. Thomas Salazar, probably mestizo, who stated his profession as a stonecutter, sold the gatera Isabel Criolla twenty fanegas of potatoes on credit. That morning he was in the market to collect his payment, and, he recalled, he and the gatera disputed the price of the potatoes.[91] The Spaniard Captain don Joseph Ponse Castillejo testified that he was involved in a business transaction with another gatera, María Sinaylín, that morning.[92] A third witness, Juan García Rubio, who declared that at the time he was a tratante, stated that he had come to the market that morning to collect payments owed to him from another group of gateras.[93]

The mestizo Blas Texada is another example of non-Indians' involvement in the market women's commerce. Although a professional key maker, when he could not find work in Quito, he traveled to the Yumbos. From this warmer, lowlands region on the western slopes of the volcano Pichincha, he transported products to the markets of Quito.[94] Texada was married to an indigenous woman and owned and lived in a complex of houses in Quito with other Indians, including members of his wife's family. His trade was probably facilitated by his connections to his wife's family, for he negotiated directly with the Indians in the Yumbos, who reportedly held him in great respect. These examples suggest that non-Indians of all social distinctions, from an unemployed key maker to an elite captain with the title *don*, were directly involved in the commerce practiced by indigenous market women. In addition, the fact that all these transactions were limited to potatoes, salt, and produce from the Yumbos indicates that even for products of basic necessity, the gateras relied on Spaniards and mestizos for both credit and provisions.

Gateras could also be employed directly by Spaniards. Such was the case of the indigenous Esperanza Chabla, who was contracted by María Jiménez in 1690 for 12 pesos a year to sell bread, biscuit (*pambazo*), peppers, salt, and other comestibles in the plaza of Guano, a pueblo near Riobamba.[95] Jiménez provided all of Chabla's merchandise, which immediately became a problem because the bread and biscuit were small and the other products of low quality, so no one wanted to buy from Chabla. When she tried to return the items to Jiménez, the latter refused to accept them, asking payment for them and allegedly overcharging Chabla for their value. Because of her poverty Chabla couldn't pay the sum of 24 pesos, so María imprisoned her in her house and physically mistreated her. Chabla sold some of her lands but was still able to pay her only 9 pesos. Jiménez allegedly treated her as a slave, demanding one of Chabla's daughters in exchange for her freedom.

In the end Chabla, using the Protector of the Indians, sued Jiménez. The decision in her favor ordered Jiménez to leave her in peace and not to collect any more money from her. The next year Jiménez' husband was arrested for illegally employing a gatera to sell bread from their house. Although there is no evidence that the indigenous woman was punished, she ran the risk of being condemned to one hundred lashes and having her head shorn.[96] As these cases show, gateras who worked as employees lost all control over their commerce, could find themselves in coercive situations, and potentially faced severe sanctions by officials.

Market women, of course, also procured their merchandise through other Indians, though such networks are harder to document. There were no legal restrictions on transactions between Indians, as there were between Indians and non-Indians. The lack of legal scrutiny of Indians' commercial relations with each other resulted in few records of their business agreements. As we saw in the last chapter, indigenous women did, however, leave testaments showing impressive multiracial networks of investment, credit, and debt, which probably included market women.

Spanish officials assumed that some products the gateras sold in the market, such as fruit and vegetables, were produced and grown by Indians. It wasn't until 1708 that suspicions arose over the indigenous origins of this commerce.[97] Spanish officials accused a group of Indian men of transporting goods owned by Spaniards to avoid paying the alcabala. Officials questioned the Indians, who regularly transported produce to the central market of Quito, because of the large quantity of fruit and vegetables in their possession. The attorney for the indigenous transporters responded that "the fruit, even if it was a lot, certainly and evidently belonged to the Indians as no Spaniard cultivated these products." And in fact, the Indians were set free and their goods returned to them on the basis of this argument.[98] Despite this association between produce and the indigenous sector of the economy, the networks that gateras used to acquire such goods, in fact, were multiethnic. As we have seen above, non-Indians frequently provided the gateras with produce. Individuals involved in this type of commerce with gateras could even be quite wealthy. In 1701 the Spanish doña Juana Méndez de la Higuera, for example, stated in her will that she owned several houses and estancias of wheat. She also had lands devoted to growing corn, potatoes, and other vegetables and was involved in business relations with various indigenous women.[99]

Although none of the gateras' commerce seems to have exclusive indigenous origins, the women's networks did include Indians who were professional dealers in large quantities of merchandise. As we have seen, indigenous men regularly transported salt, fruit, and vegetables, as well as sheep, into the city of Quito. Gateras also dealt with people who provisioned the market women in more casual and sporadic transactions. As for many of the Spaniards we have seen, selling merchandise to the market women was not necessarily a primary occupation but could be an activity engaged in occasionally or as part of a broader economic strategy based on investments, loans, and commercial transactions, which could include market women. The indigenous Pedro Franco, for example, was not a tratante by profession but combined his stated occupation of farm laborer with transporting peppers, guayabas, and other comestibles on his back from the village of Perucho to sell in the city of Quito.[100] Not all Indians who were involved in the gateras' commerce were as poor as Franco. In 1655, for example, when the indigenous doña Juana Tosi dictated her will, she ran an impressive economic network, which included two houses and several estancias of corn and cattle. She also left a long list of debtors, including one gatera who owed her 20 pesos and another who owed her 5 pesos from a larger debt for a sack of coca.[101]

Gateras also provisioned their stock through family networks. This was the case of another group of indigenous women who sold mutton in Quito. Their husbands, indigenous transporters who drove sheep into Quito, stated that they bought the animals from other Indians, killed the sheep in their houses, and gave the meat and fat to their wives to sell in the city's markets.[102] Another example that suggests a family network of trade relations is that of María Cuxipamba, who lived in Quito but regularly went to the pueblo Cotocollao, on the outskirts of the city, to pick up comestibles from her mother.[103] Catalina Barona, one of the salt sellers mentioned above, was probably provisioned by her husband, who, at the time she testified, was in the Yumbos, a region which specialized in salt production.[104]

Market women thus provisioned themselves in a number of ways. They bought from professional dealers, as well as from those who more occasionally came to the market with items to sell the vendors. In addition, some women received their merchandise through family networks. The evidence that there were men who collected debts from the women in the market and the presence of market women as debtors in testaments indicate that the women were given products on credit to be repaid once the merchandise was sold. Spaniards also employed gateras, albeit illegally, in which case the employers provided all the women's stock. Both Spaniards and Indians were involved in all aspects of the production, transportation, and wholesale of merchandise, despite the government's attempt to maintain separate Spanish and indigenous economies. In fact, the same product could be procured in different ways, as with the Andean potato, which both Spanish and indigenous traders proffered to the women. The evidence is even clearer with mutton: it could be bought from indigenous tratantes who themselves bought from other Indians, or the women could buy sheep from local Spanish haciendas and kill the animals themselves, or the vendors' husbands could simply give it to them to sell in the market. As we can see, market women had to be astute in the logistics of acquiring their merchandise and in arranging the credit they needed. Their racial status, as Indians, facilitated the gateras' access to multiethnic networks to run their businesses and legalized the participation of Indians and non-Indians in those networks.

Jurisdictional Disputes

As we have seen, indigenous market women not only were active in the economy but used litigation to impose their interests on the legal structure that regulated their commerce. However, even when the laws were not in their favor, the market women often continued to ply their trade with little interference from officials. Contrarily, though the gateras' commercial activities were determined to be legal by royal authorities, the women could still face fines and imprisonment by individual local authorities. Thus although gateras were generally successful in changing commercial law to favor their economic interests, they had to negotiate, like all others in Spanish America, between the various bureaucracies and individuals who shared jurisdictions over the enforcement of these laws. Multiple interests converged around the women's commerce. First, as pulperos in the city of Quito complained, market women were frequently protected by powerful interests in the city government, important persons of wealth, and owners of haciendas from whom the women bought their merchandise. Second, as we've seen, there was a structural ambiguity between the laws formulated by the Royal Audiencia and compliance with them at the level of the cities and pueblos. Finally, city councils themselves did not always control their appointed tax collectors, who had personal reasons of their own for collecting the sales tax. The power struggles between different agencies and individuals over the control and enforcement of the alcabala could either favor or injure the interests of the market women.

Pulperos consistently and bitterly complained that city council members were committing tax fraud through the gateras. In 1670, in fact, the pulperos formally appealed to the royal government to appoint tax collectors who were not connected to the city council.[105] The pulperos argued that the gateras bought their items from Spanish haciendas and were then favored by officials appointed by hacienda owners who controlled the city council. As we've seen, in fact, there is ample evidence that the Spaniards were deeply involved in the women's commerce. From the first lawsuit by the pulperos in 1642 through the end of the century, officials were accused of ignoring the illegal activities of market women. The negligence of city officials in regulating the women's commerce was so pronounced that in 1667 the Audiencia ruled that any official who did not comply with the court's mandates would be fined 20 pesos.[106]

The Audiencia's reliance on local officials to enforce royal laws created problems throughout the district. In 1687, for example, in the pueblo of Sanbisa near Quito, the pulperos claimed that the gateras procured their merchandise through the local haciendas and that the women had even received a license from the local magistrate to sell items that were prohibited by royal authorities.[107] In Cotocollao, near Quito, there weren't even any pulperos to complain because no one wanted to rent the royally licensed pulpería, due to the uncontrolled commercial activity of the pueblo's residents. The investigation by royal authorities revealed that several members of the ruling indigenous family were selling prohibited products from their houses and in the streets.[108]

Conflicts between local and royal authorities, of course, were not new. Indeed, the shared jurisdiction over the alcabala made disputes between city councils and the Audiencia structurally unavoidable. In many instances local concerns could coincide with the economic interests of the market women, but this was not always the case. In 1691 Captain Juan de Tena Berrio, familiar (agent) of the Inquisition and a merchant who had paid for the rights to collect the sales tax in Quito, was accused of breaking royal laws by permitting his collectors to levy the alcabala on all products Indians brought into the city. Indians first brought suit against the captain in 1689; two years later, in 1691, the attorney for the Indians was so enraged by the captain's stalling techniques that he demanded that the captain be fined 1,000 pesos for continuing to disobey royal mandates.[109] In 1708 the indigenous men who transported produce to the plaza mayor of Quito were also subjected by city tax collectors to paying the alcabala, despite royal mandates exempting their commerce. Earlier, in 1699, the Audiencia had clearly prohibited the city from collecting the sales tax from indigenous people, mandating that the property of men taxed be returned and that any city official who disobeyed be fined 200 pesos and jailed.[110]

The wayward practices of the city's tax collectors could bring them into conflict with the city itself. When the indigenous women who sold mutton were jailed in 1685 for refusing to pay the alcabala, it was revealed that the city's administrator of the alcabala had been using his own arbitrary system of tax assessment and collection, rather than obeying royal law, which completely exempted the women from paying the tax. The administrator, Captain don Antonio Laso de la Vega, stated that he used "regulated discretion" in collecting the tax, considering the poverty of the Indians and often only collecting what the Indians wanted to pay.[111] The Indians' attorney, not satisfied with this vague response, requested that the city council itself account precisely for the practices and laws observed in taxing the animals and meat sold by Indians in the city. The city council responded by stating that it had never permitted the captain to collect the alcabala from the Indians who sold mutton or pork and that it had notified him in 1684 that collecting from Indians was prohibited, under penalty of 50 pesos for any official who disobeyed.

Of obvious concern to the city council was the fact that the price of meat had doubled since the captain had started arbitrarily collecting the alcabala from Indians, driving many indigenous vendors to quit the occupation altogether and reducing the amount of meat in the city.[112] The potential for conflict between the cabildo and those to whom it leased the rights to administer the alcabala was great. It was normally merchants who paid to collect the alcabala; their expectation of profit from their investment and, perhaps, their interest in driving up the prices of food and other items in the city ran counter to the cabildo's expressed objective of ensuring through the tax's administration that "the citizens not be burdened, the poor be alleviated and the Indians not be subjected to extortion."[113]

Wherever jurisdictions overlapped, disputes between authorities could affect the market women. The Quito District was divided into corregimientos (subdistricts) and conflicts also occurred at this level over the women's commerce. In Riobamba a dispute arose regarding Captain Sergeant Major don Bernabé Pérez de Villaroel, who had paid the crown 2,001 pesos for the position of *fiel ejecutor,* a lifetime appointment which, in addition to giving him a permanent seat as regidor (alderman) in the Riobamba cabildo, granted him authority over weights, measures, and standards in all commercial activities in the villa and the corregimiento.[114] The fiel ejecutor was challenged by the *maestro de campo* Isidro Sáenz, who was also the lieutenant governor of the corregimiento and acting *alcalde ordinario* (appointed magistrate on the city council).

The focus of the conflict was, again, women who sold mutton in the gato of the villa, but this time their meat and not they had been thrown in jail, or, more precisely, the lieutenant governor had seized the women's merchandise and distributed it to the poor in jail, claiming that the city council had prohibited the women from vending meat.[115] Both officials asserted their authority at the provincial level of the corregimiento, the fiel ejecutor legitimating his control through the royal government and the lieutenant governor through the Riobamba City Council. In his lawsuit against the lieutenant governor, the fiel ejecutor claimed that by seizing the gateras' merchandise, city justices had usurped his authority to regulate economic activities within the city and province.

This jurisdictional dispute seems to have been a common occurrence, because the former fiel ejecutor, who died in office, had successfully litigated against the last two corregidores (governors), don Baltasar Pinto de Guevara and don Juan Manrique de Lara, over power to regulate the province's commercial activities.[116] The case in 1680 was also resolved favorably for the fiel ejecutor when, after the lieutenant governor referred the issue to the city council, the latter voted to confirm the priority of the fiel ejecutor in authorizing commercial activities.[117] The gateras had served as a point of departure for an ongoing jurisdictional dispute between the royal and city governments over control at the level of the corregimiento. In the legal resolution of this power struggle between elite men and their administrations, the indigenous women's commerce, transformed into a symbol of commercial control, was allowed to continue in the gato of Riobamba.

Provincial Market Women

This examination has focused mainly on the legal dilemmas surrounding the definition of market women's merchandise. The determination of what kinds of products the women legally could sell, of course, affected gateras in the entire district. But whereas the legal battles of the gateras of Quito were completely dominated by this issue, the market women in the provinces also were embroiled in disputes over the regulation of the locations where they could legally vend their merchandise. There is no record that the location of vendors was ever cause for dispute in the city of Quito. Indeed, it seems that most if not all of the gateras sold their wares in the central plazas designated as gatos. There were advantages for the women in the large city of Quito in being centrally gathered in more or less permanent locations. It was in the plaza where stable relations with customers were formed, where business transactions were conducted, and where the products from the provinces were delivered. These economic advantages probably outweighed the other consequence of centralized commerce, which was the constant vigilance by government authorities. Outside the city of Quito, however, conflicts arose over regulating the locations where vendors sold because in the smaller pueblos the women avoided the centralized control of the plazas by selling in the towns' streets, doorways, and houses.

Typical of the battles over where market women could legally vend their merchandise is the case of the indigenous gateras of Sanbisa, an outlying pueblo of Quito, who sold bread, chicha, and other comestibles at the entrance to the pueblo on the main road. In 1687 don Miguel del Barco, a citizen of Quito who owned the royally licensed pulpería of Sanbisa, brought a lawsuit against the indigenous women vendors to force them to return to the pueblo's official marketplace. In his lawsuit he stated that there already was an ordinance prohibiting vendors from selling outside the plaza but that local officials failed to enforce the mandate. Two years later he was still litigating against the gateras, complaining that officials continued to allow the gateras to sell in the village streets.[118]

It seems to have been a common occurrence in the smaller pueblos for women to choose to sell outside the central plaza, preferring instead to vend their wares on the public roads and streets. One possible explanation is that in more rural areas, especially those near larger cities, customers passing through were more dependent on commercialized and prepared food than the residents, who presumably relied on their own production. In addition, those products which would have been of interest to rural populations—processed items, such as cheese, sugar, candles, and soap, or imported goods from Spain, such as wine—were transported from Quito, and their commerce was legally confined to the pueblo's government-licensed pulpería. Women selling such items thus had good reason to avoid the intense scrutiny of the central plazas in small communities and instead opt to vend their wares on the highways at the pueblo's entrance or surreptitiously from houses or doorways.

Lying outside the city of Quito, Cotocollao is an example of such a pueblo. Cotocollao depended on Quito as a market for its primary products and, in turn, imported processed goods from the metropolis. Examination of the commercial strategies of the market women in Cotocollao indicates that many avoided the central plaza, instead selling a broad spectrum of goods on the highway and in houses. There is evidence that the women received protection from the local elite, the reigning Pizuli *caci-cazgo* (dynastic family), as well as from royal authorities who refused to enforce mandates that limited the kinds of products the women could sell and that confined the vendors to Cotocollao's main plaza. Information on the market women of Cotocollao comes from a murder case which occurred in the pueblo in 1694 and an official inquiry into the commercial practices of the pueblo's residents in 1701.

The primary witnesses that Sunday in 1694, when the indigenous Pedro Franco murdered Gregorio de Alvarado, also indigenous, were women either involved in the transport of goods to Quito or selling in the highway and houses of Cotocollao.[119] The economic networks that tied the pueblo to Quito were shown by one of the first witnesses in the case, the forty-five-year-old, indigenous María Cuxipamba, mentioned above, who came from Quito that Sunday to her mother's house in Cotocollao in order to get "cosas comestibles."[120] We have already mentioned the case of doña Francisca Puzuli, who was accused of selling in the public street in Cotocollao in 1701. Of importance here is that her husband, Manuel Gamarra, supplied her trading stock from an illegal pulpería in their house, where among other things he sold bread, cheese, sugar, soap, and tobacco that he had reportedly brought from Quito.[121] Cotocollao thus fits our model of a typical secondary population center, exporting primary products to the capital and importing more elaborate goods.

In the murder case Franco's defense was that he was drunk at the time of the killing and therefore should not be held responsible.[122] Important witnesses in this defense strategy were two women: a street vendor, who claimed to have seen that he was inebriated, and the woman who sold him the chicha. The mestizo Francisca Rodríguez, married to a Spaniard, was selling "comestibles" in the street at the pueblo's entrance that Sunday.[123] The other witness, the indigenous Pascuala Llapsa, is noted as selling comestibles from her house, in addition to prepared food and chicha. Llapsa catered to Indians who passed through the pueblo. Franco had gone to Quito with peppers, guayabas, and other products from Perucho and was returning home through Cotocollao; he stopped at Llapsa's house to eat and drink because she was "well known." He was joined by other Indians, who also came to Llapsa's establishment to drink chicha. Llapsa testified that Franco drank a lot of chicha that day.[124] The records also mention the existence of a public market in the plaza of Cotocollao, where the women could have conducted their commerce. Another witness testified that later the widow of the murdered Alvarado, the indigenous Juana Sánchez, went to the public plaza and sold things that Franco had been carrying with him, property she had earlier denied taking.[125]

Seven years later the royal government, concerned that no one wanted to rent the officially licensed pulpería of Cotocollao, investigated the commercial activities of the pueblo's residents.[126] At that time witnesses claimed that the indigenous Rufina Tituasán had run a pulpería from her house a year earlier but for lack of profit stopped and began to sell in the public street.[127] Residents also testified, as mentioned above, that the mestizo doña Francisca Pizuli was also selling in the street and that her husband, Manuel Gamarra, ran a pulpería from their house. In addition, one witness claimed that don Cristóbal Pizuli was selling *aguardiente* (cane liquor) together with a "white man" who lived in his house.[128]

It is notable that in both 1694 and 1701 the women vendors mentioned all sold on the highway that ran through the pueblo. In the case of Tituasán, who formerly sold from her house, it is clear that she found selling on the highway more profitable. The only woman mentioned who sold from her house, Pascuala Llapsa, ran a kind of restaurant/tavern in addition to selling comestibles. Although local Indians frequented her establishment, it is evident that she, like the other women vendors, catered to travelers passing through the pueblo. Unlike the market women in Quito, who found economic advantages in being centrally located despite the increased supervision of their commerce by officials, market women in the smaller pueblos had little to gain from being confined to a central location. By selling in the highway the women gained customers, provisioning travelers passing through the pueblo. In addition, being dispersed, their illegal commerce was less noticeable and easier for authorities to ignore.

There is much evidence that officials did tend to overlook the women selling in the highway, despite the fact that their commerce was legally prohibited. The indigenous authorities in Cotocollao were aware of the illegal commerce in the pueblo but were complicit or actively implicated in much of it. The alcalde ordinario had identified all the persons involved in unsanctioned commerce but had done nothing to impede their activities.[129] The caciques in the Pizuli family were deeply involved in all economic aspects of the pueblo. The market woman Francisca Rodríguez, mentioned above in the murder case of 1694, sold in the public street near the house of doña Juana Pizuli.[130] In the investigation of 1701, the caciques don Pedro and don Tomás Pizuli both testified about their knowledge of the commercial activities of the pueblo.[131] As we have seen, doña Francisca Pizuli sold on the street, and don Cristóbal Pizuli sold aguardiente. An official witness to all the testimonies in the investigation was don Juan Pizuli. Despite the evidence that many members of the Pizuli family were directly involved in illegal commerce, no one was arrested. In fact, the royal authorities ignored all the reported illegal activities except for the pulpería of Manuel Gamarra. His property was seized, whereas the market women on the highway were left alone to sell their goods.

In the pueblo of Guano, near Riobamba, attempts to regulate the town's commerce disintegrated into accusations of physical violence, abuse of power, and theft, formalized in various lawsuits between 1691 and 1692. In the first lawsuit María de Guzmán, who also went by María Jácome, accused Juan de Avilés, who owned the town's legal pulpería in addition to being a tratante and *juez de desagravios* (justice of the peace), of stealing her property, mistreating her, and illegally imprisoning her in the private jail that he kept in his house. That same year Avilés brought his own criminal suit against Guzmán for disrespectable behavior and also sued her husband, Josef de Escobar, for illegal commercial activities.[132] In 1692 the pueblo's *cacicas* (female indigenous rulers) criminally charged Guzmán; Escobar, her husband; and her sister, Manuela de Castro, with abusing the town's Indians. The rancor of the elite indigenous women was so great by this time that they tried to have all Spaniards, mestizos, blacks, and mulattos expelled from the town.[133]

Guzmán and Escobar were mentioned above in regards to their practice of illegally employing indigenous women to sell their merchandise. The pair's relationship with the gateras was the crux of the major dispute in Guano over where selling could take place. Legally, there were only two places where commerce could occur, the royally licensed pulpería and the central plaza or gato. Guzmán and Escobar, by running an illegal pulpería and employing gateras to sell out of houses and in the streets, were thus breaking all the rules. Although the two certainly seem to have attracted a lot of animosity in Guano, their economic activities were actually part of the general dispersal of irregular commerce throughout the pueblo. Officials and witnesses repeatedly reported that residents were allowing or employing gateras to sell in their doorways and in the streets.

Royal authorities asserted that the wayward economic practices of the town's residents encouraged moral disorder in the indigenous women vendors. In January of 1691 the royal courts mandated that "gateras should sell only in the main plaza [plaza pública] because they are selling on various streets in Guano to the detriment of the Christian doctrine, because the indigenous women, under the pretext that they are in the houses and serving Spaniards, don't attend catechism where they can be taught the mysteries of our Holy Catholic Faith." The courts ordered that the indigenous women sell only in the plaza and that they attend catechism on all required days every week. Gateras who disobeyed this ordinance were to receive one hundred lashes and have their hair cut; individuals who impeded the objective of this law were to be fined 25 pesos and incarcerated for ten days.[134] To the consternation of officials, the enterprising spirit of the residents triumphed over the Holy Spirit; the indigenous women continued to vend their wares in all parts of the pueblo.

At the end of the seventeenth century, Guano was a pueblo filled with hostility and violence, caused primarily by conflicts over the regulation of the residents' commercial activities. The main representative of Spanish justice in the pueblo, the deputy corregidor and acting judge, also owned the only legal pulpería in the town and used his authority primarily to discourage and punish those who encroached upon his economic interests. The gateras, aided and abetted by other residents, avoided the central plaza at all costs, risking physical punishment and public shame to continue selling in the pueblo's streets and houses. The Spanish government's reaction to the defiance of laws for centralizing commerce was to link the perceived economic chaos with religious disobedience. In an attempt to morally justify and strengthen its control over commerce, it sought to enforce the religious indoctrination of the gateras. The indigenous elite defined the problem in racial terms, believing that the economic pursuits of non-Indians were responsible for the town's problems and that racial segregation would restore order. Neither of these solutions favored the interests of the gateras, whose rejection of the plaza was probably increased by the added element of moral control and whose economic transactions were often with non-Indians. Neither Spanish law nor the proposals of the indigenous elite were successful; the gateras continued selling outside of the main plaza as provisioners and employees of the town's racially mixed population.

Conclusion

In her study of Indians in colonial Lima, Lowry comments that "the striking thing about the gateras is that though they performed a job both vital to city welfare and highly public, they are virtually invisible in the documents." She notes that indigenous women in general seldom appear in colonial documents, with the exception of service contracts and testaments.[135] The market women in the Quito District appear to be quite different from their counterparts in the viceregal capital. Far from being invisible, the women used their gender and racial status to extend their economic activities, provoking conflicts with pulperos and government officials. As women the gateras did not pay the tribute owed by indigenous males. As Indians they were exempt from paying the colonial sales tax, the alcabala. With no official financial obligations, with different sources of supply, and with lower overhead, the women sold their merchandise at lower prices than the pulperos, who maintained fixed establishments and were burdened with a number of economic and military obligations to the crown. Commercial competition between the gateras and pulperos was at the core of more than eighty years of litigation and appeals to royal authorities to change the content, interpretation, and enforcement of commercial law in the Audiencia of Quito. As litigants indigenous women enjoyed another racial advantage: access to free legal representation by the Protector of the Indians. These attorneys were extremely successful at promoting the agendas of the market women, effectively redefining how racial difference constructed the colonial economy.

Colonial society was formally divided into separate republics, the Republic of the Indians and the Republic of the Spaniards. This division was expressed in the economy through the development of parallel economies marked in the seventeenth century by the application of the alcabala, the royally imposed sales tax, on the basis of race. In 1642, when our records begin, Indians were exempt from the tax because of the combination of their racial status and the kind of merchandise they were legally allowed to sell, mainly produce which they grew themselves. Any products other than produce grown by the Indians themselves were liable to be taxed and thus illegal for them to sell. By the end of the century, however, the indigenous market women successfully redefined how the alcabala was administered. The gateras' tax exemption was extended to all their commercial activities; as indigenous women retail sellers, they were able to sell any item regardless of where the item had been produced or by whom. The gateras thus subverted the intent of the Spanish-imposed racial label *Indian,* which was originally designed to limit their economic activities. Instead, the women used their racial status as Indians to expand the scope of their commercial enterprises. The legal success of the gateras in extending their commercial rights not only benefited them as market women but was also used as a precedent for broadening the economic rights of Indians in general throughout the district.

Indigenous women and their supporters were therefore successful at changing the official content and interpretation of commercial law. However, the women's commerce was affected not only by legislation; the commercial success of the gateras also depended on their agility in aligning their interests with the various authorities charged with enforcing commercial law codes. Conflicts of interest between royal and local agencies and disputes between local authorities themselves all affected how the women operated their businesses. Despite early legal limitations on indigenous market women's economic activities, evidence shows that the gateras continued to sell prohibited items with the approbation of local authorities. It is plausible that, as the pulperos complained, the women were protected by the hacienda owners who controlled the city council, from whom the women procured at least a part of their merchandise. Their later legal success can thus be seen as the official legitimization of a commercial liberty they already enjoyed in practice. Toward the end of the century, however, despite laws that protected the women's commerce and exempted them from the alcabala, tax collectors still tried to levy the tax on the indigenous vendors and their suppliers. There is some evidence that merchants were increasingly involved in the collection of the alcabala at the end of the century, paying the city council for the right to appoint tax collectors. In at least one example, the desire to profit economically from his control over tax collection brought a merchant into confrontations with both the Royal Audiencia and the Quito cabildo, both of which questioned his attempts to illegally collect the alcabala from indigenous persons.

Jurisdictional disputes also determined the scope of the economic activities of women vendors in the provinces. Despite royal legislation that prohibited them from selling outside of central plazas, gateras outside of Quito commonly chose to sell in streets and from houses instead of in the officially designated market. Although the women were not successful in legally challenging the regulation of their vending locations, in practice their dispersed commerce was supported by local populations and officials. Despite laws that would punish the women with severe physical punishment and public shame and their accomplices with fines and incarceration, vending in streets, doorways, and houses was a common practice outside of Quito.

Finally, it is important to note that this female-dominated occupation was not regulated by gender-specific legislation or practices. No woman was asked to present contracts or licenses from her husband, and none of the litigants noted their marital status. The right of the gateras as women to run businesses and to litigate was never contested. Throughout the women's battles with male officials and shop owners, it is their race and not their gender which drove the discourse over their rights to engage in commercial activities. It was as women that they filled the markets and streets vending their wares, but it was as Indians that they protected their economic interests and that they, rather than their nonindigenous counterparts, entered the historical record.

CHAPTER 6

Conclusion

Onion Tales

In 1469 Isabella, queen of Castile, married Ferdinand, king of Aragon. Many scholars consider the marriage of these two powerful monarchs to be the most important event in Spanish history, the event, in fact, which created for the first time a unified Spain.[1] The institution of marriage in Iberian tradition, however, though it might indeed connect the destinies of spouses, did not connect their worldly possessions. Like all other married women, Isabella retained her individual name and title, in her case queen of Castile. She also retained possession of her estate, which was the Kingdom of Castile. Castile was far larger territorially then Ferdinand's Kingdom of Aragon, contained over four times the population, and was the most economically dynamic of the two kingdoms. The two kingdoms remained distinct; each kingdom retained its own fueros, or special privileges given to specific groups; standards and systems of justices; political orders; militias; and even coinage.

Through his marriage to Isabella, Ferdinand never became a legitimate ruler of Castile, even at the death of Isabella. When Isabella died in 1504 she, as all parents did, individually bequeathed her estate to her child. Isabella transferred her legitimate possession of the Kingdom of Castile to her daughter Juana and not to Ferdinand. Juana, however, was increasingly insane and therefore incapable of ruling Castile. Ferdinand ruled Castile in Juana's name until his own death in 1516. He confronted much internal opposition in Castile; his status as husband of the former ruler and father to the new ruler did not give him a legitimate claim to Castile. Castile and Aragon would not share a legitimate ruler until the accession of Juana's son, Charles I, in 1516. He inherited the rulership of both kingdoms through his mother, the legitimate heir of both Isabella and Ferdinand. Family law, indeed, had a great impact on the formation of the Spanish state.

Recognizing that although their marriage eternally united their individual souls, it did little to unite their two kingdoms, Isabella and Ferdinand turned to religion. In fact, one of the few elements that the two kingdoms had in common was that each of their rulers was Catholic. Capitalizing on their shared Catholicism, Isabella and Ferdinand declared their intention to unite and expand their kingdoms by imposing religious orthodoxy throughout their realms. Rome responded by granting them a papal bull to create an Inquisition into heresy that began in Castile in 1480, and in Aragon in 1482. Using religious unity as a way to unite their kingdoms socially and politically, the monarchs institutionalized the Inquisition with grave consequences for many of their subjects. Isabella's secretary estimated that by 1490, 2,000 Judaizers (Jewish converts to Christianity who were suspected of continuing to practice the Jewish faith in secret) had been burned and 15,000 others punished in attempts to reconcile them with the true faith. Isabella and Ferdinand's campaign of religious intolerance culminated in the taking of Granada in 1492 and a decree that all remaining Jews convert to Catholicism or leave Spanish domains. For their efforts in promoting Catholicism, the monarchs were pronounced "Athletes of Christ" by the Pope.[2]

Would the Athletes, however, carry the torch of the Inquisition in their leap across the Atlantic Ocean? The year 1492 is also, of course, infamous for Columbus' first voyage to what would eventually be called America. The incorporation of most of the territory of the American continents into Spanish domains would seem an opportune moment for the Spanish Monarchy to extend its authority through its control over the Inquisition. However, despite the opposition of many religious authorities, the crown always refused to include Indians in the jurisdiction of the Inquisition.[3]

Authority over religious beliefs in Spanish America would not be centralized. Spaniards, blacks, mestizos, and mulattos would be subject to the Inquisition, but the majority of the population, the Indians, were placed under the jurisdiction of the archbishop. This division ensured myriad jurisdictional conflicts. Most parishes, with special papal dispensation, were under the authority of the regular clergy, such as the Dominicans, Franciscans, and Mercedarians, and these orders competed among themselves to increase their jurisdictional authority over the indigenous population. By giving ultimate religious authority over the indigenous population to the archbishop, however, secular religious authorities also had jurisdiction over these same indigenous populations. The religious beliefs of Indians and non-Indians would not be monitored by one centralized authority but would be divided into separate and parallel organizations. At a critical juncture in Spain's history, then, when the monarchs had the opportunity to centralize the only aspect of their authority that was universally legitimate throughout their domains—the Royal Inquisition—the crown opted instead to create another parallel jurisdiction and thus ensure bureaucratic rivalries and dissension.

Spain did not depend on a centralized figure or institution for its unity. Like slicing into an onion, analyzing the mechanisms of power in Spanish society reveals layers of authority held together through tension instead of by a central core. There is a large body of evidence in the early Latin American field demonstrating that social stability was, in fact, guaranteed through decentralized power relations. The government itself was composed of multiple hierarchies with overlapping and competing jurisdictions. Vertical authority was systematically disrupted through the actions of subordinates, who influenced and impeded the implementation of laws. The potential of the monarch to exercise centralized control over this network was limited through the need of the crown to legitimate its demands within a system of reciprocity and to balance the objectives of the metropolis with local political and economic concerns. The objective of this decentralized system was to facilitate responses to changing situations and to prevent any individual or group from consolidating a position of absolute control.

Father Fiction

This book has argued that this tendency to multiply and diversify, rather than to unify and centralize, was a cultural characteristic of Spanish American colonial society that also defined the logic of family structure. Family members were joined in a union that created shared domains of interest while preserving the interests of individuals. The potential for husband/fathers to consolidate positions of patriarchal authority was recognized by society. But rather than viewing semiautonomous, male-headed households as elements of social stability, the colonial government viewed patriarchy as disruptive to a social order that culturally and institutionally undermined all forms of centralized control. In order to check the possible formation of patriarchal authority within the family, wives were legally empowered to defend their interests against their husbands. Spanish courts upheld women's property and legal rights through a large body of gender legislation that applied to all racial groups.

In property suits between husbands and wives, the government consistently gave higher priority to the preservation and enlargement of women's property than to the preservation of male authority in the family. Within marriage, wives and husbands retained private estates while sharing equally in community property. A wife's property registered in a notarized dowry contract was secured by legally obligating her husband and his estate for its value. Husbands legally managed their wives' estates, though their use of their wives' property was restricted, and at no time could husbands, creditors, or the government treat the property as belonging to the husband. In order to alienate his wife's dowry property or make it indebted, a husband needed her license for that specific transaction. Without her license a wife's estate was not liable for her husband's debts to private creditors or government agencies; nor could her property be seized by the government for crimes committed by her husband. Individual estates remained so distinct, in fact, that spouses loaned each other money and expected to be reimbursed. Women who sued to defend their dowries against the claims of husbands, creditors, and the government usually won their suits.

Although a wife legally needed her husband's license to engage in economic transactions or to litigate, even more important for the validation of a woman's economic contracts was the requirement that the transaction financially benefit her estate. Negotiations that were not financially favorable were invalid even if a husband had authorized the transaction, and many contracts made by wives were valid without their husbands' licenses. Husbands could not use their authority to obligate their wives to enter contracts with others or with themselves. A wife was not expected to obligate herself or her property as an act of obedience. In fact, a wife's contracts were legally valid only if she understood the nature of the specific transaction and the expected financial benefit to her estate; understood her general rights as a married woman and the laws protecting her; and finally, on the basis of this knowledge, entered the agreement of her own free will. Any use of authority on the part of the husband to coerce his wife legally invalidated the contract.

The legal system recognized the family not as a male-headed unit but as the union of distinct individuals. Wives maintained juridical identities separate from their husbands', and a husband could represent his wife in legal and economic transactions only on the basis of a notarized license granted by her. The same licensing process also allowed wives to represent their husbands in official business. The legal system recognized that a wife's interests could diverge substantially from her husband's, and therefore wives had legal recourse to defend themselves against their spouses.

Abuse of Power

The same rationale that permitted women to defend their economic assets from the mismanagement or intentional plunder of husbands also supported women's actions against abusive and adulterous men who threatened their security. Far from being considered male prerogatives, domestic violence and adultery were defined as criminal offenses. Although the church also condemned such behavior, it lacked official mechanisms for censuring or punishing spouses for their misconduct. The only official action the church could take to resolve marital discord was to dissolve the union temporally or permanently, an action that the church deemed as threatening to the sanctity of marriage in general and to the church's institutional legitimacy, as its control over marriage was based on its definition as a sacred and inviolable union of the souls of men and women. For women who suffered from the consequences of their husbands' physical violence and adultery, the church was therefore not a practical recourse because such male misconduct was rarely considered sufficient reason for dissolving the marriage.

Women had the option, however, of suing their husbands for domestic violence and adultery in the criminal justice system. There women found almost immediate relief; husbands were often jailed for the course of the suit. If found guilty, men faced potentially severe punishments, including imprisonment, confiscation of their property, fines, loss of office, forced labor, and long exiles. Prosecution for domestic violence, like physical assault in general, depended on the claimant's willingness to pursue the suit. In suits concerning adultery, however, the government prosecuted husbands not only on the basis of their wives' formal complaints but also independently. Illicit lovers picked up by city patrols could be directly prosecuted by government officials. In addition, the government could continue the prosecution of a man accused of adultery even if his wife had pardoned him and desisted from pursuing the case. Severe judgments against husbands had an equally disruptive effect on the economic survival and stability of women and children. Unlike many other types of crimes, adultery was considered an offense against the government, and the government felt compelled to prosecute it.

The testimony of witnesses in suits brought by wives against husbands demonstrates that physical abuse and adultery were not tolerated. In many cases, men and women intervened to stop a husband's violence against his wife and to publicly berate a husband for his illicit sexual relationships and abandonment of his wife. The public reputations of men could, in fact, be diminished on the basis of their relationships with their wives. Neighbors and acquaintances volunteered incriminating information about husbands, denounced men to authorities, and even aided in finding and arresting wayward husbands. Community censure of violent and unfaithful men was not, therefore, only an informal pressure exercised on men. Women who complained publicly about their husbands and aroused the interest of neighbors had a much better chance of winning their suits. Community involvement was thus also an element in the formal mechanisms used to prosecute men; on the basis of a wife's formal complaint and the corroborative testimony of a few neighbors, a husband could find himself in jail and his property confiscated.

The government and society recognized the potential of married men to consolidate their power within their families and become patriarchs. But husbands were the object of community vigilance and the targets of criminal prosecutions precisely to prevent them from forming enclaves subject to their personal authority. Not only could married men be prosecuted by their wives and the government; they could also face criminal complaints by women they seduced. In cases of seduction single women, even with questionable backgrounds, had a much greater chance of success against married men than did women who sued single men for breaking marriage promises. The government felt more compelled to take action against potential patriarchs than against unmarried men who did not yet pose a threat to the decentralized power relations that guaranteed social stability.

This research suggests that relations between women and men were not predominantly structured according to a model of patriarchy. The organization of the state was based on a concept of power as being produced and constrained within a network of relations that decentralized positions of authority. The family was similarly structured; the potential for men to use the family as a bastion of power was viewed as a threat not only to women but also to the public well-being. The permeability of the family to state and community intervention limited men's ability to transform themselves into patriarchs. Men did not have ultimate authority over family resources or the destinies of family members; nor were wives expected to endure their husbands' physical aggression and adulterous relations as male prerogatives. The paradigm of patriarchy cannot explain women's status within society and the family, women's use of governmental mechanisms, or women's economic activities.

Money Matters

Women involved themselves in a broad range of economic activities that were essential to the district of Quito. Through ownership, management, investment, and labor, women from both Spanish and indigenous sectors, married and single, operated very independently from men. In textile manufacturing, the dominant industry in Quito, women owned some of the largest mills and ran smaller operations out of their houses. Women also formed part of the labor force in textile production. Both Spanish and indigenous women invested in the domestic and interregional marketing of textiles. In addition to provisioning by street marketing, women also owned and managed pulperías or small shops; owned and sold livestock; and were also involved in the processing of livestock. Quite a bit of the district's agricultural and urban property was owned by women. Women of all racial backgrounds were extremely important in the movement of capital in both large and small amounts throughout the district. Especially noteworthy in this regard were indigenous women who loaned out both large and small sums of money to Spaniards, to blacks, and to other indigenous persons. Women also worked in low-status, traditionally female occupations such as domestic service, bread baking, and chicha brewing. Although these kinds of workers seemed vulnerable to exploitation, the panaderas, like other women in other occupations, were able to reach extralegal accords with officials to circumvent laws that were unfavorable to their businesses.

The provisioning of cities and provincial towns in markets and streets was exclusively the domain of women. There is no mention of a male street vendor in the district of Quito during the seventeenth century. With the complete exception of Spanish women, women of all other racial backgrounds were involved in street marketing. It is clear, however, that indigenous women, commonly referred to as gateras, dominated this profession. Indeed, indigenous women had advantages over others in marketing. As women, they did not pay the tribute owed to the crown by Indian men. As Indians, they were exempt from paying the sales tax, the alcabala, levied on the economic transactions of all other groups in society. With little overhead, different supply channels, and no financial obligations to the government, the gateras were able to undercut the prices of merchandise sold in the pulperías, or small grocery shops, whose owners and administrators were burdened by, among other things, a number of taxes and fees.

The unique legal and economic situation of the gateras generated legal conflicts between them and shop owners and government officials, who wanted to limit the women to selling produce and reserve the sale of more expensive finished and imported goods to the government-controlled and -taxed pulperías. Although the commerce of indigenous women in other parts of Spanish America seems to have been limited to produce or other items of low financial value typically produced within the indigenous sector, the gateras in the Quito District sold a wide variety of elaborated and imported merchandise. In legal battles that ran continuously through the second half of the seventeenth century, the pulperos challenged the gateras by using commercial law that divided the economy into racially distinct sectors. Race as a fiscal category, rather than discussions over the women's gender or marital status, drove the debates over the women's commerce. The gateras tenaciously defended their economic activities through their appointed attorneys, the Protector of the Indians. Although the gateras were poor, illiterate, and unable to speak Spanish, they consistently won their suits and progressively broadened their rights to sell all types of merchandise, both inside and outside the central market plazas. Their success at redefining the fiscal status of Indians was used by men and women throughout the region to expand indigenous economic rights. Even when their merchandise was officially prohibited, the gateras were skilled at using the endemic conflicts between different government agencies to reach extralegal accords that permitted them to continue their activities.

The records of the legal conflicts that surrounded the gateras during the second half of the seventeenth century not only document the women's insistence on selling where and what they wanted but also indicate some of the mechanisms they used to run their enterprises. Men and women of varying racial heritages and social statuses were involved in market women's commerce, supplying them with credit and merchandise and investing in the production and transportation of products sold in the markets. Official attempts to impose barriers between the indigenous sector, associated with subsistence items, and the Spanish sector, which emphasized refined and imported goods, were generally not successful. Spaniards and mestizos were involved in all aspects of the women's trade; even the Andean potato could be acquired through Spanish networks. The records also suggest that the careers of market women spanned many years and that they tended to specialize in particular products. In fact, the loyalties of the women seemed to be based on the kinds of products they sold, rather than on any group consciousness as market women.

The Question

This study documents the lives of women living in colonial Spanish America as wives, mothers, property owners, entrepreneurs, and legal adversaries. In many ways, their stories are not new; other scholars, researching other women in different times and places in colonial Spanish America have shown forcefully that women were not only active but essential in creating and maintaining colonial society. But this study asks a different question about these women's lives than most works. Research on women in this field, recognizing the breadth of women's activities, intrinsically organizes itself around the question of how women gained fleeting moments of authority in a traditional patriarchal society. This study turns this question around and asks: What kind of society made it possible for women to act independently, even when this caused conflict with the men around them?

In answering this question, this research shows that women's independence was not exceptional but was culturally necessary in a society that thrived on difference, competition, and even conflict. Elements that are normally seen as disruptive to centralized authority were instead the basis of social stability in Spanish America, at least through the seventeenth century. At every level of society, mechanisms were institutionalized that undermined the possibility of any individual or group from consolidating authority. Spanish colonial society had very different rules from our own; in some respects those rules are mirror opposites of what constitutes for us social stability. It is, of course, always wise to remember that when we enter other cultures we should perhaps leave what we know as truth behind and be very wary about the kinds of questions we ask. As Lewis Carroll, famous for imagining contrary worlds, cautions: "Do we decide questions at all? We decide answers, no doubt, but surely the questions decide us."[4]

Notes

Preface

1. María's story was shared with me when I first arrived in Quito in 1995. The actual woman, who has been given the fictitious name María, prefers to remain anonymous. Information on Ventura, whose full name is doña Ventura de Zárate, comes from Criminales, 9 September 1685, Archivo Nacional del Ecuador, Quito (hereafter, ANE/Q).

2. FLACSO, (http://www.eurosur.org/FLACSO/mujeres/ecuador/legi-3.htm) (accessed 14 June 2001).

3. Astrid Müller, *Por pan y equidad: Organizaciones de mujeres ecuatorianas* (Quito: Ediciones Abya-Yala, 1994), 41.

4. Müller, *Por pan y equidad,* 59–60.

5. Unidad de Modernización Judicial de la Comisión Andina de Juristas, (http://www.cajpe.org.pe/RIJ/Bases/mujer/1.htm) (accessed 13 June 2001).

Introduction

1. C. H. Haring, *The Spanish Empire in America* (1945; reprint, New York: Harcourt Brace Jovanovich, 1975), 86. Cathryn L. Lombardi and John V. Lombardi, with K. Lynn Stoner, *Latin American History: A Teaching Atlas* (Madison: Univ. of Wisconsin Press, 1983), 29.

2. John Leddy Phelan, *The Kingdom of Quito in the Seventeenth Century: Bureaucratic Politics in the Spanish Empire* (Madison: Univ. of Wisconsin Press, 1967), 3, 46.

3. Suzanne Austin Alchon, *Native Society and Disease in Colonial Ecuador* (Cambridge, England: Cambridge Univ. Press, 1991), 57–99; Henry F. Dobyns, "An Outline of Andean Epidemic History to 1720," *Bulletin of the History of Medicine* 37 (1963): 493–515; Linda A. Newson, "Old World Epidemics in Early Colonial Ecuador," in "Secret Judgements of God": *Old World Disease in Colonial Spanish America,* ed. N. David Cook and W. George Lovell (Norman: Univ. of Oklahoma Press, 1991), 84–112.

4. John Super, "Partnership and Profit in the Early Andean Trade: The Experiences of Quito Merchants, 1580–1610," *Journal of Latin American Studies* 2 (1979): 265–281.

5. Adám Szásdi, "The Economic History of the Diocese of Quito, 1616–1787," *Latin American Research Review* 21 (1986): 267.

6. Between 1601 and 1700, the production of Potosí dropped by almost two-thirds. See Carlos Sempat Assadourian, *El sistema de la economía colonial: El mercado interno, regiones y espacio económico* (Mexico City: Editorial Nueva Imagen, 1983), 140. Kenneth J. Andrien attributes the cause of the fiscal crisis in the viceroyalty to corrupt and inefficient crown policies: *Crisis and Decline: The Viceroyalty of Peru in the Seventeenth Century* (Albuquerque: Univ. of New Mexico Press, 1985). For the economy of Quito, see Robson Brines Tyrer, *Historia demográfica y económica de la Audiencia de Quito: Población indígena e industria textil, 1600-1800* (Quito: Banco Central del Ecuador, 1988), 190.

7. Christiana Borchart de Moreno, "Circulación y producción en Quito: De la colonia a la república," *Siglo XIX* 14 (1993): 73–97. For Quito's early economic diversification, see John Super, "Empresarios quiteños en 1580–1620," *Revista del Archivo Histórico del Guayas* 16 (1979): 5–20.

8. The functioning of the textile industry is examined in a special edition of the *Revista Ecuatoriana de Historia Económica* 2:4 (1988), by contributors Manuel Miño Grijalva, Javier Ortíz de la Tabla Ducasse, Alexandra Kennedy Troya, and Carmen Fauria Roma. See also Phelan, *Kingdom of Quito,* 66–84.

9. See Super, "Partnership and Profit in the Early Andean Trade," for an analysis of how merchants overcame the geographical challenges to establishing an Andean and trans-Atlantic trading network.

10. Martin Minchom, *The People of Quito, 1690-1810: Change and Unrest in the Underclass* (Boulder, Colo.: Westview Press, 1994), 21.

11. Phelan, *Kingdom of Quito,* 49.

12. See Ricardo Descalzi de Castillo, *La Real Audiencia de Quito claustro en los Andes: Siglo XVI* (Barcelona: I.G. Seix y Barral Hnos., S.A., 1978), 210, for the original creation of indigenous parishes. See also Hugo Burgos Guevara, *Primeras doctrinas en la Real Audiencia de Quito 1570-1640: Estudio preliminar y transcripción de las relaciones eclesiales y misionales de los siglos XVI y XVII* (Quito: Ediciones Abya-Yala, 1995), 185.

13. For Lima see Lyn Brandon Lowry, "Forging an Indian Nation: Urban Indians under Spanish Colonial Control (Lima, Peru, 1535-1765)," Ph.D. dissertation, Department of History, Univ. of California, Berkeley, 1991. For Mexico City see Andrés Lira, *Comunidades indígenas frente a la ciudad de México, Tenochtitlán y Tlatelolco, sus pueblos y barrios, 1812-1919* (Mexico City: Colegio de México, 1983).

14. For an interesting study of the cultural adaptations made by Indians and Spaniards in sixteenth-century Quito, see Frank Salomon, "Indian Women of Early Colonial Quito as Seen through Their Testaments," *Americas* 44 (1988): 325–342.

15. The Bourbon Crown's attempts to centralize authority at the expense of local autonomy fomented unrest in the Audiencia of Quito. For urban insurrections in the jurisdiction of the Audiencia of Quito during the eighteenth century, see Anthony McFarlane, "The 'Rebellion of the Barrios': Urban Insurrection in

Bourbon Quito," *Hispanic American Historical Review* 69 (1989): 283–330; for indigenous revolts see Segundo Moreno Yánez, *Sublevaciones indígenas en la Audiencia de Quito: Desde comienzos del siglo XVIII hasta finales de la colonia* (Quito: PUCE, 1977).

16. Although there is evidence of individuals of African descent living in the region, they appear infrequently in the sources used for this study and therefore remain largely outside of the focus of this book.

17. There is still an open-ended debate over the role of economic/class factors in determining ethnic/racial categories. A classic study in this debate is by Magnus Morner, "Economic Factors and Stratification in Colonial Spanish America with Special Regard to the Elites," *Hispanic American Historical Review* 63:2 (May 1983): 335–369. See also John K. Chance and William B. Taylor, "Estate and Class in a Colonial City: Oaxaca in 1792," *Comparative Studies in Society and History* 12:4 (October 1977): 454–487, and the response to this study by Robert McCaa, Stuart B. Schwartz, and Arturo Grubessich, "Race and Class in Colonial Latin America: A Critique," *Comparative Studies in Society and History* 21:3 (July 1979): 421–433. An important work analyzing racial relations in colonial Mexico City is by R. Douglas Cope, *The Limits of Racial Domination: Plebian Society in Colonial Mexico City, 1660–1720* (Madison: Univ. of Wisconsin Press, 1994). Patricia Seed analyzes the 1753 census of Mexico City in "Social Dimensions of Race: Mexico City, 1753," *Hispanic American Historical Review* 62:4 (1982): 569–606. For colonial Guatemala see Christopher H. Lutz, *Santiago de Guatemala, 1541–1773: City, Caste, and the Colonial Experience* (Norman: Univ. of Oklahoma Press, 1994). For an interesting analysis of racial categories in colonial Brazil, see Muriel Nazzari, "Vanishing Indians: The Social Construction of Race in Colonial São Paulo," *Americas* 57:4 (April 2001): 497–524.

18. Elizabeth Anne Kuznesof, "Ethnic and Gender Influences on 'Spanish' Creole Society in Colonial Spanish America," *Colonial Latin American Review* 4:1 (1995): 153–176, 165.

19. Olivia Harris, "Ethnic Identity and Market Relations: Indians and Mestizos in the Andes," in *Ethnicity, Markets, and Migration in the Andes: At the Crossroads of History and Anthropology*, ed. Brooke Larson and Olivia Harris, with Enrique Tandeter (Durham, N.C.: Duke Univ. Press, 1995), 351–390, 354. It should be added that the definition of being nonnative also carried specific economic obligations for the colonial state.

20. Minchom, *People of Quito*, 153–200.

21. The distinction between racial categories and racial identities is important for researchers to recognize. Because racial categories, like other social categories in colonial society, had legal consequences, there could be compelling reasons for individuals to claim particular definitions for themselves, despite how they felt about who they were, their identities. See Stuart B. Schwartz, "Colonial Identities and the *Sociedad de Castas*," *Colonial Latin American Review* 4:1 (1995): 185–201, especially 186–187.

22. This work argues that the weight of gender or racial definitions will vary for individuals situationally and that our analyses should give importance to the categories the subjects of our research deploy. Irene Silverblatt makes a similar argu-

ment in her caution to researchers not to use gender or other often-used categories uncritically as frameworks for analysis. See Irene Silverblatt, "Lessons of Gender and Ethnohistory in Mesoamerica," *Ethnohistory* 42:4 (1995): 639–650, 647. For an alternative analysis of the connections between race and gender in colonial Spanish America, see Kuznesof, "Ethnic and Gender Influences," 156. Kuznesof argues that gender was a more important indicator of social status than was race for women prior to 1570, at which time race increasingly became the dominant category. Contrarily, Schwartz suggests that gender will never become "an analytical tool as effective as class or other forms of social status" in colonial society. See Schwartz, "Colonial Identities," 187. For an enlightening analysis of how modern economic forces affect indigenous women's racial identity in Peru, see Marisol de la Cadena, "Women Are More Indian: Ethnicity and Gender in a Community Near Cuzco," in *Ethnicity, Markets, and Migration in the Andes: At the Crossroads of History and Anthropology*, ed. Brooke Larson and Olivia Harris, with Enrique Tandeter (Durham, N.C.: Duke Univ. Press, 1995), 329–348.

23. Haring, *Spanish Empire*.

24. John Phelan, "Authority and Flexibility in the Spanish Imperial Bureaucracy," *Administrative Science Quarterly* 5 (1960); Phelan, *Kingdom of Quito*.

25. Although many scholars continue to believe that gender roles are inherently stable, I am indebted here to the work of Patricia Seed, whose study of the colonial Spanish American family demonstrates that husbands and fathers gained increasing authority over their wives and children in the latter part of the colonial period. See Patricia Seed, *To Love, Honor, and Obey in Colonial Mexico* (Stanford, Calif.: Stanford Univ. Press, 1988).

26. Bartolomé de Las Casas, *A Short Account of the Destruction of the Indies*, trans. Nigel Griffin (1542; reprint, London: Penguin Books, 1992).

27. Numerous scholars have been influential in revising the history of indigenous peoples in Spanish America. See, for example, Charles Gibson, *The Aztecs under Spanish Rule: A History of the Indians of the Valley of Mexico, 1519–1810* (Stanford, Calif.: Stanford Univ. Press, 1964); William B. Taylor, *Drinking, Homicide, and Rebellion in Colonial Mexican Villages* (Stanford, Calif.: Stanford Univ. Press, 1979); Steve J. Stern, *Peru's Indian Peoples and the Challenge of Spanish Conquest: Huamanga to 1640*, 2d ed. (Madison: Univ. of Wisconsin Press, 1993); Karen Spalding, *Huarochirí: An Andean Society under Inca and Spanish Rule* (Stanford, Calif.: Stanford Univ. Press, 1984); James Lockhart, *The Nahuas after the Conquest: A Social and Cultural History of the Indians of Central Mexico, Sixteenth through Eighteenth Centuries* (Stanford, Calif.: Stanford Univ. Press, 1992); Karen Powers, *Andean Journeys: Migration, Ethnogenesis, and the State in Colonial Quito* (Albuquerque: Univ. of New Mexico Press, 1995).

28. Stern, "Prologue: Paradigms of Conquest. History, Historiography, and Politics," in *Peru's Indian Peoples*, xxi–liii.

29. Silverblatt expresses a similar view: "Might the use of terms like patriarchy, unless very specifically grounded, conceal just the kinds of differences that have, historically, made a difference?" See Silverblatt, "Lessons of Gender and Ethnohistory," 647.

Chapter One

1. Earnst Troeltsch, *The Social Teaching of the Christian Churches,* trans. Olive Wyon (1931; reprint, New York: Harper, 1960), 1:186–315 passim, 418. Quoted in Richard Boyer, "Women, *La Mala Vida,* and the Politics of Marriage," in *Sexuality and Marriage in Colonial Latin America,* ed. Asunción Lavrin (Lincoln: Univ. of Nebraska Press, 1992), 252.

2. Theodore Meyer, *Die christlich-ethischen sozial Principien und die Arbeiterfrage* (1904). Quoted in Boyer, "Women, *La Mala Vida,* and the Politics of Marriage," 252.

3. Historians of women in early Spanish America almost ubiquitously use a patriarchal paradigm in their analysis. For example, see the recent work of Jenny Londoño, *Entre la sumisión y la resistencia: Las mujeres en la Audiencia de Quito* (Quito: Ediciones Abya-Yala, 1997). Two important works on women in colonial Mexico in this regard are Richard Boyer, *Lives of the Bigamists: Marriage, Family, and Community in Colonial Mexico* (Albuquerque: Univ. of New Mexico Press, 1995), and Steve J. Stern, *The Secret History of Gender: Women, Men, and Power in Late Colonial Mexico* (Chapel Hill: Univ. of North Carolina Press, 1995). Stern, while showing a more nuanced vision of women's status, still includes women's use of the legal system as part of a strategy he identifies as "the multiplication of patriarchs." Boyer concludes that women were subjugated absolutely to fathers and husbands. Curiously, he legitimizes this view by claiming that women were considered perpetual minors under Spanish legislation, citing the work of Sylvia Arrom as the source for this information. Arrom's study, however, demonstrates that women were never considered minors in colonial legislation. See Silvia Marina Arrom, *The Women of Mexico City, 1790–1857* (Stanford, Calif.: Stanford Univ. Press, 1985), 57–58. Representative scholarship on the Andean region includes Irene Silverblatt, *Moon, Sun, and Witches: Gender Ideologies and Class in Inca and Colonial Peru* (Princeton, N.J.: Princeton Univ. Press, 1987), and Luis Martín, *Daughters of the Conquistadores* (Albuquerque: Univ. of New Mexico Press, 1983). For a strikingly different perspective on gender relations in colonial Spanish America, see Patricia Seed, *To Love, Honor, and Obey.* Seed asserts that the development of patriarchy coincides with growing political centralization during the Bourbon Monarchy in the mid-eighteenth century. Lisa Sousa's research suggests that gender roles were complementary rather than patriarchal in indigenous communities in southern Mexico. See Lisa Mary Sousa, "Women and Crime in Colonial Oaxaca: Evidence of Complementary Gender Roles in Mixtec and Zapotec Societies," in *Indian Women of Early Mexico,* ed. Susan Schroeder, Stephanie Wood, and Robert Haskett (Norman: Univ. of Oklahoma Press, 1997), 199–214. General social historians of early Spanish America have long seen women's relative independence and assertiveness; for them, patriarchy is hardly a factor. See, for example, James Lockhart, *Spanish Peru, 1532–1560: A Social History,* 2d ed. (Madison: Univ. of Wisconsin Press, 1994), 169–192.

4. Joan Scott, in her now classic essay, "Gender: A Useful Category of Historical Analysis," in *Gender and the Politics of History* (New York: Columbia Univ. Press, 1988), 34.

5. Quoted in Sarah S. Hughes, "Beyond Eurocentrism: Developing World Women's Studies," *Feminist Studies* 18 (1992): 401.

6. Ruth Behar, "Rage and Redemption: Reading the Life Story of a Mexican Marketing Woman," *Feminist Studies* 16 (1990): 230-231.

7. The imposition of metahistorical concepts such as patriarchy on distinct cultures has been widely critiqued as a Western hegemonic practice. See, for example, Daphne Patai, *Brazilian Women Speak* (New Brunswick, N.J.: Rutgers Univ. Press, 1988); Teresa de Lauretis, "Eccentric Subjects: Feminist Theory and Historical Consciousness," *Feminist Studies* 16 (1990): 115-150; Irvin Cemil Schick, "Representing Middle Eastern Women: Feminism and Colonial Discourse," *Feminist Studies* 16 (1990): 345-380. For the use of postcolonial criticism and the need to promote multiple, coexisting histories, see "The Postcolonial Critic: Homi Bhabha Interviewed by David Bennett and Terry Collits," 47-63, and Dipesh Chakrabarty, "Subaltern Studies and Critique of History," 105-134, both in *arena* 96 (Spring 1991).

8. MacEwen Scott, "Women in Latin America: Stereotypes and Social Science", *Bulletin of Latin American Research* 5 (1986): 22.

9. Boyer, *Lives of the Bigamists,* 63, 96. Boyer uses the work of Nancy Cott on eighteenth-century Massachusetts, John Stuart Mill's nineteenth-century characterization of women as bond servants to their husbands, Deborah Gray White's study of female slaves in the United States, and Edward Shorter's study of English and French family structures as the basis for his observation that women, as perpetual minors, were little more than indentured servants to fathers and husbands in colonial Spanish America.

10. Arrom, *Women of Mexico City,* 53-97. Arrom provides an analysis of the legal situation of women in Spain and Spanish America "for the entire colonial period," relying heavily on documentation from the later centuries, thus implying a legal continuity for women when, in fact, legislation changed throughout the colonial period.

11. See Peter Laslett, "Introduction: The History of the Family," in *Household and Family in Past Time,* ed. Peter Laslett and Richard Wall (Cambridge, England: Cambridge Univ. Press, 1972), 8. The nuclear or simple family structure is defined as containing one married couple and their children.

12. Peter Laslett, "Family and Household as Work Group and Kin Group: Areas of Traditional Europe Compared," in *Family Forms in Historic Europe,* ed. Richard Wall, Jean Robin, and Peter Laslett (Cambridge, England: Cambridge Univ. Press, 1983), 513-563.

13. Richard Wall assumes male headship in family units that contain adult men. Female headship only occurs in family units that do not contain men, such as would occur for single women or widows. See Richard Wall, "Introduction," in *Family Forms in Historic Europe,* ed. Richard Wall, Jean Robin, and Peter Laslett (Cambridge, England: Cambridge Univ. Press, 1983), 39. J. Hajnal, in establishing "household formation rules," also finds that the husband usually heads the household and comments that there is not even an accepted term for referring to a couple who are jointly in charge of households. See J. Hajnal, "Two Kinds of Pre-industrial Household Formation Systems," in *Family Forms in Historic Europe,*

ed. Richard Wall, Jean Robin, and Peter Laslett (Cambridge, England: Cambridge Univ. Press, 1983), 69.

14. Edward Shorter, *The Making of the Modern Family* (New York: Basic Books Inc., 1975), 72–78. Lawrence Stone, *The Family, Sex and Marriage in England, 1500–1800* (New York: Harper and Row, 1979).

15. The *Journal of Family History,* for example, devoted two issues to reviewing recent trends in Iberian family history. See David I. Kertzer and Caroline Brettel, "Advances in Italian and Iberian Family History," *Journal of Family History* 12: 1–3 (1987): 87–120, and William A. Douglass, "Iberian Family History," *Journal of Family History* 13:1 (1988): 1–12.

16. Pierre Vilar, *La familia en la España mediterránea (siglos XV–XIX)* (Barcelona: Editorial Crítica, 1987), 21–26. See also Ruth Behar and David Frye, "Property, Progeny, and Emotion: Family History in a Leonese Village," *Journal of Family History* 13:1 (1988): 13–32. Their work seeks to expand on Laslett's schema of the nuclear family structure by showing "how a family form apparently so universal must be understood within the local cultural/historical context that gives it meaning" (14–15). James Casey notes that "if families did tend to live apart, they cooperated very closely, and often one needs to get beyond the censuses in order to perceive this underlying reality." James Casey, *Early Modern Spain: A Social History* (New York: Routledge, 1999), 211.

17. Vilar, *La familia en la España,* 31. For a discussion of the economic and political effects of primogeniture and partibility in early modern Europe, see Jack Goody, *The Development of the Family and Marriage in Europe* (Cambridge, England: Cambridge Univ. Press, 1983), 18–123.

18. Goody discusses how the advancement of inheritance to the woman through the dowry integrated the new conjugal unit into the larger kin network by encouraging her natal family's interest in the marriage and the offspring it produced. Goody, *Development of the Family,* 258–259. The practice of men's families' advancing inheritance in the form of a donation at the time of marriage also reinforced the integration of individual households into a larger network of interests and responsibilities.

19. Behar and Frye, "Property, Progeny, and Emotion," 16.

20. See Stern, *Secret History,* 311. Other examples of this methodological tendency by researchers include Boyer, *Lives of the Bigamists,* 230; Arrom, *Women of Mexico City,* 76–77; Asunción Lavrin and Edith Couturier, "Las mujeres tienen la palabra: Otras voces en la historia colonial de México," *Historia Mexicana* 31 (1981): 279.

21. Stern, *Secret History,* 311. See also Ann Zulawski, "Social Differentiation, Gender, and Ethnicity: Urban Indian Women in Colonial Bolivia, 1640–1725," *Latin American Research Review* 25 (1990): 97; Arrom, *Women of Mexico City,* 77; Boyer, *Lives of the Bigamists,* 163, 230.

22. Casey, *Early Modern Spain,* 87–110. Gustavo Villapalos Salas and José María Castán Vázquez provide an articulate discussion of various civil, ecclesiastic, and military jurisdictions legally recognized by Isabel and Fernando in *Justicia y monarquía: Puntos de vista sobre su evolución en el reinado de los Reyes Católicos. Discurso leído el día 16 de junio de 1997 en su recepción pública como académico*

de número (Madrid: Real Academia de Jurisprudencia y Legislación, 1997), 185–252. For the legal description of feudalism in England, see Sir William Blackstone (1723–1780), *Commentaries on the Laws of England*, ed. Thomas M. Cooley (Chicago: Callaghan and Co., 1899), "Feudalism," bk. 2, chap. 4.

23. When the crown devalued the currency in 1651, local populations in Spain revolted until the crown restored the currency to its old value. Casey, *Early Modern Spain*, 135–136.

24. In 1639 customs agent Marcos Antonio Bisse, for example, was suspended from his position in the Spanish port of Alicante for collecting royally mandated shipping taxes "in such an excessive fashion that no man can be found, native or foreigner, willing to do business in that port." Casey, *Early Modern Spain*, 76–77.

25. Casey, *Early Modern Spain*, 87. Casey is commenting on the work of José Ortega y Gasset, *España invertebrada: Bosquejo de algunos pensamientos históricos* (Madrid: Calpe, 1921).

26. Andrien, *Crisis and Decline*, 43–75.

27. Phelan, "Authority and Flexibility," 59.

28. Clarence Haring, *Spanish Empire*, 113.

29. Phelan, *Kingdom of Quito*, 18–22.

30. Libro de cabildos de Quito, 21 May 1644. In *Libro de cabildos de la Ciudad de Quito*, ed. Jorge A. Garcés G., Publicaciones, no. 30 (1638–1648; reprint, Quito: Archivo Municipal de Quito, 1960) (hereafter, *Libro de cabildos de Quito*, Garcés); "Nómbrase a don Francisco de Villegas Santamaría y Pedro Vásquez Feijóo, para que preparen el pliego de peticiones a su majestad por intermedio de su delegado en España Juan Rodríguez."

31. Phelan, "Authority and Flexibility," 53–54; Haring, *Spanish Empire*, 113.

32. For a succinct analysis of the imposition of the alcabala in Peru and the revolt against the crown that occurred in Quito, see Bernard Lavalle, "La rebelión de las alcabalas," *Revista de Indias* 44 (1984): 141–201.

33. The alcabala generated conflicts in Spain as well. Desperate for money, in 1575 Philip II attempted to triple the alcabala in Spain. Local populations rebelled, and royal officials refused to collect the new amounts. Only after two years of negotiation was the king able to collect a part of the tax increases. Casey, *Early Modern Spain*, 135.

34. Letter from the viceroy to don Felipe II, 24 April 1592. Quoted in Bernard Lavalle, "La rebelión," 144. "Decimos y afirmamos que no concedimos ni consentimos ni queremos sujetarnos a pagarla [la alcabala] ni la pagaremos agora ni en ningún tiempo ésta ni otra ninguna, por quanto en la conquistación destos nuestros reinos el Rey nuestro señor no gastó nada ni dispendió nada."

35. Phelan, *Kingdom of Quito*, 84.

36. Phelan, "Authority and Flexibility," 48–49.

37. Phelan, "Authority and Flexibility," 49.

38. Phelan, "Authority and Flexibility," 57.

39. For the operation of decentralization in the Quito district, see Phelan, *Kingdom of Quito*, especially 19, 22, 27, 82, 119–146.

40. Criminales, 25 October 1696, ANE/Q, fols. 1–9.

41. Silvia Cogollos Amaya and Martín Eduardo Vargas Poo, "Las discusiones

en torno a la construcción y utilidad de los 'dormitorios' para los muertos: Santafé, finales del siglo XVIII," in *Inquisición, muerte y sexualidad en la Nueva Granada*, ed. Jaime Humberto Borja Gómez (Bogotá: Editorial Ariel, 1996), 143-167. Londoño notes that the first cemetery in the jurisdiction of the Audiencia of Quito was constructed at the end of the eighteenth century: *Entre la sumisión y la resistencia*, 47-48.

42. See the legal commentary of don José Vicente y Caravantes in don Sancho Llamas y Molina and don José Vicente y Caravantes, *Comentario crítico, jurídico, literal, a las ochenta y tres Leyes de Toro* (Madrid: Imprenta de Gaspar y Roig, 1853), 105-109; hereafter Toro.

43. Seed, *To Love, Honor, and Obey*, 299.

44. Lockhart, *Spanish Peru*, 1994, 175-176.

45. Rev. H. J. Schroeder, *Canons and Decrees of the Council of Trent* (London: B. Herder Book Co., 1941) (hereafter, Trent), chap. 1, 183-185; Seed, *To Love, Honor and Obey*, 32-40. See also Goody, *Development of the Family*, 146-151.

46. Toro, Law 53.

47. Trent, chap. 9.

48. Seed, *To Love, Honor and Obey*, 34.

49. Seed, *To Love, Honor and Obey*, 255.

50. Seed, *To Love, Honor and Obey*, 35. See also Goody, *Development of the Family*, 151.

51. Seed, *To Love, Honor and Obey*, 285.

52. Seed, *To Love, Honor and Obey*, 204.

53. Florencia E. Mallon, "Patriarchy in the Transition to Capitalism: Central Peru, 1830-1950," *Feminist Studies* 13 (1987): 379-407, 389. Mallon situates her study of gender relations in the early republican era of Peru within what she describes as the tradition of Spanish American patriarchal relations. Other studies which imply that fathers legally controlled marriages throughout the colonial period are Stern, *Secret History*, 16, 95; Zulawski, "Social Differentiation," 98; and Elinor Burkett, "In Dubious Sisterhood: Class and Sex in Spanish Colonial South America," *Latin American Perspectives* 4 (1977), 20. Like Seed, other authors recognize that the status of women changed in the late colonial period as male authority increased. See, for example, the work of Muriel Nazzari, "Parents and Daughters: Change in the Practice of Dowry in São Paulo (1600-1770)," *Hispanic American Historical Review* 70:4 (1990): 639-665; Linda Lewin, "Natural and Spurious Children in Brazilian Inheritance Law from Colony to Empire: A Methodological Essay," *Americas* (January 1992): 351-396; Deborah E. Kanter, "Native Female Land Tenure and Its Decline in Mexico, 1750-1900," *Ethnohistory* 42:4 (Fall 1995): 607-626.

54. Boyer, *Lives of the Bigamists*, 43.

55. For a discussion on marriage practices that treat women as gift property, see Lewis Hyde, *The Gift, Imagination and the Erotic Life of Property* (New York: Vintage Books, 1983), especially chap. 6 (93-108), "A Female Property." See also Goody, "From Brideprice to Dowry?" in *Development of the Family*, 240-261.

56. Norma Basch, *In the Eyes of the Law* (Ithaca, N.Y.: Cornell Univ. Press, 1982), 53.

57. Norma Basch, *In the Eyes of the Law,* 49. For the legal doctrine of coverture, see Blackstone, *Commentaries on the Laws of England,* bk. 1, chap. 15, "Of Husband and Wife," especially sec. 3, "Effects of Marriage on Status." "By marriage, the husband and wife are one person in law: that is, the very being or legal existence of the woman is suspended during the marriage, or at least is incorporated and consolidated into that of the husband [also referred to as her baron or lord]; under whose wing, protection, and cover she performs everything" (442).

58. Linda A. Pollock's research, focusing on the relationship between siblings in an elite English family, suggests that women had more autonomy and a larger field of operation outside of the framework of marriage. Linda A. Pollock, "Rethinking Patriarchy and the Family in Seventeenth-Century England," *Journal of Family History* 23:1 (January 1998): 3-28.

59. Common Law specifies that because wives are prohibited from contracting, "a man cannot grant any thing to his wife, or enter into covenant with her; for the grant would be to suppose her separate existence; and to covenant with her would be only to covenant with himself." Blackstone, *Commentaries on the Laws of England,* bk. 1, chap. 15, sec. 3, "Disability to Contract" (442).

60. Blackstone, *Commentaries on the Laws of England,* bk. 2, chap. 32, sec. 2, "Capacity to Make a Will" (497-500). Wives are included with minors, the insane, and felons as classes of individuals prohibited from making a testament.

61. Blackstone, *Commentaries on the Laws of England,* bk. 2, chap. 29, sec. 6, "Title by Marriage." "Whatever personal property belonged to the wife, before marriage, is by marriage absolutely vested in the husband" (433). However, it should be added that English legislation included the provision of equity, in which the disadvantaged could appeal to the royal courts for treatment based on fairness rather than legal strictness. By the seventeenth century, the concept of equity could ameliorate the situations of wives, usually those of the upper class, who sought to gain control over their property. But equity was still a legal exception; wives' ability to control property was seen as a rupture in the normal course of law. Basch, *In the Eyes of the Law,* 21-27. For a legal description of the Court of Equity, see Blackstone, *Commentaries on the Laws of England,* bk. 3, chap. 27 (429-442).

62. Blackstone, *Commentaries on the Laws of England,* bk. 1, chap. 15, sec. 3 (443).

63. Basch, *In the Eyes of the Law,* 17, 54-55. See also Peggy Rabkin, *Fathers to Daughters: The Legal Foundations of Female Emancipation* (Westport, Conn.: Greenwood Press, 1980), 19. For the legal description of *dower* under Common Law, see Blackstone, *Commentaries on the Laws of England,* bk. 2, chap. 8, sec. 4, "Dower" (129-140). For inheritance law see Blackstone, *Commentaries on the Laws of England,* bk. 2, chap. 14, sec. 2, "Males Preferred before Females" (213-214), and sec. 3, "Primogeniture" (215-216). For inheritance patterns see Jan De Vries, *The Economy of Europe in an Age of Crisis, 1600-1750* (New York: Cambridge Univ. Press, 1984), 63, 76, 223.

64. See, for example, the surnames of the legitimate children of doña Beatriz del Corral and her husband, Alonso de Ruanes: doña Juana de Aguilar, doña Francisca del Corral, doña Ana de Aguilar, and doña Margarita de Carranza. Of their

four daughters, three have different surnames, and none carries the surname of their father. Testament of doña Beatriz del Corral, 1 Notaría, 23 January 1648, ANE/Q, fols. 1-5. Doña Margarita de Carranza later changed her surname to her mother's. See testament of doña Margarita de Corral, 1 Notaría, vol. 181, 1654, ANE/Q, fols. 455-456.

65. Lockhart, *Spanish Peru*, 173-174.

66. Nazzari's research on naming practices in Brazil also suggests the correlation between the use of husbands' and fathers' surnames by wives and children and increasing male authority in the family. Muriel Nazzari, *Disappearance of the Dowry: Women, Families, and Social Change in São Paulo, Brazil (1600-1900)* (Stanford, Calif.: Stanford Univ. Press, 1991), 140-142.

67. Seed, *To Love, Honor, and Obey*, 167. Seed claims that this growing trend toward centralization of power coincides with the growth of capitalism and economic rationalism. "Capitalism, or more accurately the changes in attitudes about control of property and acquisitiveness that accompanied capitalism, provided for the reevaluation of the role of fathers by stressing the significance of their economic function and by strengthening their authority as consequence of their management not only of the immediate family's well-being but also of its ambitions within new realms of economic activity" (235).

68. Seed, *To Love, Honor, and Obey*, 133.

69. Joan Scott also supports this view that gender relations reflect and inform political order in "Gender: A Useful Category of Historical Analysis," 28-50.

Chapter Two

1. For examples of loans between wives and husbands, see the testament of Juan de Rueda, whose second wife loaned him 100 pesos, which he wanted paid to her through his estate, 1 Notaría, vol. 181, 1651, ANE/Q, fols. 191-200; and the testament of doña María Brava de Quintanilla, who requested that her third husband be reimbursed from her estate for his officially notarized loan to her of 1,200 pesos, 1 Notaría, vol. 269, 1700, ANE/Q, folios not numbered. In addition, see the testament of the indigenous doña Francisca Pillafaña, *cacica principal* (female indigenous ruler) of the pueblo of Guayllabamba, who asked her executors to collect a 50-peso debt from her Spanish husband for her estate, 1 Notaría, vol. 181, 1654, ANE/Q, fols. 508-511. All specifically used the term *préstamo* (loan) for the money exchanged between spouses, although perhaps in consideration of their marriage, the loans were apparently interest free.

2. On emancipation see Partidas, P.1:21, P.3.2:7, P.6.1:13, P.6.16:12-21; *Fuero Real del Rey Don Alonso El Sabio* (Madrid: La Imprenta Real, 1836) (hereafter, Fuero Real), bk. 1, Title XI, Law 8; Toro, Law 47.

3. Eugene H. Korth, and Della M. Flusche, "Dowry and Inheritance in Colonial Spanish America: Peninsular Law and Chilean Practice," *Americas* 43 (1987): 395-410.

4. Boyer, *Lives of the Bigamists*, 63. According to Boyer, husbands' control over their spouses' dowries is another manifestation of husbands' "uncontested 'juris-

diction' over wives." Zulawski finds that a wife's impact on the use of her dowry was limited to when the marriage ended either through legal dissolution or, more usually, through death; see "Social Differentiation," 98. Burkett considers women the passive carriers of dowries directly controlled by elite men for transferring capital within endogamous social networks. "In Dubious Sisterhood," 20, 24.

5. See, for example, Lockhart, *Spanish Peru,* 176; Lavrin and Couturier, "Las mujeres tienen la palabra," 283; Asunción Lavrin and Edith Couturier, "Dowries and Wills: A View of Women's Socioeconomic Role in Colonial Guadalajara and Puebla, 1640-1857," *Hispanic American Historical Review* 50:2 (1979): 280-304; Susan Migden Socolow, *The Merchants of Buenos Aires, 1778-1810: Family and Commerce* (Cambridge, England: Cambridge Univ. Press, 1978), 34-53, and "Acceptable Partners: Marriage Choice in Colonial Argentina, 1778-1810," in *Sexuality and Marriage in Colonial Latin America,* ed. Asunción Lavrin (Lincoln: Univ. of Nebraska Press, 1989), 209-251.

6. Linda Lewin, "Natural and Spurious Children," 351-396.

7. Nazzari, *Disappearance of the Dowry.*

8. Nazzari, *Disappearance of the Dowry,* 149-161.

9. For Lewin, Portuguese family relations were clearly different from the "traditional" European family model. She critiques researchers for using Anglo-American concepts of family organization for interpreting Brazilian family structure. Lewin, "Natural and Spurious Children," 353, 358.

10. Nazzari, *Disappearance of the Dowry,* 3-27.

11. For example, when the mestizo Anastasia Gutiérrez de Villapardo married Baltasar de Trujillo, neither of them claimed any capital, 1 Notaría, vol. 181, 1652, ANE/Q, fols. 305-307. The Spanish Juana Viera and her husband, Melchor Hernández, similarly lacked property when they married, 1 Notaría, vol. 169, 1641, ANE/Q, fols. 375-376.

12. See, for example, the testament of doña Juana Suárez Pavón, in which she declares that because her family was poor her husband, Francisco Montenegro, who possessed a sizable fortune, presented her with a dowry at the time of their marriage, 1 Notaría, vol. 247, 1684, ANE/Q, folios not numbered. This form of dowry reversal was not uncommon in Spanish America, where men of new wealth sought respectability by connecting themselves to families of high social status. See Lockhart, *Spanish Peru,* 175-176.

13. Many women claimed that they owned houses and land at the time of their marriage. See 1 Notaría, vol. 174, 1644, ANE/Q, fols. 378-381, testament of Juana Gascón; 1 Notaría, vol. 181, 1651, ANE/Q, fols. 233-235, testament of Inés Durán.

14. Partidas, P.4.3:1-5; Trent, chap. 1.

15. 1 Notaría, vol. 181, 1654, ANE/Q, fols. 494-497, testament of María Gómez.

16. Deborah Kanter's research on indigenous female land tenure in the Toluca Valley shows that Indians were fully incorporated into the Spanish legal tradition of partible inheritance and female property rights. Indigenous women used Spanish law to protect their property rights, and Spanish courts defended women's land claims against indigenous men who contested female landholdings. Her research suggests that juridical changes in the late colonial and republican periods

increased male authority by restricting the property rights of women, including the indigenous women in her study, who, by the Porfiriato, only rarely held land in their communities. See Kanter, "Native Female Land Tenure," 607–626.

17. For an overview of Spanish colonial legislation concerning women, see Korth and Flusche, "Dowry and Inheritance," 395–410. An overview of Spanish colonial legislation prevailing in the late-eighteenth and early-nineteenth centuries can be found in Arrom, *Women of Mexico City*, 53–97. Other works consulted that discuss the general development of Spanish legislation are Luis Gómez Morán, *La mujer en la historia y en la legislación* (Madrid: Gobierno de Audiencia Territorial, 1942); Mariano López Alarcón and Rafael Navarro-Valls, *Curso de derecho matrimonial canónico y concordado* (Madrid: Editorial Tecnos, 1984). For the Fuero Juzgo see *Fuero Juzgo en latín y castellano, cortejado con los más antiguos y preciosos códices* (Madrid: La Real Academia Española, 1815); hereafter, Fuero Juzgo. For the Fuero Real, see the full citation given in Chapter 1, Note 42. For the Siete Partidas see Francisco López Estrada and María Teresa López García-Berdoy, eds., *Las Siete Partidas: Antología* (Madrid: Editorial Castalia, 1992); D. Francisco Martínez Marina, *Ensayo histórico-crítico sobre la legislación de los Reinos de León y Castilla, especialmente sobre el código de las Siete Partidas*, 2 vols. (Madrid: Imprenta de D. E. Aguado, 1834); Esteban Martínez Marcos, *Las causas matrimoniales en las Partidas de Alfonso El Sabio* (Salamanca, Spain: Graficesa, 1966); Marilyn Stone, *Marriage and Friendship in Medieval Spain: Social Relations according to the Fourth Partida of Alfonso X* (New York: Peter Lang, 1990). For the Leyes de Toro, see the full citation given in Chapter 1, Note 42; Villapalos Salas and Castán Vázquez, *Justicia y Monarquía*, especially chap. 5, "El Nuevo ordenamiento privado, penal y procesal," 253–316. For the Council of Trent, see Trent; Martin Chemnitz, *Examination of the Council of Trent*, vol. 2, trans. Fred Kramer (1522–1586; reprint, St. Louis: Concordia, 1986).

18. The basic right of women to hold property was established by the Fuero Juzgo, bk. 4, Title II, Laws 1, 9, and Title V, Law 1, and was reaffirmed through law and practice throughout the colonial period. For rights of married women and property, see Toro, Laws 50–62.

19. Legislation outlining the dowry and its custody can be found in Partidas, P.3.18:87; P.4.11:1, 7, 17–22, 25–26, 29–32; P.5.13:33; and Toro, Laws 17, 22–23, 25–26, 29, 53.

20. Legislation concerning the arras: Partidas, P.3.18:87; P.4.11:1, 7; Toro, Laws 50–52.

21. Korth and Flusche, "Dowry and Inheritance," 401.

22. Korth and Flusche, "Dowry and Inheritance," 401. Laws concerning the husband's responsibilities for his wife's estate after her death are found in Partidas, P.4.11:30, 31.

23. Dowry contracts are quite common and are identical in format. The example used is the dowry contract of doña Luciana de Avila y Torres, whose dowry was provided by her aunt, María Mejía, 1 Notaría, vol. 161, 1638, ANE/Q, fols. 14–19. For other examples see dowry contracts of doña Ursula Fraile de Andrade, 1 Notaría, vol. 258, 1686, ANE/Q, fols. 367–370; doña Lucía de Ruanes, 1 Notaría, vol. 169, 1641, ANE/Q, fols. 336–338.

24. Goody, *Development of the Family,* 258.

25. Boyer, *Lives of the Bigamists,* 110.

26. The right of wives to sue husbands for the return of dowry property is defined in Partidas, P.4.XI:29.

27. Matrimoniales, 29 August 1680, ANE/Q.

28. Matrimoniales, 2 March 1672, ANE/Q.

29. Legislation defined daughters' dowries and donations to sons as anticipated inheritances; Partidas, P.6.15:3; Toro, Laws 17, 22–23, 25–27.

30. Criminales, 1 April 1682, ANE/Q.

31. Matrimoniales, 20 September 1700, ANE/Q.

32. Partidas, P.4.17:8, does not actually grant fathers the right to eat their children. As Stone notes, this partida explains the rights of fathers in the thirteenth century to sell or pawn children in times of necessity by describing that in the Fuero Real "it is written that if a man were trapped in a castle and dying of hunger, he might sooner eat his son than give up the castle without the order of his lord." The Fuero Real, however, contains no such provision about a father eating his son. Stone, *Marriage and Friendship,* 99.

Quotation from attorney in Matrimoniales, 20 September 1700, ANE/Q.

33. Toro, Law 77.

34. Criminales, 24 December 1691, ANE/Q (1692).

35. 1 Notaría, vol. 181, 1651, ANE/Q, fols. 191–200, testament of Juan de Rueda.

36. Lockhart, *Spanish Peru,* 37, 176.

37. For information on the relative status of the titles *don* and *doña* in early Spanish Peru, see Lockhart, *Spanish Peru,* 172–173.

38. Community and individual property rights within marriage are explained in Toro, Laws 14–29, 51, 54, 60, 77, 78.

39. All of Partida 6 is devoted to rights of inheritance and testaments. See also Toro, Laws 3–9, 17–28, 31–36, 49, 54. In rare cases, a family could receive a license from the crown in order to leave all of the inheritance to a single heir, the first-born child, be it daughter or son (*mayorazgo,* or primogeniture), Toro, Laws 41–46.

40. Toro, Law 55.

41. Toro, Laws 56, 57, 59.

42. An example of such a license is the power of attorney between Antonio Rodríguez and Juana de Hoyones Lescano, giving her license to engage in all civil and ecclesiastical suits and economically manage "what belonged to her." 1 Notaría, vol. 161, 1638, ANE/Q, fols. 321–323.

43. 1 Notaría, vol. 161, 1638, ANE/Q, fols. 212–213. Another example is the power of attorney between Pablo Sánchez and his wife, doña Luisa de Navárez, giving her license to legally and economically represent both of them. 1 Notaría, vol. 169, 1642, ANE/Q, fols. 463–434.

44. Toro, Law 58.

45. Toro, Law 57.

46. Toro, Law 55.

47. Obligación que hazen doña Francisca de Moreta y doña Jacoba de Moreta, 1 Notaría, vol. 169, 1648, ANE/Q, fols. 284–289.

48. Toro, Laws 70–75 give family members precedence in sales of family property.

49. Toro, Law 61.

50. The legal precedent cited was Partidas, P.6.12:3, which prohibited married women from acting as guarantors except in specific situations, such as when the contract was to the women's specific advantage.

51. Vicente y Caravantes, *Comentario*, 315–334 (Commentary on Toro, Law 61).

52. Partidas, P.5.12:2, permitted women to renounce the legal protection of their private estates.

53. 1 Notaría, 9 January 1657, ANE/Q, fols. 1–9, Imposición de Censo, Juan Cristóbal de Arce and doña Josefa Zambrana (1656).

54. The specific text reads: "Renunciando como expresamente renuncio las leyes de *duobus reis devendi* y el autentica presente *cobdice hocita de fide jusoribus* y el beneficio de la division y escursion de personas y vienes, y todas las demas leyes fueros y derechos de la mancomunidad como en ellas y en cada una de ellas se contiene."

55. The text in Spanish reads: "y la dicha doña Josepha Zambrana, renuncio la ley del senado jurisconsulto beleyano que aprobo el emperador Justiniano Leys de Toro y Partidas de Madrid que son en favor de las mugeres, de cuio efecto y remedio le abise yo el escribano, y como enterada en ellas las renuncio y aparto de su auxilio y favor, y por ser casada juro a Dios, y a la Cruz de haver por firme esta Escriptura, y no ir contra ella, por su docte, arras, ni otros derechos, ni alegara que fue forsada por su marido, ni otra persona, antes declara que la ortorga de su libre voluntad, por ser en su utilidad y probecho."

56. Casas, 19 July 1625, ANE/Q, fols. 16–18.

57. Toro, Law 55.

Chapter Three

1. Maestro Francisco de la Vega's testimony reads: "esta dicha mujer legitima llego mas de dies o doce veces a este testigo siendo cura a quejarse como el dicho su marido unas veces entraba tan colerico contra ella que le puso muchas veces las manos por haber dado quejas a los vecinos que le quitaba todo lo que tenia para dar lo a la dicha Maria de Castillo y entendiendo la dicha mujer del dicho Antonio Carrillo hallaba alguna ampara en el dicho cura theniente le respondio este testigo que en todas occasiones que no era justicia para remediarlo y que asi le dijo este testigo acudiese a las reales justicias que ellas eran quienes remediaban esas cosas." Criminales, 4 November 1662, ANE/Q, fol. 52.

2. See Asunción Lavrin, "Introduction: The Scenario, the Actors, and the Issues," in *Sexuality and Marriage in Colonial Latin America*, ed. Asunción Lavrin (Lincoln: Univ. of Nebraska Press, 1989), 3.

3. See, for example, Ruth Behar, "Sexual Witchcraft, Colonialism, and

Women's Powers: Views from the Mexican Inquisition," in *Sexuality and Marriage in Colonial Latin America,* ed. Asunción Lavrin (Lincoln: Univ. of Nebraska Press, 1989), 178-206, and Richard Boyer, "Women, *La Mala Vida,* and the Politics of Marriage," 252-286.

4. Partidas, P.4.2:1.

5. Partidas, P.4.9 and P.4.10; and The Council of Trent, Session 24, 1563, "Concerning Matrimony": canons 4-9 treat dissolution of marriage. See also Arrom, *Women of Mexico City,* 208-209; Natalia León Galarza, *La primera alianza. El matrimonio criollo: Honor y violencia conyugal. Cuenca 1750-1800* (Quito: Nueva Editorial, 1997), 59-60.

6. Partidas, P.7.17:1. The legislation reads: "porque del adulterio que hiciese ella puede venir al marido muy gran daño, pues si se empreñase de aquel con quien hizo el adulterio, vendría el hijo extraño heredero en uno con sus hijos, lo que no occuria a la mujer del adulterio que el marido hiciese con otra."

7. León, *La primera alianza,* 96-97.

8. Arrom, *Women of Mexico City,* 228-229.

9. Matrimoniales, 11 September 1724, ANE/Q.

10. Matrimoniales, 11 September 1724, ANE/Q, fol. 10.

11. Nancy van Deusan's study of divorce cases in Lima between 1650 and 1700 indicates that the number of marital litigation suits increased during this period. Although women made up 95 percent of the litigants, the majority dropped their suits, perhaps because of the difficulties mentioned. See Nancy van Deusan, "Determining the Boundaries of Virtue: The Discourse of Recogimiento among Women in Seventeenth-Century Lima," *Journal of Family History* 22:4 (October 1997): 373-389.

12. According to Goody, *Development of the Family,* 167, although marriage had been considered a sacrament since the beginning of the thirteenth century, it was not so declared until the sixteenth century in the Council of Trent, when the church claimed exclusive rights to determine marriage validity (Trent, Canon 1). The thirteenth-century Partidas recognized what was essentially self-marriage; relationships in which individuals exchanged marriage vows and physically consummated their union were considered valid marriages (Partidas, P.4.1:2-4).

13. Goody, *Development of the Family,* 45.

14. Sousa's work with criminal records in southern Mexico demonstrates that even indigenous women living outside of Spanish centers used the criminal justice system to resolve their conflicts with men. Sousa, "Women and Crime in Colonial Oaxaca."

15. Criminal records are also being used to revise the history of domestic violence in England. Whereas other studies have relied on divorce cases to show that only extreme forms of spousal abuse were prosecuted, the work of Jennine Hurl-Eamon, using recognizances, shows that wives could prosecute even a relatively minor incident of violence. The complaints that wives brought before justices of the peace, even if they did not go to trial, forced accused husbands to post a substantial bond and to pay a fee and appear at a summons. If a husband did not comply with the process, he risked losing his bond, incurring fines, and undergoing imprisonment. See Jennine Hurl-Eamon, "Domestic Violence Prosecuted: Women

Binding over Their Husbands for Assault at Westminster Quarter Sessions, 1685–1720," *Journal of Family History* 26:4 (October 2001): 435–454.

16. According to Shorter (*The Making of the Modern Family*, 50–51) central European governments also intervened in family relations to enforce public morality. However, the primary objective of that intervention was to reinforce the authority of husbands and fathers through laws that targeted the sexual behavior of women.

17. See, for example, Indiferente 536, 19 November 1618, Archivo General de los Indies (AGI), Libro 2, fol. 145. "Que no se de licencia a ningun hombre casado para venir a estos reinos si no fuere con conocimiento de causa y por tiempo limitado." Quoted in Richard Konetzke, ed., *Colección de documentos para la historia de la formación social de Hispanoamérica, 1493–1810* (Madrid: Consejo Superior de Investigaciones Científicas, 1958), 2:229.

18. Descalzi del Castillo, *La Real Audiencia de Quito*, 176–177.

19. Descalzi, *La Real Audiencia de Quito*, 204.

20. Descalzi, *La Real Audiencia de Quito*, 222.

21. Fondo Esp., vol. 1, 1625, ANE/Q, fol. 63; Fondo Esp., vol. 6, 1646, ANE/Q, fol. 10; Fondo Esp., vol. 8, 1672, ANE/Q, fol. 131.

22. Civiles, 27 February 1695, ANE/Q, fols. unnumbered.

23. Criminales, 23 June 1699, ANE/Q, fols. unnumbered.

24. Criminales, 26 August 1680, ANE/Q, fols. 3–4.

25. Criminales, 2 January 1680, ANE/Q, fol. 1.

26. Criminales, 2 January 1680, ANE/Q, fol. 2.

27. Criminales, 4 March 1662, ANE/Q, fol. 52.

28. Criminales, 2 January 1680, ANE/Q, fol. 3.

29. Criminales, 28 June 1636, ANE/Q.

30. Criminales, 30 June 1636, ANE/Q. The file is misdated; the actual date of the suit is 27 June 1636. For another example of a married woman bringing criminal charges in her own name against a third party, see Criminales, 22 March 1691, ANE/Q. Doña Francisca Arias de la Vega, legitimate wife of Diego Rodríguez Zambrana, sued Francisco de Paredes and his mulatto servant Pedro for assault and robbery. Both men were jailed and their property seized.

31. Criminales, 28 June 1636, ANE/Q, fols. 1–2, 11.

32. Criminales, 2 January 1680, ANE/Q, fol. 2.

33. Criminales, 5 March 1695, ANE/Q, fol. 96.

34. Criminales, 14 January 1697, ANE/Q.

35. For examples of women granting pardons, see 1 Notaría, vol. 169, 1640, ANE/Q, fols. 140–41: Ursula Pérez, mestizo in indigenous clothing, pardons the death of her husband, Pedro de Veredia; 1 Notaría, vol. 181, 1650, ANE/Q, fol. 25: Magdalena Proaño, free mulatto, pardons the death of her brother, Francisco Rodríguez; 1 Notaría, vol. 181, 1651, ANE/Q, fol. 237: María Flores, mestizo in indigenous clothing, pardons the death of her son, Juan Jiménez Garido; 1 Notaría, vol. 181, 1651, ANE/Q, fol. 568: the married María Zambrano renounces the Leyes de Toro and the Partidas and pardons the death of her mother, Bárbara Sangochimbo.

36. Criminales, 30 March 1662, ANE/Q.

37. Criminales, 30 March 1662, ANE/Q, fols. 1-7.
38. Criminales, 30 March 1662, ANE/Q, fols. 9-14.
39. Criminales, 30 March 1662, ANE/Q, fols. 17-24.
40. Criminales, 30 March 1662, ANE/Q, fol. 31.
41. Criminales, 30 March 1662, ANE/Q, fol. 43.
42. Criminales, 30 March 1662, ANE/Q, fols. 55-58.
43. Francisco Tomás y Valiente, *El derecho penal de la monarquía absoluta (siglos XVI-XVII-XVIII)* (Madrid: Editorial Tecnos, 1969), 397-405.
44. Twinam's insightful study of perceptions of honor and illegitimacy among colonial Spanish American elites shows that the belief that the marriage promise legitimated sexual relations was common and linked to the older tradition, codified in the Partidas, that allowed couples to effectively marry by exchanging vows without the intervention of clerics. See Ann Twinam, *Public Lives, Private Secrets: Gender, Honor, Sexuality, and Illegitimacy in Colonial Spanish America* (Stanford, Calif.: Stanford Univ. Press, 1999), especially 36-41.
45. Criminales, 13 May 1676, ANE/Q.
46. Criminales, 19 January 1694, ANE/Q.
47. Seed's research on disputes over breach of marriage promises suggests that ecclesiastical courts also increasingly refused to enforce these oral agreements. Seed links the devaluing of women's testimony in these cases with the lack of respect accorded oral testimony and the greater reliance on written documents in the late colonial period. In this situation men were less inclined to keep their spoken promises, and the sexual honor of women, which depended on men's fulfillment of their word, was increasingly put at risk. Patricia Seed, "Marriage Promises and the Value of a Woman's Testimony in Colonial Mexico," *Journal of Women in Culture and Society* 13:21 (1988): 253-276.
48. Criminales, 16 November 1691, ANE/Q.
49. Criminales, 16 November 1691, ANE/Q, fol. 7.
50. Criminales, 21 August 1692, ANE/Q.
51. Criminales, 21 August 1692, ANE/Q, fols. 21-22.
52. Criminales, 27 September 1661, ANE/Q.
53. Criminales, 27 September 1661, ANE/Q, fol. 2.
54. Criminales, 27 September 1661, ANE/Q, fol. 1.

Chapter Four

1. Arrom, *Women of Mexico City*, 154. Women's strong presence in the colonial economy generally is accepted by historians in the early Latin American field. Some works focusing on the economic activities of women include Lockhart, *Spanish Peru*; Elinor Burkett, "Indian Women and White Society: The Case of Sixteenth-Century Peru," *Latin American Women: Historical Perspectives*, ed. Asunción Lavrin (Westport, Conn.: Greenwood, 1978), 101-128. Asunción Lavrin, in this same book, documents the active participation of married and single women in the colonial Mexican economy: "In Search of the Colonial Woman in Mexico: The Seventeenth and Eighteenth Centuries," 3-22. See also Borchart, "Circula-

ción y producción en Quito"; and Ann Zulawski, *They Eat from Their Labor: Work and Social Change in Colonial Bolivia* (Pittsburgh: Univ. of Pittsburgh Press, 1995).

2. "Informe del Presidente Lope Antonio de Munive, 1681," cited in Javier Ortíz de la Tabla, "El obraje colonial ecuatoriano: Aproximación a su estudio," *Revista Ecuatoriana de Historia Económica* 2 (1988): 74.

3. Ortíz de la Tabla, "El obraje colonial," 63-142. He has constructed genealogical charts for the leading obraje-owning families in the Quito region, from which the following information is drawn.

4. Criminales, 22 January 1686, ANE/Q.

5. 1 Notaría, vol. 269, 1700, ANE/Q, fols. 23-25.

6. It should be noted that literacy also was not common among the general population of men. The use of estate administrators by elites and the availability of notaries for the general population made literacy in individuals less important in commercial relations in this period than it would be later.

7. Criminales, 19 June 1693, ANE/Q.

8. Criminales, 19 June 1693, ANE/Q, fol. 16.

9. Criminales, 19 June 1693, ANE/Q, fol. 15.

10. Criminales, 19 June 1693, ANE/Q, fol. 3.

11. Ortíz de la Tabla, "El obraje colonial," 78. The cacica doña Joana Rosa Conda also claimed that Indians were fleeing the region surrounding Achimbo because of the cruel treatment in the pueblo's obraje. See Criminales, 19 June 1693, ANE/Q, fol. 2.

12. Ortíz de la Tabla, "El obraje colonial," 77.

13. Forced work in obrajes was a standard and accepted form of punishment for non-Indians. Royal law, however, prohibited using this punishment for Indians. Corregidores legally could not condemn Indians to work in obrajes and, instead, were to ensure that conditions in the obraje were healthy and that workers were treated humanely. See Royal Cedula: Audiencia of Lima 573, 16 April 1655, AGI, Libro 24, fol. 352. Quoted in Konetzke, *Colección de documentos*, 2:461-462. Such regulations, as these cases show, were not enforced in Quito.

14. Ortíz de la Tabla, "El obraje colonial," 131-133.

15. Criminales, 22 January 1686, ANE/Q.

16. Criminales, 19 June 1693, ANE/Q, fol. 3.

17. Among those sentenced to work in obrajes for crimes they had committed were even Spanish men. See, for example, the case of Manuel López de Hinojosa, sentenced to work in an obraje in Quito for a robbery he committed, Criminales, 13 February 1695, ANE/Q.

18. Criminales, 19 June 1693, ANE/Q, fols. 1-3.

19. Criminales, 19 June 1693, ANE/Q, fol. 16.

20. Corregidores were royal appointees. These officials were appointed by the crown in Spain or by either the viceroy or the president of the Audiencia in America. See Haring, *Spanish Empire*, 128-130.

21. The practice of giving workers advances on their salaries was apparently common for obrajes in both New Spain (Mexico) and Peru and traditionally has been seen by historians as a mechanism to coercively retain workers in "debt peon-

age." For an example of this view, see Manuel Miño Grijalva, "La manufactura colonial: Aspectos comparativos entre el obraje andino y el novohispano," *Revista Ecuatoriana de Historia Económica* 2 (1988): 38-45. The research of other scholars, however, suggests that debt peonage was not commonly practiced in the colonial period. See James Lockhart and Stuart B. Schwartz, *Early Latin America: A History of Colonial Spanish America and Brazil* (Cambridge, England: Cambridge Univ. Press, 1985), 141-146. They specifically discuss the potential use of debt peonage for obrajes and find that debt was not an effective means of retaining workers. My own research supports their findings; although obraje owners frequently did advance earnings, this practice was combined with more coercive methods to retain workers, often through physical restraint.

22. Ortíz de la Tabla, "El obraje colonial," 74, mentions the widespread phenomenon of these small, usually itinerant operations in the Quito region.

23. 1 Notaría, vol. 269, 1701, ANE/Q, folios numbered incorrectly, testament of doña Joana Méndez de la Higuera.

24. 1 Notaría, vol. 175, ANE/Q, 1644, fols. 73-76, testament of Gerónima de Tamayo.

25. 1 Notaría, vol. 169, 1641, ANE/Q, fols. 226-227.

26. 1 Notaría, vol. 169, 1641, ANE/Q, fols. 351-353.

27. 1 Notaría, vol. 181, 1652, ANE/Q, fols. 347-348.

28. 1 Notaría, vol. 161, 1637, ANE/Q, fols. 241-42, 263-64, 470-471.

29. Carn. y Pulp., 14 June 1642, ANE/Q fol. 4.

30. Carn. y Pulp., 5 December 1669, ANE/Q.

31. Jay Kinsbruner's study of eighteenth- and nineteenth-century pulperías shows that there was great local variation in the gender coding of particular economic activities in Spanish America. Although he notes that all the pulperías in Santiago, Chile, and Paucartambo, Peru, were run by women, very few women owned or operated pulperías in the city of Puebla, Mexico City, Caracas, and Buenos Aires, the focus of his research. See Jay Kinsbruner, *Petty Capitalism in Spanish America: The Pulperos of Puebla, Mexico City, Caracas, and Buenos Aires* (Boulder, Colo.: Westview Press, 1987).

32. Criminales, 26 July 1671, ANE/Q, fol. 41.

33. Criminales, 23 January 1679, ANE/Q.

34. Carn. y Pulp., 14 June 1642, ANE/Q, fol. 4.

35. Criminales, 13 September 1690, ANE/Q, fol. 6.

36. José Toribio Medina, ed., *Cosas de la colonia*, 1952, 88-90, quoted in Kinsbruner, *Petty Capitalism*, 14. In Ann Zulawski's study of indigenous women in colonial Bolivia, she mentions two indigenous women who ran pulperías in Potosí and La Plata. Ann Zulawski, *Indian Women and the Market Economy in Colonial Bolivia* (New York: Consortium of Columbia Univ. Institute of Latin America and Iberian Studies and New York Univ. Center for Latin American and Caribbean Studies, 1988), 8, 11. Although both Kinsbruner and Zulawski found evidence of Indians managing pulperías, there is no evidence that any Indian owned or operated a pulpería in seventeenth-century Quito.

37. 1 Notaría, vol. 248, 1687, ANE/Q, folios not numbered, testament of Tomasa Sánchez. It is possible that her father was the same Gerónimo Sánchez men-

tioned above as the deceased husband of the mestizo pulpera María de Eraso, but as this was a common name, it is impossible to be certain.

38. 1 Notaría, vol. 185, 1647, ANE/Q, fols. 371-372, testament of Gerónima Morales.

39. For an analysis of the interplay of personal interests and public policy in the provisioning of cities in commodities considered of primary necessity, such as wheat, maize, and meat, see Eric Van Young, *Hacienda and Market in Eighteenth-Century Mexico: The Rural Economy of the Guadalajara Region, 1675-1820* (Berkeley: Univ. of Calif. Press, 1981), 43-103. Also see Lutz, *Santiago de Guatemala,* 144-152.

40. Repartición de semanas para el abasto de carne a la ciudad, Actas, 14 February 1659, 13 February 1661, 1 January 1662, 1 February 1663, ANE/Q. Cited in Londoño, *Entre la sumisión y la resistencia,* 174.

41. Lockhart, *Spanish Peru,* 180.

42. 1 Notaría, vol. 169, 1641, ANE/Q, fols. 409-410.

43. 1 Notaría, vol. 174, 1645, ANE/Q, fols. 547-550, testament of Catalina Sánchez.

44. 1 Notaría, vol. 169, 1642, ANE/Q, fols. 457-459.

45. 1 Notaría, Protocoles, vol. 269, 1700, ANE/Q, folios not numbered, testament of María de Mendiola india.

46. Criminales, 4 February 1662. ANE/Q.

47. Lockhart, *Spanish Peru,* 180.

48. 1 Notaría, vol. 161, 1638, ANE/Q, fols. 299-300, 303-308.

49. 1 Notaría, vol. 161, 1638, ANE/Q, fols. 40-42.

50. 1 Notaría, vol. 174, 1645, ANE/Q, fol. 479.

51. 1 Notaría, vol. 169, 1642, ANE/Q, fols. 552-553.

52. 1 Notaría, vol. 161, 1638, ANE/Q, fols. 358-359.

53. 1 Notaría, vol. 172, 1642, ANE/Q, fol. 266.

54. 1 Notaría, vol. 169, 1642, ANE/Q, fols. 504-506.

55. 1 Notaría, vol. 269, 1699, ANE/Q, folios not numbered, testament of doña Tomasa de Fonseca y Ponce.

56. 1 Notaría, vol. 174, 1644, ANE/Q, fols. 378-381, testament of Juana Gascón.

57. 1 Notaría, vol. 257, 1674, ANE/Q, fols. 140-141, testament of Mariana de Torres.

58. Criminales, 16 November 1691, ANE/Q.

59. 1 Notaría, vol. 181, 1650, ANE/Q, fols. 127-180, testament of Isabel de Castillo.

60. 1 Notaría, vol. 181, 1655, ANE/Q, fols. 538-542, testament of doña Leonor Carxatigua india.

61. 1 Notaría, vol. 181, 1655, ANE/Q, fols. 646-650, testament of doña Juana Tosi india.

62. 1 Notaría, vol. 269, ANE/Q, folios not numbered, testament of María de Mendiola india.

63. 1 Notaría, vol. 184, 1647, ANE/Q, fols. 306-308, testament of Francisca Chuitiguay.

64. 1 Notaría, vol. 181, 1648, ANE/Q, fols. 14–16, testament of Ana Marchin india.

65. See Diego González Holguín, *Vocabulario de la lengua Qquichua* (1608; reprint, Quito: Corporación Editora Nacional, 1993), 110: "China: Criada, moça de servicio." The ultimate origin of the word remains uncertain. It appears in other Spanish American areas with the same meaning, and some feel it may originally have been Spanish.

66. 1 Notaría, vol. 161, 1649, ANE/Q, fol. 323, testament of Lucía Nasipansa india.

67. Criminales, 16 November 1691, ANE/Q, fol. 4.

68. See, for example, 1 Notaría, vol. 269, ANE/Q, folios not numbered, testament of María de Mendiola india. She lent money to two indigenous panaderas. The gender and racial categories of bread bakers varied by region. In colonial Guatemala, for example, Lutz found evidence of both men and women bread bakers from all racial groups, including Spaniards. Lutz, *Santiago de Guatemala*, 146–147.

69. Conflicts between city councils and bread bakers over the quality and quantity of bread sold raged throughout Spanish America. For Guatemala see Lutz, *Santiago de Guatemala*, 146–147. For Mexico see Van Young, *Hacienda and Market*, 68.

70. *Libro de cabildos de Quito*, March 7, 1654, in *Libro de cabildos de la Ciudad de Quito*, ed. Gustavo Chiriboga C., Publicaciones, no. 32 (1650–1657; reprint, Quito: Archivo Municipal de Quito, 1969); hereafter, *Libro de cabildos de Quito*, Chiriboga.

71. *Libro de cabildos de Quito*, August 27, 1654, Chiriboga.

72. *Libro de cabildos de Quito*, February 5, 1655, Chiriboga.

73. González Holguín, *Vocabulario de la lengua Qquichua*, 18. "Aka: El açua o chicha." Indigenous women were in charge of the preparation of chicha throughout the Andes. For chicheras in Lima see Lowry, "Forging an Indian Nation," 228.

74. Bernabé Cobo, *Historia del Nuevo Mundo*, 2 vols. (Madrid: Real Academia de Historia, 1956).

75. Criminales, 25 May 1694, ANE/Q.

76. Carn. y Pulp., 24 January 1687, ANE/Q.

77. 1 Notaría, vol. 269, 1701, ANE/Q, folios not numbered, testament of doña Juana Méndez de la Higuera.

78. Criminales, 16 November 1691, ANE/Q, fol. 4.

79. 1 Notaría, vol. 269, 1701, ANE/Q, folios not numbered, testament of doña Juana Méndez de la Higuera.

Chapter Five

1. Carn. y Pulp., 14 June 1642, ANE/Q, fol. 8 (1654): "[S]in que sea justo que el interes que pretenden los tratantes en los dichos jeneros ay a de ser con perjuizio y daño de las yndias que tienen la misma libertad y el mismo derecho que ellos para poder bender estos jeneros."

2. Carn. y Pulp., 16 March 1662, ANE/Q, fol. 4: "[Q]ue no se puede impedir que vendamos los frutos de nuestras haziendas, quitandonos la libertad que el derecho natural y de las gentes nos consede."

3. See, for an example, Autos Acordados, 23 February 1656, ANE/Q, fol. 25, an ordinance prohibiting vendors in the marketplace from accepting valuable items in exchange for their wares. Also see Carn. y Pulp., 14 June 1642, ANE/Q, fol. 1, litigation between pulperos and gateras.

4. John Murra first proposed the concept of "ecological archipelagos" in 1955. For a recent overview of his theory on Andean vertical control over resources, see "Did Tribute and Markets Prevail in the Andes before the European Invasion?" in *Ethnicity, Markets, and Migration in the Andes: At the Crossroads of History and Anthropology*, ed. Brooke Larson and Olivia Harris, with Enrique Tandeter (Durham, N.C.: Duke Univ. Press, 1995), 57-72.

5. Murra, "Tribute and Markets," 61.

6. Roswith Hartman: "Mercados y ferias prehispánicas en el área andina," *Boletín de la Academia Nacional de Historia* 54 (1971): 214-235; Udo Oberem, "Trade and Trade Goods in the Ecuadorian Montaña," trans. Alegonda M. Schokkenbroek, in *Native South Americans*, ed. Patricia J. Lyon (Boston: Little Brown, 1974), 346-357; Frank Salomon, *Native Lords of Quito in the Age of the Incas: The Political Economy of North Andean Chiefdoms* (Cambridge, England: Cambridge Univ. Press, 1986). Enrique Mayer claims that there was a pre-Incaic market tradition in the area of Cuzco, which was curtailed by the Incan administration. See Enrique Mayer, "El trueque y los mercados en el imperio incaico," in *Los campesinos y el mercado*, ed. Enrique Mayer, Sidney W. Mintz, and G. William Skinner (Lima: PUCE, 1974), 13-50.

7. Salomon, *Native Lords of Quito*, 98-99. Steve Stern, however, dismisses the importance of a market system in pre-Hispanic Quito, and Susan Ramírez completely rejects the evidence of an indigenous tradition of trade. See Steve J. Stern, "The Variety and Ambiguity of Native Andean Intervention in European Colonial Markets," 73-100, and Susan Ramírez, "Exchange and Markets in the Sixteenth Century: A View from the North," 134-164; both in *Ethnicity, Markets, and Migration in the Andes: At the Crossroads of History and Anthropology*, ed. Brooke Larson and Olivia Harris, with Enrique Tandeter (Durham, N.C.: Duke Univ. Press, 1995).

8. Salomon, *Native Lords of Quito*, 99; *Libro de cabildos de Quito*, 20 May 1535, cited in Descalzi, *La Real Audiencia de Quito*, 64.

9. *Libro de cabildos de Quito*, 21 June 1535, cited in Descalzi, *La Real Audiencia de Quito*, 69.

10. Diego González Holguín, *Vocabulario de la lengua Qquichua*, 138: "Katu: Mercado de cosas de comer." The standard term for market in the Quito District in the seventeenth century was usually *gato*. See, for example, Criminales, 19 June 1693, ANE/Q, fol. 2. Lowry, "Forging an Indian Nation," 229-233, presents evidence that the terms *gato* and *gatera* were also used in Lima in the seventeenth century.

11. 1 Notaría, Juicios, 6 August 1701, ANE/Q, fol. 4.

12. Partidas, P.4.14:3.

13. Partidas, P.4.15:1. See also Toro, Laws 9–13. The Spaniards had a legal gradation for children born outside of marriage. The first category, "hijo natural," was quite common and relatively socially acceptable and included the right to inherit from one's parents, though not equally with legitimate children. Those who fell in the category of "hijo espurio" were considered "vile," with no rights to their parents' inheritance.

14. Carn. y Pulp., 14 June 1642, ANE/Q, fol. 8 (1654).

15. Salomon, *Native Lords of Quito*, 102–106.

16. Salomon, *Native Lords of Quito*, 102–103.

17. Salomon, *Native Lords of Quito*, 105–106.

18. Criminales, 25 November 1665, ANE/Q, fol. 38. The colonial definition for the term *tratante* varies according to region. In Mexico tratantes were often associated with interregional trade of domestic products. In the Quito District, tratante meant any kind of small-scale dealer. The pulperos interchangeably referred to themselves as "pulperos," as "tratantes en pulperías," and simply as "tratantes." Indians never described themselves as tratantes, though their attorneys often did so. Indians who transported goods, bought goods for resale, or sold retail were referred to as "tratantes," "negociantes," "comerciantes," and "contratantes." Market women, however, were never referred to as tratantes.

19. Criminales, 19 December 1690, ANE/Q, fol. 12.

20. The active participation of Andean Indians in commercial activities has been well documented. See, for example, Steve Stern, "Early Spanish-Indian Accommodation in the Andes," in *The Indian in Latin American History: Resistance, Resilience, and Acculturation,* ed. John E. Kicza (Wilmington, Del.: Scholarly Resources, 1993). For information on the commercial activities of indigenous women in Spanish urban centers, see Burkett, "Indian Women and White Society"; Frank Salomon, "Indian Women of Early Colonial Quito"; Ann Zulawski, *Indian Women and the Market Economy.*

21. A royal mandate issued in 1656, for example, was directed at mestiza, indigenous, mulatto, and black women who sold in the plaza mayor of Quito. The punishment for disobeying the mandate was gender specific, one hundred lashes in the plaza and streets plus one year of prison and service in the *recogimiento* of Santa Marta, a convent where women lawbreakers were sent. See Autos Acordados, 1656, ANE/Q, fol. 25; the reference is to "mestizas, indias, mulatas y negras que venden en el mercado de la plaza mayor de esta dicha ciudad."

22. The *Recopilación* (Libro VI, Título 5, Ley 19, 1618), cited in Haring, *Spanish Empire,* 264. Haring notes that in most provinces in Mexico, contrarily, indigenous women were subject to paying this tax.

23. Haring, *Spanish Empire,* 56.

24. Mestizos, 8 June 1695, ANE/Q, cited in Minchom, *People of Quito,* 108.

25. Salomon, *Native Lords of Quito,* 101.

26. Criminales, 19 June 1693, ANE/Q, fol. 2.

27. Criminales, 25 November 1665, ANE/Q.

28. Criminales, 20 December 1691, ANE/Q, fol. 15 (Guano).

29. Carn. y Pulp., 14 June 1642, ANE/Q, fol. 2.

30. Carn. y Pulp., 14 June 1642, ANE/Q, fol. 3.

31. Carn. y Pulp., 14 June 1642, ANE/Q, fol. 3.

32. Lowry, "Forging an Indian Nation," 230.

33. Carn. y Pulp., 14 June 1642, ANE/Q, fol. 119 (1714). Douglas Cope, in his study of urban society in colonial Mexico, mentions that in 1700 the city council attempted to close the nighttime market (*tianguillo*). Indian vendors appealed to the viceroy and were allowed to continue selling indispensable foodstuffs, such as *atole* (cornmeal mush), tortillas, and bread. Cope, *The Limits of Racial Domination*, 37. Lutz notes that in the early part of the eighteenth century in Guatemala City even inexpensive products, such as vegetables, flowers, and wood, were regulated, though he suggests that by this time Indians had been replaced generally by *castas* (individuals of mixed racial ancestry, and blacks) and poor Spaniards in the markets. It is unclear in his discussion what specific regulations were imposed on these products. See Lutz, *Santiago de Guatemala*, 143.

34. See Haring, *Spanish Empire*, 260, for rates of the alcabala. The practice of compounding the alcabala into a lump sum paid by the municipality was typical for principal cities in Spain and Spanish America. For this practice in Spain, see Casey, *Early Modern Spain*, 80–81.

35. See, for example, *Libro de cabildos de Quito*, June 15, 1644, Garcés: "Conoce el Cabildo el auto de la Real Audiencia sobre el Cabezón de las Alcabalas," in which the royal authorities agree to prorate the city's tax payments, fixing a sum of 14,000 pesos to be paid yearly for the next five years, in addition to stipulating a debt repayment plan for the 28,500 pesos already owed by the city to the royal treasury. For a general description of the alcabala, see Alfredo Pareja Diezcanseco, *Las instituciones y la administración de la Real Audiencia de Quito* (Quito: Editorial Universitaria, 1975), 142–148.

36. Haring, *Spanish Empire*, 270.

37. The classic study of the mechanisms and impact of the "two republic" model is by Magnus Morner, *La Corona española y los foráneos en los pueblos de indios de América*, Institute of Ibero-American Studies, Stockholm, Publication Series A, no. 1 (Stockholm: Almquist and Wiksell, 1970).

38. The crown formally recognized the noble status of indigenous rulers and their traditional authority in their communities. See, for example, Indiferente 431, 26 March 1697, AGI, Libro 44, fol. 55. Quoted in Konetzke, *Colección de documentos*, 3:66–69. Royal prohibitions against non-Indians living in indigenous pueblos were continually repeated throughout the colonial period. See, for example, Audiencia de Lima 572, 30 June 1646, AGI, Libro 22, fol. 356 (Konetzke, *Colección de documentos*, 2:401–402).

39. Criminales, 29 January 1692, ANE/Q.

40. Minchom, *People of Quito*, 102.

41. Carn. y Pulp., 14 June 1642, ANE/Q, fol. 28 (1670) and fol. 47 (1702).

42. Carn. y Pulp., 14 June 1642, ANE/Q, fols. 88–95 (1708).

43. Carn. y Pulp., 5 December 1669, ANE/Q. City-licensed pulperías are also mentioned in Carn. y Pulp., 14 June 1642, ANE/Q, fol. 8 (1654).

44. Carn. y Pulp., 14 June 1642, ANE/Q, fol. 27 (1670). The pulperos of Riobamba also complained about their financial and military obligations to the crown; see Carn. y Pulp., 23 July 1671, ANE/Q. The pulperos were a group targeted by

the Audiencia and the Quito cabildo for all kinds of mandatory "contributions." In 1599 the city mandated that the pulperos contribute 1 peso a piece in order to buy the fabric necessary for the costumes of the dancers for the feast of Corpus Christi. This decision was ratified by the Royal Audiencia. See *Libro de cabildos de Quito*, 2 June 1599, cited in José María Vargas, *Historia del Ecuador, siglo XVII* (Quito: Ed. Royal, 1982), 21.

45. Indians were not excluded from owning and operating pulperías in other areas of the viceroyalty. In Ann Zulawski's study of indigenous women in colonial Bolivia, she mentions two indigenous women who ran pulperías in Potosí and La Plata. Ann Zulawski, *Indian Women and the Market Economy*, 8, 11.

46. Criminales, 13 September 1690, ANE/Q, fol. 6.

47. Carn. y Pulp., 14 June 1642, ANE/Q, fol. 4; Carn. y Pulp., 5 December 1669, ANE/Q.

48. See, for example, Carn. y Pulp., 14 June 1642, ANE/Q, fol. 12 (1667).

49. To dramatize their dire situation, in 1642 the pulperos claimed that there were only twenty-eight pulperías operating in Quito; Carn. y Pulp., 14 June 1642, ANE/Q, fol. 3. Minchom relied on this number to indicate that there was a low level of licensed commercial activity in Quito, thus demonstrating that a large percentage of the population was provisioning itself through the markets rather than through licensed pulperías (Minchom, *People of Quito*, 106). But the terrain of retail selling in Quito was actually more complicated because of the existence of the thirty city-licensed shops. Thus, there were at least fifty-eight pulperías in Quito in 1642, and it is therefore more difficult to gauge what percentage of the population conducted their commercial activity exclusively in the market to the detriment of the pulperías.

50. Lowry, "Forging an Indian Nation," 229–233.

51. Pulp. y Carn., 14 June 1642, ANE/Q, fol. 1.

52. For examples of some of the items sold by gateras, see Pulp. y Carn., 14 June 1642, ANE/Q, fols. 1, 5, 9, 12, 14.

53. For Riobamba see Carn. y Pulp., 23 July 1671, ANE/Q, and Carn. y Pulp., 25 January 1671, ANE/Q. For smaller pueblos see 1 Notaría, Juicios, 6 August 1701, ANE/Q (Cotocollao); Carn. y Pulp. 24 January 1687, ANE/Q (Sanbisa); Criminales, 20 December 1691, ANE/Q and Criminales, 29 January 1692, ANE/Q (Guano).

54. Carn. y Pulp., 14 June 1642, ANE/Q, fols. 1–4.

55. Carn. y Pulp., 14 June 1642, ANE/Q, fol. 2.

56. Litigation in the years 1666 to 1667 mentions that the pulperos lost their case in 1654 and specifically cites the intervention of the Protector of the Indians as the cause: Carn. y Pulp., 14 June 1642, ANE/Q, fol. 14 (1667). For the pulperos' definition of what the gateras were allowed to sell, see Carn. y Pulp., 14 June 1642, ANE/Q, fol. 13.

57. Carn. y Pulp., 14 June 1642, ANE/Q, fol. 14 (1667).

58. Haring, *Spanish Empire*, 275.

59. Cheryl Pomeroy, *La sal en las culturas andinas* (Quito: Mundo Andino, 1986), 45–46.

60. Pomeroy, *La sal en las culturas andinas*, 49–53.

61. Pomeroy, *La sal en las culturas andinas*, 49–53. The evidence is so inconclusive that Pomeroy is forced to extrapolate from information on indigenous communities in Guatemala, Mexico, and Cuzco in order to strengthen her argument.

62. Haring, *Spanish Empire*, 275.

63. See, for example, litigation in 1678 between male salt dealers, who claimed to be horneros themselves, and officials collecting the alcabala, who claimed that the men were transporting salt owned by Spaniards. The indigenous men admitted that Spaniards were investing in the transportation: Carn. y Pulp., 14 June 1642, ANE/Q, fols. 48, 61 (1678). Mineral salt was produced from ponds with high salinity in which the water was collected, filtered, and then baked in clay cone-shaped vessels; thus salt producers were called horneros (bakers). See Pomeroy, *La sal en las culturas andinas*, 8–9, for techniques of salt production.

64. Carn. y Pulp., 14 June 1642, ANE/Q, fol. 17 (1667).

65. Carn. y Pulp., 14 June 1642, ANE/Q, fols. 17–19.

66. Criminales, 24 February 1665, ANE/Q.

67. Criminales, 24 February 1665, ANE/Q, fols. 2–4.

68. Criminales, 24 February 1665, ANE/Q, fols. 28–29 (1678).

69. Carn. y Pulp., 14 June 1642, ANE/Q, fol. 13 (1667). The pulperos claimed that the indigenous vendors came to Quito illegally and that they should be in their own communities, occupying themselves in growing vegetables and other legitimate activities in order to pay their tributes instead of encroaching on the trade of the pulperos.

70. Carn. y Pulp., 14 June 1642, ANE/Q, fol. 22 (1667).

71. Carn. y Pulp., 14 June 1642, ANE/Q, fol. 24 (1667).

72. Carn. y Pulp., 14 June 1642, ANE/Q, fol. 24 (1667).

73. Carn. y Pulp., 14 June 1642, ANE/Q, fol. 25 (1668).

74. Carn. y Pulp., 14 June 1642, ANE/Q, fols. 57–58 (1677).

75. Carn. y Pulp., 14 June 1642, ANE/Q, fol. 73 (1679).

76. Carn. y Pulp., 14 June 1642, ANE/Q, fol. 32 (1685).

77. Carn. y Pulp., 14 June 1642, ANE/Q, fol. 2 (1642), fol. 5 (1654), fol. 9 (1667).

78. Carn. y Pulp., 14 June 1642, ANE/Q, fol. 8 (1654).

79. Autos Acordados, 1656, ANE/Q, fol. 25.

80. Carn. y Pulp., 14 June 1642, ANE/Q, fol. 17 (1667).

81. Haring, *Spanish Empire*, 289–291.

82. Tyrer, *Historia demográfica y económica de la Audiencia de Quito*, 192.

83. *Libro de cabildos de Quito*, 23 May 1646, Garcés.

84. *Libro de cabildos de Quito*, 4 November 1654, Chiriboga.

85. Carn. y Pulp., 14 June 1642, ANE/Q, fols. 7–8 (1654).

86. Criminales, 5 July 1695, ANE/Q.

87. Carn. y Pulp., 14 June 1642, ANE/Q, fols. 31–52 (1685–1687).

88. Carn. y Pulp., 14 June 1642, ANE/Q, fols. 61, 68 (1679).

89. Carn. y Pulp., 14 June 1642, ANE/Q, fols. 69–72.

90. Carn. y Pulp., 14 June 1642, ANE/Q, fol. 73.

91. Criminales, 25 November 1665, ANE/Q, fol. 3.

92. Criminales, 25 November 1665, ANE/Q, fol. 32.

93. Criminales, 25 November 1665, ANE/Q, fol. 38.

94. Criminales, 5 August 1695, ANE/Q.

95. Criminales, 29 January 1692, ANE/Q, fols. 14–15.

96. Criminales, 20 December 1691, ANE/Q, fol. 20.

97. Carn. y Pulp., 14 June 1642, ANE/Q, fols. 88–95 (1708).

98. Carn. y Pulp., 14 June 1642, ANE/Q, fols. 90, 94 (1708).

99. 1 Notaría, vol. 269, 1701, ANE/Q, fols. 10–15 (documents not sequentially numbered), testament of doña Juana Méndez de la Higuera.

100. Criminales, 25 May 1694, ANE/Q, fol. 1.

101. 1 Notaría, vol. 181, 1655, ANE/Q, fols. 646–650.

102. Carn. y Pulp., 14 June 1642, ANE/Q, fol. 57 (1677).

103. Criminales, 25 May 1694, ANE/Q, fol. 4.

104. Criminales, 25 October 1696, ANE/Q, fol. 8.

105. Carn. y Pulp., 14 June 1642, ANE/Q, fol. 27 (1670).

106. Carn. y Pulp., 14 June 1642, ANE/Q, fol. 15 (1667).

107. Carn. y Pulp., 24 January 1687, ANE/Q, fol. 1.

108. 1 Notaría, Juicios, 6 August 1701, ANE/Q.

109. Carn. y Pulp., 14 June 1642, ANE/Q, fols. 42–43 (1691).

110. Carn. y Pulp., 14 June 1642, ANE/Q, fols. 91–94 (1699).

111. Carn. y Pulp., 14 June 1642, ANE/Q, fols. 31–34 (1685).

112. Carn. y Pulp., 14 June 1642, ANE/Q, fols. 36–38 (1685).

113. Carn. y Pulp., 14 June 1642, ANE/Q, fol. 36 (1685). Merchants were very involved with the alcabala. They were responsible for guaranteeing the city's payment to the royal treasury and are also listed as administrators and deputies of the alcabala, positions that were leased out by the city council. See Carn. y Pulp., 14 June 1642, ANE/Q, fol. 33 (1685), for merchants as deputies. The use of merchants as public officials in Quito alarmed the crown. In its request to the Audiencia for an explanation of this practice, the crown stressed the conflict of interest between the profit motivations of merchants and the well-being of the city. See Audiencia de Quito 209, 3 May 1605, AGI, Libro 1, fol. 176. Quoted in Konetzke, *Colección de documentos*, 2:72.

114. Carn. y Pulp., 25 January 1680, ANE/Q, fols. 3–4, Contract with the royal government for the appointment of fiel ejecutor.

115. Carn. y Pulp., 25 January 1680, ANE/Q, fols. 1–2.

116. Carn. y Pulp., 25 January 1680, ANE/Q, fol. 5.

117. Carn. y Pulp., 25 January 1680, ANE/Q, fols. 5–7.

118. Carn. y Pulp., 24 January 1687, ANE/Q.

119. Criminales, 15 May 1694, ANE/Q.

120. Criminales, 15 May 1694, ANE/Q, fol. 4.

121. Notaría, Juicios, 6 August 1701, ANE/Q, fol. 4.

122. Criminales, 25 May 1694, ANE/Q, fols. 22–23. Pedro's excuse that he was drunk was not accepted, and he was condemned to be hanged.

123. Criminales, 25 May 1694, ANE/Q, fol. 19.

124. Criminales, 25 May 1694, ANE/Q, fols. 3–4, 19.

125. Criminales, 25 May 1694, ANE/Q, fols. 6–7.

126. 1 Notaría, Juicios, 6 July 1701, ANE/Q, fol. 1.

127. 1 Notaría, Juicios, 6 July 1701, ANE/Q, fols. 3-5.

128. 1 Notaría, Juicios, 6 July 1701, ANE/Q, fol. 3. This is the only instance I have seen of the term *hombre blanco* used in the documentation for this project. The standard term is *español*.

129. 1 Notaría, Juicios, 6 July 1701, ANE/Q, fol. 4.

130. Criminales, 25 May 1694, ANE/Q, fol. 19.

131. 1 Notaría, Juicios, 6 July 1701, ANE/Q, fols. 4-5.

132. Criminales, 20 December 1691, ANE/Q.

133. Criminales, 29 January 1692, ANE/Q.

134. Criminales, 20 December 1692, ANE/Q, fol. 14.

135. Lowry, "Forging an Indian Nation," 225, 232.

Chapter Six

1. See Peter Bakewell, *A History of Latin America: Empires and Sequels, 1450-1930* (Malden, Mass.: Blackwell Publishers Inc., 1997), 47-56.

2. Bakewell, *History of Latin America,* 51.

3. On indigenous peoples in Peru and religious extirpations, see Nicholas Griffiths, *The Cross and the Serpent: Religious Repression and Resurgence in Colonial Peru* (Norman: Univ. of Oklahoma Press, 1996).

4. Lewis Carroll, *Alice's Adventures in Wonderland,* preface and notes by James R. Kincaid (Berkeley: Univ. of California Press, 1982), 8.

Bibliography

Abbreviations

ANE/Q	Archivo Nacional del Ecuador, Quito
Fuero Juzgo	As seen in *Fuero Juzgo en latín y castellano*
Fuero Real	As seen in *Fuero Real del Rey Don Alonso El Sabio*
Partidas	The Siete Partidas, as seen in López Estrada and López García-Berdoy, *Las Siete Partidas: Antología,* and Martínez Marina, *Ensayo histórico-crítico*
Toro	The Laws of Toro, as seen in Llamas y Molina and Vicente y Caravantes, *Comentario*
Trent	The Laws of Trent, as seen in Rev. H. J. Schroeder, *Canons and Decrees*

Sessions of the municipal council of Quito are referred to using the title of the published collection (see the two *Libro de cabildos de la Ciudad de Quito* citations below) in the form *Libro de cabildos de Quito,* the date of the session, and the name of the editor.

Laws are referred to by the paragraph or section of the original collection, not by the page in the published edition. "P." after "Partidas" refers to the specific Partida, not to a page number. For example, P.4.1:2 indicates Partida 4, Title 1, Law 2.

Archival Sources

Archivo Nacional del Ecuador, Quito (ANE/Q)
Sections: Autos Acordados; Carnicerías y Pulperías (Carn. y Pulp.); Civiles; Criminales; Esclavos; Fondo Especial (Fondo Esp.); Matrimoniales; 1 Notaría: Protocolos and Juicios

In the ANE/Q, documents are sometimes grouped together within one file and are collectively labeled by the date of the earliest document. In such cases, for purposes of clarity, the actual date of the document has been included in parentheses, in addition to the date which labels the file.

Parenthetical place-names refer to the location where events in the document take place, in order to clarify that the document originates from a pueblo outside the city of Quito.

Published Materials

Alchon, Suzanne Austin. *Native Society and Disease in Colonial Ecuador.* Cambridge, England: Cambridge Univ. Press, 1991.

Andrien, Kenneth J. *Crisis and Decline: The Viceroyalty of Peru in the Seventeenth Century.* Albuquerque: Univ. of New Mexico Press, 1985.

Arrom, Silvia Marina. *The Women of Mexico City, 1790–1857.* Stanford, Calif.: Stanford Univ. Press, 1985.

Bakewell, Peter. *A History of Latin America: Empires and Sequels, 1450–1930.* Malden, Mass.: Blackwell Publishers Inc., 1997.

Basch, Norma. *In the Eyes of the Law.* Ithaca, N.Y.: Cornell Univ. Press, 1982.

Behar, Ruth. "Sexual Witchcraft, Colonialism, and Women's Powers: Views from the Mexican Inquisition." In *Sexuality and Marriage in Colonial Latin America,* ed. Asunción Lavrin. Lincoln: Univ. of Nebraska Press, 1989, 178–206.

———. "Rage and Redemption: Reading the Life Story of a Mexican Marketing Woman." *Feminist Studies* 16 (1990): 223–258.

Behar, Ruth, and David Frye. "Property, Progeny, and Emotion: Family History in a Leonese Village." *Journal of Family History* 13:1 (1988): 13–32.

Bennett, David, and Terry Collits. "The Postcolonial Critic: Homi Bhabha Interviewed." *arena* 96 (Spring 1991): 47–63.

Blackstone, Sir William. *Commentaries on the Laws of England,* ed. Thomas M. Cooley. 1723–1780; reprint, Chicago: Callaghan and Co., 1899.

Borchart de Moreno, Christiana. "Circulación y producción en Quito: De la colonia a la república." *Siglo XIX* 14 (1993): 73–97.

Boyer, Richard. "Women, *La Mala Vida,* and the Politics of Marriage." In *Sexuality and Marriage in Colonial Latin America,* ed. Asunción Lavrin. Lincoln: Univ. of Nebraska Press, 1989, 252–286.

———. *Lives of the Bigamists: Marriage, Family, and Community in Colonial Mexico.* Albuquerque: Univ. of New Mexico Press, 1995.

Burgos Guevara, Hugo, ed. *Primeras doctrinas en la Real Audiencia de Quito, 1570–1640: Estudio preliminar y transcripción de las relaciones eclesiales y misionales de los siglos XVI y XVII.* Quito: Ediciones Abya-Yala, 1995.

Burkett, Elinor. "In Dubious Sisterhood: Class and Sex in Spanish Colonial South America." *Latin American Perspectives* 4 (1977): 18–26.

———. "Indian Women and White Society: The Case of Sixteenth-Century Peru." In *Latin American Women: Historical Perspectives,* ed. Asunción Lavrin. Westport, Conn.: Greenwood, 1978, 101–128.

Cadena, Marisol de la. "Women Are More Indian: Ethnicity and Gender in a Community Near Cuzco." In *Ethnicity, Markets, and Migration in the Andes:*

At the Crossroads of History and Anthropology, ed. Brooke Larson and Olivia Harris, with Enrique Tandeter. Durham, N.C.: Duke Univ. Press, 1995, 329–348.

Carroll, Lewis. *Alice's Adventures in Wonderland,* preface and notes by James R. Kincaid. Berkeley: Univ. of California Press, 1982.

Casey, James. *Early Modern Spain: A Social History.* New York: Routledge, 1999.

Chakrabarty, Dipesh. "Subaltern Studies and Critique of History." *arena* 96 (Spring 1991): 105–134.

Chance, John, and William B. Taylor, "Estate and Class in a Colonial City: Oaxaca in 1792." *Comparative Studies in Society and History* 12:4 (October 1977): 454–487.

Chemnitz, Martin. *Examination of the Council of Trent,* vol. 2, trans. Fred Kramer. 1522–1586; reprint, St. Louis: Concordia, 1986.

Cobo, Bernabé. *Historia del nuevo mundo.* 2 vols. Madrid: Real Academia de Historia, 1956.

Cogollos Amaya, Silvia, and Martín Eduardo Vargas Poo. "Las discusiones en torno a la construcción y utilidad de los 'dormitorios' para los muertos: Santafé, finales del siglo XVIII." In *Inquisición, muerte y sexualidad en la Nueva Granada,* ed. Jaime Humberto Borja Gómez. Bogotá: Editorial Ariel, 1996, 143–167.

Cope, Douglas. *The Limits of Racial Domination: Plebian Society in Colonial Mexico City, 1660–1720.* Madison: Univ. of Wisconsin Press, 1994.

Descalzi del Castillo, Ricardo. *La Real Audiencia de Quito claustro en los Andes: Siglo XVI.* Barcelona: I.G. Seix y Barral Hnos., S.A., 1978.

Dobyns, Henry F. "An Outline of Andean Epidemic History to 1720." *Bulletin of the History of Medicine* 37 (1963): 493–515.

Douglass, William A. "Iberian Family History." *Journal of Family History* 13:1 (1988): 1–12.

FLACSO (Facultad Latino Americano de Ciencias Sociales). <http://www.eurosur.org/FLACSO/mujeres/ecuador/legi-3.htm> (accessed 14 June 2001).

Fuero Juzgo en latín y castellano, cotejado con los más antiguos y preciosos códices. Madrid: La Real Academia Española, 1815.

Fuero Real del Rey Don Alonso El Sabio. Madrid: La Imprenta Real, 1836.

Gibson, Charles. *The Aztecs under Spanish Rule: A History of the Indians of the Valley of Mexico, 1519–1810.* Stanford, Calif.: Stanford Univ. Press, 1964.

Gómez Morán, Luis. *La mujer en la historia y en la legislación.* Madrid: Gobierno de Audiencia Territorial, 1942.

González Holguín, Diego. *Vocabulario de la lengua Qquichua.* 1601; reprint, Quito: Corporación Editora Nacional, 1993.

Goody, Jack. *The Development of the Family and Marriage in Europe.* Cambridge, England: Cambridge Univ. Press, 1983.

Griffiths, Nicholas. *The Cross and the Serpent: Religious Repression and Resurgence in Colonial Peru.* Norman: Univ. of Oklahoma Press, 1996.

Hajnal, J. "Two Kinds of Pre-industrial Household Formation Systems." In *Family Forms in Historic Europe,* ed. Richard Wall, Jean Robin, and Peter Laslett. Cambridge, England: Cambridge Univ. Press, 1983, 65–104.

Haring, C. H. *The Spanish Empire in America.* 1947; reprint, New York: Harcourt Brace Jovanovich, 1975.

Harris, Olivia. "Ethnic Identity and Market Relations: Indians and Mestizos in the Andes." In *Ethnicity, Markets, and Migration in the Andes: At the Crossroads of History and Anthropology,* ed. Brooke Larson and Olivia Harris, with Enrique Tandeter. Durham, N.C.: Duke Univ. Press, 1995, 351–390.

Hartman, Roswith. "Mercados y ferias prehispánicas en el área andina." *Boletín de la Academia Nacional de Historia* 54 (1971): 214–235.

Hughes, Sarah S. "Beyond Eurocentrism: Developing World Women's Studies." *Feminist Studies* 18 (1992): 389–404.

Hurl-Eamon, Jennine. "Domestic Violence Prosecuted: Women Binding over Their Husbands for Assault at Westminster Quarter Sessions, 1685–1720." *Journal of Family History* 26:4 (October 2001): 435–454.

Hyde, Lewis. *The Gift, Imagination and the Erotic Life of Property.* New York: Vintage Books, 1983.

Kanter, Deborah E. "Native Female Land Tenure and Its Decline in Mexico, 1750–1900." *Ethnohistory* 42:4 (Fall 1995): 607–626.

Kennedy Troya, Alexandra, and Carmen Fauria Roma. "Obrajes en la Audiencia de Quito: Tilipulo." *Revista Ecuatoriana de Historia Económica* 4:2 (1988): 143–220.

Kertzer, David I., and Caroline Brettel. "Advances in Italian and Iberian Family History." *Journal of Family History* 12:1–3 (1987): 87–120.

Kinsbruner, Jay. *Petty Capitalism in Spanish America: The Pulperos of Puebla, Mexico City, Caracas, and Buenos Aires.* Boulder, Colo.: Westview Press, 1987.

Konetzke, Richard, ed. *Colección de documentos para la historia de la formación social de Hispanoamérica, 1493–1810,* vols. 1–3. Madrid: Consejo Superior de Investigaciones Científicas, 1958.

Korth, Eugene H., and Della M. Flusche. "Dowry and Inheritance in Colonial Spanish America: Peninsular Law and Chilean Practice." *Americas* 43 (1987): 395–410.

Kuznesof, Elizabeth Anne. "Ethnic and Gender Influences on 'Spanish' Creole Society in Colonial Spanish America." *Colonial Latin American Review* 4:1 (1995): 153–176.

Las Casas, Bartolomé de. *A Short Account of the Destruction of the Indies,* trans. Nigel Griffin. 1542; reprint, London: Penguin Books, 1992.

Laslett, Peter. "Introduction: The History of the Family." In *Household and Family in Past Time,* ed. Peter Laslett and Richard Wall. Cambridge, England: Cambridge Univ. Press, 1972, 1–73.

———. "Family and Household as Work Group and Kin Group: Areas of Traditional Europe Compared." In *Family Forms in Historic Europe,* ed. Richard Wall, Jean Robin, and Peter Laslett. Cambridge, England: Cambridge Univ. Press, 1983, 513–563.

Lauretis, Teresa de. "Eccentric Subjects: Feminist Theory and Historical Consciousness." *Feminist Studies* 16 (1990): 115–150.

Lavalle, Bernard. "La rebelión de las alcabalas." *Revista de Indias* 44 (1984): 141–201.

Lavrin, Asunción. "In Search of the Colonial Woman in Mexico: The Seventeenth and Eighteenth Centuries." In *Latin American Women: Historical Perspectives,* ed. Asunción Lavrin. Westport, Conn.: Greenwood, 1978, 3–22.

———. "Introduction: The Scenario, the Actors, and the Issues." In *Sexuality and Marriage in Colonial Latin America,* ed. Asunción Lavrin. Lincoln: Univ. of Nebraska Press, 1989, 1–43.

Lavrin, Asunción, and Edith Couturier. "Dowries and Wills: A View of Women's Socioeconomic Role in Colonial Guadalajara and Puebla, 1640–1857." *Hispanic American Historical Review* 50:2 (1979): 280–304.

———. "Las Mujeres tienen la palabra: Otras voces en la historia colonial de México." *Historia Mexicana* 31 (1981): 278–313.

León Galarza, Natalia. *La primera alianza. El matrimonio criollo: Honor y violencia conyugal. Cuenca: 1750–1800.* Quito: Nueva Editorial, 1997.

Lewin, Linda. "Natural and Spurious Children in Brazilian Inheritance Law from Colony to Empire: A Methodological Essay." *Americas* (January 1992): 351–396.

Libro de cabildos de la Ciudad de Quito, ed. Jorge A. Garcés G. Publicaciones, no. 30. 1638–1646; reprint, Quito: Archivo Municipal de Quito, 1960.

Libro de cabildos de la Ciudad de Quito, ed. Gustavo Chiriboga C. Publicaciones, no. 32. 1650–1657; reprint, Quito: Archivo Municipal de Quito, 1969.

Lira, Andrés. *Comunidades indígenas frente a la ciudad de México, Tenochtitlán y Tlatelolco, sus pueblos y barrios, 1812–1919.* Mexico City: Colegio de México, 1983.

Llamas y Molina, don Sancho, and don José Vicente y Caravantes. *Comentario crítico, jurídico, literal, a las ochenta y tres Leyes de Toro.* 2 vols. Madrid: Imprenta de Gaspar y Roig, 1853.

Lockhart, James. *The Nahuas after the Conquest: A Social and Cultural History of the Indians of Central Mexico, Sixteenth through Eighteenth Centuries.* Stanford, Calif.: Stanford Univ. Press, 1992.

———. *Spanish Peru, 1532–1560: A Social History,* 2d ed. Madison: Univ. of Wisconsin Press, 1994.

Lockhart, James, and Stuart B. Schwartz. *Early Latin America: A History of Colonial Spanish America and Brazil.* Cambridge, England: Cambridge Univ. Press, 1985.

Lombardi, Cathryn L., and John V. Lombardi, with K. Lynn Stoner. *Latin American History: A Teaching Atlas.* Madison: Univ. of Wisconsin Press, 1983.

Londoño, Jenny. *Entre la sumisión y la resistencia: Las mujeres en la Real Audiencia de Quito.* Quito: Abya-Yala, 1997.

López Alarcón, Mariano, and Rafael Navarro-Valls. *Curso de derecho matrimonial canónico y concordado.* Madrid: Editorial Tecnos, 1984.

López Estrada, Francisco, and María Teresa López García-Berdoy, eds. *Las Siete Partidas: Antología.* Madrid: Editorial Castalia, 1992.

Lowry, Lyn Brandon. "Forging an Indian Nation: Urban Indians under Spanish Colonial Control (Lima, Peru, 1535–1765)." Ph.D. dissertation. Department of History, Univ. of California, Berkeley, 1991.

168

Lutz, Christopher H. *Santiago de Guatemala, 1541-1773: City, Caste, and the Colonial Experience.* Norman: Univ. of Oklahoma Press, 1994.

MacEwen Scott, Alison. "Women in Latin America: Stereotypes and Social Science." *Bulletin of Latin American Research* 5 (1986): 21-27.

Mallon, Florencia E. "Patriarchy in the Transition to Capitalism: Central Peru, 1830-1950." *Feminist Studies* 13 (1987): 379-407.

Martín, Luis. *Daughters of the Conquistadores.* Albuquerque: Univ. of New Mexico Press, 1983.

Martínez Marcos, Esteban. *Las causas matrimoniales en las Partidas de Alfonso El Sabio.* Salamanca, Spain: Graficesa, 1966.

Martínez Marina, D. Francisco. *Ensayo histórico-crítico sobre la legislación de los Reinos de León y Castilla, especialmente sobre el código de las Siete Partidas.* 2 vols. Madrid: Imprenta de D. E. Aguado, 1834.

Mayer, Enrique. "El trueque y los mercados en el imperio incaico." In *Los campesinos y el mercado,* ed. Enrique Mayer, Sidney W. Mintz, and G. William Skinner. Lima: PUCE, 1974, 13-50.

McCaa, Robert, Stuart B. Schwartz, and Arturo Grubessich, "Race and Class in Colonial Latin America: A Critique." *Comparative Studies in Society and History* 21:3 (July 1979): 421-433.

McFarlane, Anthony. "The 'Rebellion of the Barrios': Urban Insurrection in Bourbon Quito." *Hispanic American Historical Review* 69 (1989): 283-330.

Minchom, Martin. *The People of Quito, 1690-1810: Change and Unrest in the Underclass.* Boulder, Colo.: Westview Press, 1994.

Miño Grijalva, Manuel. "La manufactura colonial: Aspectos comparativos entre el obraje andino y el novohispano." *Revista Ecuatoriana de Historia Económica* 4:2 (1988): 13-62.

Moreno Yánez, Segundo. *Sublevaciones indígenas en la Audiencia de Quito: Desde comienzos del siglo XVIII hasta finales de la Colonia.* Quito: PUCE, 1977.

Morner, Magnus. *La Corona española y los foráneos en los pueblos de indios de América.* Institute of Ibero-American Studies, Stockholm, Publication Series A, no. 1. Stockholm: Almquist and Wiksell, 1970.

———. "Economic Factors and Stratification in Colonial Spanish America with Special Regard to the Elites." *Hispanic American Historical Review* 63:2 (May 1983): 335-369.

Müller, Astrid. *Por pan y equidad: Organizaciones de mujeres ecuatorianas.* Quito: Ediciones Abya-Yala, 1994.

Murra, John V. "Did Tribute and Markets Prevail in the Andes before the European Invasion?" In *Ethnicity, Markets, and Migration in the Andes: At the Crossroads of History and Anthropology,* ed. Brooke Larson and Olivia Harris, with Enrique Tandeter. Durham, N.C.: Duke Univ. Press, 1995, 57-72.

Nazarri, Muriel. "Parents and Daughters: Change in the Practice of Dowry in São Paulo (1600-1770)." *Hispanic American Historical Review* 70:4 (1990): 639-665.

———. *Disappearance of the Dowry: Women, Families, and Social Change in São Paulo, Brazil (1600-1900).* Stanford, Calif.: Stanford Univ. Press, 1991.

————. "Vanishing Indians: The Social Construction of Race in Colonial São Paulo." *Americas* 57:4 (April 2001): 497–524.

Newson, Linda A. "Old World Epidemics in Early Colonial Ecuador." In *"Secret Judgements of God": Old World Disease in Colonial Spanish America*, ed. N. David Cook and W. George Lovell. Norman: Univ. of Oklahoma Press, 1991, 84–112.

Oberem, Udo. "Trade and Trade Goods in the Ecuadorian Montaña," trans. Alegonda M. Schokkenbroek. In *Native South Americans*, ed. Patricia J. Lyon. Boston: Little Brown, 1974, 346–357.

Ortega y Gasset, José. *España invertebrada: Bosquejo de algunos pensamientos históricos* (Madrid: Calpe, 1921).

Ortíz de la Tabla Ducasse, Javier. "El obraje colonial ecuatoriano: Aproximación a su estudio." *Revista Ecuatoriana de Historia Económica* 4:2 (1988): 63–142.

Pareja Diezcanseco, Alfredo. *Las instituciones y la administración en la Real Audiencia de Quito*. Quito: Editorial Universitaria, 1975.

Patai, Daphne. *Brazilian Women Speak*. New Brunswick, N.J.: Rutgers Univ. Press, 1988.

Phelan, John Leddy. "Authority and Flexibility in the Spanish Imperial Bureaucracy." *Administrative Science Quarterly* 5 (1960): 47–65.

————. *The Kingdom of Quito in the Seventeenth Century: Bureaucratic Politics in the Spanish Empire*. Madison: Univ. of Wisconsin Press, 1967.

Pollock, Linda A. "Rethinking Patriarchy and the Family in Seventeenth-Century England." *Journal of Family History* 23:1 (January 1998): 3–28.

Pomeroy, Cheryl. *La sal en las culturas andinas*. Quito: Mundo Andino, 1986.

Powers, Karen. *Andean Journeys: Migration, Ethnogenesis, and the State in Colonial Quito*. Albuquerque: Univ. of New Mexico Press, 1995.

Rabkin, Peggy A. *Fathers to Daughters: The Legal Foundations of Female Emancipation*. Westport, Conn.: Greenwood Press, 1980.

Ramírez, Susan. "Exchange and Markets in the Sixteenth Century: A View from the North." In *Ethnicity, Markets, and Migration in the Andes: At the Crossroads of History and Anthropology*, ed. Brooke Larson and Olivia Harris, with Enrique Tandeter. Durham, N.C.: Duke Univ. Press, 1995, 134–164.

Salomon, Frank. *Native Lords of Quito in the Age of the Incas: The Political Economy of North Andean Chiefdoms*. Cambridge, England: Cambridge Univ. Press, 1986.

————. "Indian Women of Early Colonial Quito as Seen through Their Testaments." *Americas* 44 (1988): 325–342.

Schick, Irvin Cemil. "Representing Middle Eastern Women: Feminism and Colonial Discourse." *Feminist Studies* 16 (1990): 345–380.

Schroeder, Rev. H. J., trans. *Canons and Decrees of the Council of Trent*. London: B. Herder Book Co., 1941.

Schwartz, Stuart B. "Colonial Identities and the *Sociedad de Castas*." *Colonial Latin American Review* 4:1 (1995): 185–201.

Scott, Joan. "Gender: A Useful Category of Historical Analysis." In *Gender and the Politics of History*. New York: Columbia Univ. Press, 1988, 28–50.

Seed, Patricia. "Social Dimensions of Race: Mexico City, 1753." *Hispanic American Historical Review* 62:4 (1982): 569–606.

———. *To Love, Honor, and Obey in Colonial Mexico.* Stanford, Calif.: Stanford Univ. Press, 1988.

———. "Marriage Promises and the Value of a Woman's Testimony in Colonial Mexico." *Signs, Journal of Women in Culture and Society* 13:21 (1988): 253–276.

Sempat Assadourian, Carlos. *El sistema de la economía colonial: El mercado interno, regiones y espacio económico.* Mexico City: Editorial Nueva Imagen, 1983.

Shorter, Edward. *The Making of the Modern Family.* New York: Basic Books, Inc., 1975.

Silverblatt, Irene. *Moon, Sun, and Witches: Gender Ideologies and Class in Inca and Colonial Peru.* Princeton, N.J.: Princeton Univ. Press, 1987.

———. "Lessons of Gender and Ethnohistory in Mesoamerica." *Ethnohistory* 42:4 (1995): 639–650.

Socolow, Susan Migden. *The Merchants of Buenos Aires, 1778-1810: Family and Commerce.* Cambridge, England: Cambridge Univ. Press, 1978.

———. "Acceptable Partners: Marriage Choice in Colonial Argentina, 1778–1810." In *Sexuality and Marriage in Colonial Latin America,* ed. Asunción Lavrin. Lincoln: Univ. of Nebraska Press, 1989, 209–251.

Sousa, Lisa Mary. "Women and Crime in Colonial Oaxaca: Evidence of Complementary Gender Roles in Mixtec and Zapotec Societies." In *Indian Women of Early Mexico,* ed. Susan Schroeder, Stephanie Wood, and Robert Haskett. Norman: Univ. of Oklahoma Press, 1977, 199–214.

Spalding, Karen. *Huarochirí: An Andean Society under Inca and Spanish Rule.* Stanford, Calif.: Stanford Univ. Press, 1984.

Stern, Steve J. *Peru's Indian Peoples and the Challenge of Spanish Conquest: Huamanga to 1640,* 2d ed. Madison: Univ. of Wisconsin Press, 1993.

———. "Early Spanish-Indian Accommodation in the Andes." In *The Indian in Latin American History: Resistance, Resilience, and Acculturation,* ed. John E. Kicza. Wilmington, Del.: Scholarly Resources, 1993, 21–49.

———. *The Secret History of Gender: Women, Men, and Power in Late Colonial Mexico.* Chapel Hill: Univ. of North Carolina Press, 1995.

———. "The Variety and Ambiguity of Native Andean Intervention in European Colonial Markets." In *Ethnicity, Markets, and Migration in the Andes: At the Crossroads of History and Anthropology,* ed. Brooke Larson and Olivia Harris, with Enrique Tandeter. Durham, N.C.: Duke Univ. Press, 1995, 73–100.

Stone, Lawrence. *The Family, Sex and Marriage in England, 1500-1800.* New York: Harper and Row, 1979.

Stone, Marilyn. *Marriage and Friendship in Medieval Spain: Social Relations according to the Fourth Partida of Alfonso X.* New York: Peter Lang, 1990.

Super, John. "Partnership and Profit in the Early Andean Trade: The Experiences of Quito Merchants, 1580-1610." *Journal of Latin American Studies* 2 (1979): 265–281.

———. "Empresarios quiteños en 1580-1620." *Revista del Archivo Histórico del Guayas* 16 (1979): 5–20.

Szásdi, Adám. "The Economic History of the Diocese of Quito, 1616–1787." *Latin American Research Review* 21 (1986): 266–275.

Taylor, William B. *Drinking, Homicide, and Rebellion in Colonial Mexican Villages.* Stanford, Calif.: Stanford Univ. Press, 1979.

Tomás y Valiente, Francisco. *El derecho penal de la monarquía absoluta (siglos XVI-XVII-XVIII).* Madrid: Editorial Tecnos, 1969.

Twinam, Ann. *Public Lives, Private Secrets: Gender, Honor, Sexuality, and Illegitimacy in Colonial Spanish America.* Stanford, Calif.: Stanford Univ. Press, 1999.

Tyrer, Robson Brines. *Historia demográfica y económica de la Audiencia de Quito: Población indígena e industria textil, 1600-1800.* Quito: Banco Central del Ecuador, 1988.

Unidad de Modernización Judicial de la Comisión Andina de Juristas. <http://www.cajpe.org.pe/RIJ/BASES/mujer/1.htm> (accessed 13 June 2001).

Van Deusan, Nancy. "Determining the Boundaries of Virtue: The Discourse of Recogimiento among Women in Seventeenth-Century Lima." *Journal of Family History* 22:4 (October 1997): 373–389.

Van Young, Eric. *Hacienda and Market in Eighteenth-Century Mexico: The Rural Economy of the Guadalajara Region, 1675-1820.* Berkeley: Univ. of California Press, 1981.

Vargas, José María. *Historia del Ecuador, siglo XVII.* Quito: Ed. Royal, 1982.

Vilar, Pierre. *La familia en la España mediterránea (siglos XV-XIX).* Barcelona: Editorial Crítica, 1987.

Villapalos Salas, Gustavo, and José María Castán Vázquez. *Justicia y monarquía: Puntos de vista sobre su evolución en el reinado de los Reyes Católicos. Discurso leído el día 16 de junio de 1997 en su recepción pública como académico de número.* Madrid: Real Academia de Jurisprudencia y Legislación, 1997.

Vries, Jan De. *The Economy of Europe in an Age of Crisis, 1600-1750.* New York: Cambridge Univ. Press, 1984.

Wall, Richard. "Introduction." In *Family Forms in Historic Europe,* ed. Richard Wall, Jean Robin, and Peter Laslett. Cambridge, England: Cambridge Univ. Press, 1983, 1–64.

Zulawski, Ann. *Indian Women and the Market Economy in Colonial Bolivia.* New York: Consortium of Columbia Univ. Institute of Latin American and Iberian Studies and New York Univ. Center for Latin American and Caribbean Studies, 1988.

———. "Social Differentiation, Gender, and Ethnicity: Urban Indian Women in Colonial Bolivia, 1640-1725." *Latin American Research Review* 25 (1990): 93–112.

———. *They Eat from Their Labor: Work and Social Change in Colonial Bolivia.* Pittsburgh: Univ. of Pittsburgh Press, 1995.

Index

CPSIA information can be obtained
at www.ICGtesting.com
Printed in the USA
LVHW031026020222
709717LV00001B/14

9 780292 722231